# CATHOLICISM AND HEALTH-CARE JUSTICE

# CATHOLICISM AND HEALTH-CARE JUSTICE

## Problems, Potential and Solutions

PHILIP S. KEANE, S.S.

PAULIST PRESS
New York/Mahwah, N.J.

*Book design by Theresa M. Sparacio*

*Cover design by Valerie Petro*

Library of Congress Cataloging-in-Publication Data

Keane, Philip S.
    Catholicism and health-care justice : problems, potential and solutions / by Philip S. Keane.
        p.   cm.
    Includes bibliographical references.
    ISBN 0-8091-4059-4 (alk. paper)
    1. Medicine—Religious aspects—Catholic Church.  2. Medical ethics—Religious aspects—Catholic Church.  3. Medical care—Religious aspects—Catholic Church.  I. Title.

R725.56 .K434  2001
362.1′088′22—dc21

                                                2001054567

Published by Paulist Press
997 Macarthur Boulevard
Mahwah, New Jersey 07430

www.paulistpress.com

Printed and bound in the
United States of America

# CONTENTS

To
My Sulpician Confreres
Both Living and Deceased

# ACKNOWLEDGMENTS

This book was written during my 1999–2000 sabbatical from St. Mary's Seminary in Baltimore. I first want to thank the leadership and staff of the United States Province of the Society of St. Sulpice for approving the sabbatical and arranging so many of the details. The Provincial Superior, Fr. Ronald Witherup, S.S., encouraged me throughout the process, and Mr. Joseph Reynolds was his usual indefatigable self in overseeing all of the arrangements for the sabbatical. I am also very grateful to Fr. Robert Leavitt, S.S., President-Rector, and to the administration and staff of St. Mary's, not only for providing the sabbatical year, but also for helping me maintain a schedule that permits me to be of help to many Catholic hospitals as well as attend to my first love, the teaching and spiritual formation of future priests. It has now been almost thirty years since I was first assigned to St. Mary's, and being there for so long has been one of the great joys of my life.

I want to thank the many persons in Catholic health care—leaders, doctors, nurses, and so many others—with whom I have had the opportunity to work over the years. These dedicated and loyal people have called on me for advice in the area of health-care ethics, but I cannot but feel that I have learned far more from them than they have from me. I know that my insights have a much greater richness because of my association with the good people of Catholic health care.

Special thanks go to the Sulpician community at 4210 North Charles Street, Baltimore. I lived there during the sabbatical year and was made to feel so very welcome. Family members and good friends also welcomed me during the sabbatical year, providing needed periods of rest, even though some of my hosts were dealing with tragedies such as death and serious illness. To them also, I am most grateful.

During the composition of the book, four people read the entire manuscript and made many very helpful suggestions. These four were Thomas R. Ulshafer, S.S., Patricia Smith, R.S.M., Patricia Lamoureux, and Sylvia DeVillers. My lasting thanks go to all four and to the countless others with whom I conversed about one or another aspect of the book. In spite of their help, I am sure the book has its shortcomings. These are entirely my responsibility.

Finally a word about the book's dedication. During my third of a century as a Sulpician, I have had the opportunity to be associated with outstanding major superiors and rectors, wonderful Sulpician faculty colleagues, distinguished Sulpician scholars, esteemed retired Sulpicians, and Sulpicians and candidates whom I have taught while they were seminarians. While I thought about naming some of these as individuals, I think the genius and charism of the Sulpicians—and our success as role models for future priests—has much to do with our commitment to work together as a collegial group of priests. Hence the dedication to all of my Sulpician confreres, both living and deceased, seems to be the most appropriate way to dedicate this book.

Ithaca, New York
July 4, 2000

# ABBREVIATIONS USED IN TEXT

AARP    American Association of Retired Persons

AHA     American Hospital Association

AMA     American Medical Association

BBA     Balanced Budget Act or Balanced Budget
        Amendment

CHA     Catholic Health Association

CHIP    Children's Health Insurance Program

CPR     Cardiopulmonary Resuscitation

DRG     Diagnosis Related Group

*ERD*   *Ethical and Religious Directives for Catholic Health-
        Care Services*

ERISA   Employment Retirement Income Security Act

FEHBP   Federal Employment Health Benefits Program

HEDIS   Health Plan Employer Data and Information Set

HIAA    Health Insurance Association of America

HIP     Health Insurance Program

HMO     Health Maintenance Organization

IDN         Integrated Delivery Network

IPA         Independent Practice Association

*JAMA*      *Journal of the American Medical Association*

JCAHO       The Joint Commission on the Accreditation of
            Healthcare Organizations

MRI         Magnetic Resonance Imaging

NCQA        National Commission on Quality Assurance

*NEJM*      *New England Journal of Medicine*

PHO         Physician Hospital Organization

POS         Point-of-Service

PPO         Preferred Provider Organization

WCF         Washington Commonwealth Foundation

N.B.:       This listing refers to abbreviations used through-
            out the entire book. Additional abbreviations
            used in the endnote citations are listed at the
            beginning of the notes.

# INTRODUCTION

In the early 1990s, an integrated national approach to health care in the United States seemed to be a real possibility. At that time it was important to assess an integrated approach from the viewpoint of Roman Catholic moral theology.[1] The question of an integrated national approach to health-care reform has not disappeared, and this question may revisit us again early in the new millennium. Since 1994, when President Clinton's plan for health care collapsed, there has been very rapid change in the U.S. health-care system, but this change has happened without any integrated direction. Instead, the change has occurred in a piecemeal fashion, with initiatives being taken by both for-profit and not-for-profit health-care providers, and by local, state, and national governments.

Among the many happenings in health care in recent years, three developments have been especially prominent. *First,* there has been a very rapid growth of managed-care organizations as providers of health-care services, with some reports stating that 87 percent of all health care in the United States is furnished in managed-care settings.[2] Managed care can occur in a great many different formats, so we need to see the term "managed care" as a blanket term that includes many variations. But even granting these variations, the total impact of managed care is enormous in the United States and of growing magnitude elsewhere. *Second,* there has been an equally rapid realignment of health-care services in our country through a fast-paced series of mergers, joint ventures, buyouts, and hospital closings. Much of this realignment has been necessary, because of excess health-care capacity in some geographical areas, and because of the need to configure health-care services into networks that can be efficient both in providing a meaningful continuum of services and in helping keep health-care costs down. *Third*, at the level of public policy, there has been a marked tendency for governments to enact individual pieces of legislation aimed at particular problems, such as childhood immunizations, care for poor children, and legal rights for persons covered by managed-care organizations. But at the same time, the Balanced Budget Act of 1997 (BBA) has taken away many billions of dollars of government support for health care. The result is that the individual legislative reforms can appear almost cosmetic, since the health-care system as a whole experiences greater and greater financial stress.

The Clinton plan was first introduced to the American people in 1993. Since then the number of persons in the United States without health-care insurance has risen to its current level of 44.3 million uninsured persons, as compared to the 37 million uninsured persons in 1993.[3] To state these almost unimaginable numbers as percentages, the number of uninsured persons in the United States has risen by 20 percent since 1993, while total population has risen only by 6 percent. Sixteen percent of all persons in the United States now lack any health insurance, as compared to 14 percent in 1993. The percentages are even higher if we factor out persons over sixty five, almost all of whom are covered by Medicare. A variety of factors have contributed to these numbers. But without any doubt, these figures show that some deep questions of social justice are interconnected with the three trends I have just mentioned. All of this was underlined recently by a study published by the World Health Organization, which ranks the United States only thirty-seventh among the nations of the world in terms of overall health-care quality.[4]

Within and in addition to these three trends, there are a host of other issues, including the role of the doctor as a professional; the freedom, dignity, and spiritual nature of the patient; care for the poor and the mentally ill; just treatment of health-care employees; the place and funding of medical education and research; the role of Catholic health-care providers, both as partners in new health-care ventures and as caregivers to and advocates for the poor; and the place (or lack thereof) of profit making in the delivery of health care.

This brief summary of today's health-care questions suggests that, even aside from the overarching issue of a unified national approach to health care, there are numerous weighty matters that call for serious ethical analysis. Many groups in society are capable of offering this kind of ethical analysis. The Roman Catholic moral tradition, with its legacy of rich historical reflection on health care and social justice, can be a significant partner in the dialogue about the moral state of health care in the United States today. My hope is that this book, which will be very explicitly rooted in the Catholic moral tradition, will serve as a contribution to the dialogue.

The book is organized as follows. Chapter 1 is a summary of the basic Catholic moral principles that apply to health care. This chapter covers themes such as the Catholic tradition on justice and care for the poor, the openness of Catholicism to a variety of economic systems, the rights and responsibilities of employees, the responsibilities of professionals, and the meaning of sickness and death. Chapters 2 to 5 use the viewpoint of Roman Catholic moral theology to assess the trends described above (managed care, health-care realignment, and piecemeal government interventions accompanied by major reductions in funding). Managed care is addressed in two chapters, one on its positive qualities (chapter 2) and one on its serious difficulties as a means of health-care delivery (chapter 3). The other major trends are addressed in chapters 4 and 5. Many of today's subsidiary moral issues in health care are addressed within these chapters, but some subsidiary issues (the cost of prescriptions, medical education, mental health care) are considered in chapter 6.

Finally, there is the question of the future and how health care is likely to evolve in the United States. Theological reflection, both on matters of principle and on today's specific trends, may provide some intimation about the future of health-care delivery in the United States. Chapter 7 offers some tentative conclusions about the future of U.S. health care, based upon the Catholic principles and on their applications to current health-care questions.

Several people have asked me to describe the audience for whom I am writing this book. My response is that I hope that I will be read by health-care leaders, especially Catholic leaders, and by policy makers, theologians, and ethicists. But in the writing I have sought to adopt a tone that will make the book worthwhile reading for any thoughtful person who is interested in how Catholic moral theology would assess the ethical aspects of health-care delivery in the United States today. It will of course be up to the readers to decide whether I have achieved this goal.

# Chapter 1
# A SUMMARY OF CATHOLIC PRINCIPLES
# FOR HEALTH-CARE JUSTICE

This chapter will review several key areas of Catholic thought that can offer basic principles of health-care justice. The topics to be treated are the fundamental Catholic theory of justice and the obligation to provide universal health care, Catholic economic theory with its openness to a variety of economic systems, the Catholic concern for justice in the treatment of health-care employees, health care as a vocation and a profession, and the meaning of suffering and death for the person as a whole. To begin the book, we set out a clear picture of the essential values that shape the Catholic approach to health care. We will then be in a good position to assess the three contemporary health-care developments that were mentioned in the Introduction. The chapter will conclude with a brief refection on the *Ethical and Religious Directives for Catholic Health Care Services (ERD).*[1]

## UNIVERSAL HEALTH CARE AS AN
## OBLIGATION OF JUSTICE

In recent decades, a growing number of authors have begun to assert that access to a reasonable standard of health care is an obligation in justice and a universal human right.[2] Such an assertion was not found so frequently in the past. It is easy to understand why the themes of justice and rights in the health-care context were not present in earlier times. The modern thinking on justice as entailing the responsibility of society to distribute a reasonable level of human goods to all persons dates especially from early twentieth-century sources such as John A. Ryan's classic text, *Distributive Justice,* first published in 1916.[3] The modern thinking about human rights as including obligations to provide all persons with certain basic goods began only slightly earlier, with the critiques raised by Marxism and with the publication of late nineteenth-century works such as Pope Leo XIII's encyclical *Rerum Novarum.*[4] When these works were written, the state of health care was quite primitive in comparison to today's standards. Thus, even though earlier authors spoke about rights to goods such as education, just wages, and retirement benefits, relatively little was said about health care as a right or as a matter involving obligations of justice. John XXIII was the first pope to speak about medical care as an issue of justice.[5]

Even when health care began to make great scientific advances near the beginning of the twentieth century, it was still relatively inexpensive, and malpractice lawsuits were practically nonexistent.[6] Doctors often found ways to care for patients who were poor and could not afford to pay for care. The frequent stories of moral heroism by earlier physicians show that there was an implicit notion of health care as a human right, but this implicit awareness led to rather little published scholarship on health care as a right or an obligation of justice. Today's health-care world is very different, and much more complex, both legally and financially. Doctors cannot be expected to run their own private charity systems, and there is a clear need to give explicit attention to access to health care as a matter of justice and human rights.

*Distributive Justice*

There are many elements in a complete Catholic understanding of justice and rights. We will look at a number of these elements, beginning with distributive justice, then moving to human rights, the common good, social justice, and other topics such as tax policy and health-care rationing. I begin with distributive justice because it is such a classic

Catholic term, and because, in my opinion, it has the most specific content in terms of an approach to universal health care. *Distributive justice* refers to the obligation of society to provide all of its citizens with a means to ensure that all can have access to a sufficient level of basic human goods. Surely in our times an appropriate level of health care is a basic human good that belongs to all people. There are frequent discussions of which model or canon of distributive justice ought to be used in providing health care, with Gene Outka's widely reprinted article from the 1970s perhaps the classic example.[7] Outka rejects merit, social worth, and ability to pay as grounds for health-care decision making, and his rejection of these three factors as the basis for deciding who gets what health care is well grounded and widely accepted by scholars of justice. There may be some exceptions, such as providing financial incentives to persons who take important preventive health-care measures such as stopping or avoiding smoking, or such as making certain optional health services available to those who can pay for these services. But in general, making the ability to pay the basis for providing or denying essential health services seems to be a failure in distributive justice. Similarly, the merit or goodness of persons and their usefulness to society are inadequate bases for making decisions about who gets health care. Both saints and sinners can get seriously ill, and health-care needs so very often arise before or after someone is socioeconomically useful—health-care needs occur frequently in both children and persons who have retired.

Outka's article has drawn more discussion on his final two canons for distributive justice: distributing health care according to need, or distributing it in a way that assures that all people are treated the same in terms of their basic health-care needs. Meeting everyone's needs is a very attractive model for health-care justice, but on further reflection, at least two problems emerge in connection with the need model of delivering health care. *First,* it can sometimes be difficult to determine what is a genuine health-care need and what is more of a want. Even the same health service might be a need for one person and a want for another person. *Second,* there is the fundamental problem of our basic human finitude. Even with all good will and all human effort, it may not be possible to meet every human need in the area of health care. This problem becomes all the greater when we stop to consider that health care is only one of a number of basic human goods. We also have to think about the responsibility of society to provide for other goods, such as education, housing, transportation, communication, and aesthetic human experience. In light of all of these goods, the limits of even our sophisticated modern society become all the clearer. It is not possible for even a truly just society to provide for every conceivable health-care good. And in the end, we all will have to face the fact that death is an intrinsic part of the human story.

Thoughts such as these lead to Outka's fifth canon for distributive justice, which he describes as treating similar cases similarly.[8] My view is that the fifth canon moves in the right direction. What a just society ought to do in behalf of distributive justice is to pick out a basic and solidly reasonable floor of health-care services and make sure that all citizens have access to at least these services. More than a century ago, in speaking about the living wage, Pope Leo XIII spoke about the right of all citizens to live in reasonable and frugal comfort.[9] Clearly today, a solidly reasonable floor of health-care services is part of what a person needs to live in reasonable and frugal comfort. The exact specifics of this solidly reasonable floor will depend on a variety of factors, such as the progress of medical science and the overall economic stability of the society. A global perspective is also important in determining a suitable standard of care. How can we give adequate consideration to what is just in one society if we do not consider what is happening in health care around the globe?

Debate will continue on the exact meaning of distributive justice and its implications for health care. For a full Catholic perspective, distributive justice needs to be enriched by the other themes in the Catholic approach to justice and rights. But distributive justice continues to be an especially rich concept. It clearly establishes the norm that society as a whole has the responsibility to provide all people with the means to access a basic good such as health care.

*Catholic Thinking on Human Rights*

Upon hearing the term "human rights," many people immediately think of eighteenth-century documents such as the U.S. Constitution's Bill of Rights or the French Declaration of the Rights of Man.[10] People think about human rights as entailing topics such as freedom of worship, freedom of speech, and freedom of the press. These rights are important, even though they can sometimes be associated with an excess of individualism, such as when someone shouts, "I demand my rights." This criticism does not deny the value of rights as personal liberties, but the criticism does raise the question of whether the personal liberties perspective offers a full enough approach to human rights.[11]

In the nineteenth and early twentieth centuries, Catholic thought sometimes showed a legitimate fear of the individual liberties aspect of human rights because of the concern about excess individualism. In the Vatican II and post–Vatican II period, Catholic thought has become much more open to individual liberties, especially in Pope John XXIII's encyclical *Pacem in Terris* and in Vatican II's Declaration on Religious Liberty.[12] This shift of tone should not obscure the fact that the Catholic concern for the dignity of every human person leads to another, perhaps even deeper element in the Catholic outlook on human rights. This deeper element has to do with a concept of rights not so much as protections from harm but rather as positive enhancements of the human good owed to all people by the larger society. Often one hears the term "entitlements" used to describe this aspect of human rights. The problem with the word *entitlements* is that it may obscure the fact that rights always imply correlative responsibilities. If a society is going to care for all of its citizens, there is a natural expectation, even an obligation, for every person to contribute whatever he or she can so as to foster the wholeness of society. So the concept of entitlement cannot be understood as simply absolving persons from their responsibility to help themselves and their fellow citizens. But once this qualification is understood, there is surely a deep validity to the concept that human rights call upon society not only to protect people, but also to create a climate in which people are able to access foundational human goods such as health care. Some authors have suggested the term "social rights" to describe this broader notion of human rights.[13] The terms "welfare rights" or "economic rights" are also used in this context.

In the introduction to this section, I mentioned Pope Leo XIII's *Rerum Novarum*. The enduring importance of *Rerum Novarum* is the concept of human rights implied by the obligation to pay workers a living wage. Leo XIII was surely aware of the earlier Marxist writing on workers, and he clearly rejected many aspects of Marxism, including its atheism. His concern about Marxism led him to stress certain types of human rights, such as the right to private property. But at the same time Leo XIII definitely embraced a social concept of human rights. Recent popes and Catholic scholars have treated human rights more completely than Leo XIII, but the roots for the social concept of rights can be found in *Rerum Novarum*. The concept of the living wage is a social concept because it involves the broader responsibility of society to create the conditions necessary for the payment of a living wage.

In the first several decades after the emergence of the concept of social rights, health care was only rarely mentioned. The relatively primitive state of health care a century ago is the reason why health care was absent from earlier lists of human rights. But as far back as the 1940s, major political figures such as Franklin Roosevelt and Winston Churchill began to speak of access to health care as a right.[14] The same ideal was included in the UN's Universal Declaration of Human Rights (1948). In 1963, the encyclical *Pacem in Terris* specifically mentioned medical care as a human right.[15] The United States in the 1960s experienced the passage of Medicare and Medicaid legislation. Whatever one thinks about the specific history of these two programs, their passage surely showed a changing consciousness in terms of health care as a social right.

These comments about historical figures such as Franklin Roosevelt and Pope John XXIII are indications that there were some important forbears to today's debate about health care as a human right. But it has taken the events of more recent decades to move the debate about health care as a human right to the forefront of most people's thinking. I refer to current facts such as the skyrocketing cost of health care, the pressure health-care cost places on the U.S. economy as a whole, the enormous complexity of the U.S. health-care system, and, most of all, the 44 million U.S. citizens who lack health care. Matters such as these have brought the debate about health care to the forefront, so that many persons now argue that health-care access is a human right. Not all would agree, and some would prefer to see the debate about health care kept at the level of economic management. But increasingly, people are speaking of access to health care as a human right.[16]

A point of clarification should be added here. There is no such thing as a right to *health*. Part of the human story is that a health-care crisis can strike any person at any time, regardless of age, economic status, or health habits. Efforts to maintain one's health through good health habits are important. Factors like proper nutrition, regular rest, good exercise, and clean air and water may lessen the likelihood of a health crisis. But even a person's best efforts do not remove the possibility of a health crisis, and in the end we all have to encounter the mystery of sickness and death. The right at issue, therefore, is not a right to health, but rather a right of access to a *reasonable standard* of health care. The exact content of this reasonable standard will always be a matter of ongoing debate and assessment. Many factors (the state of medical science and of the economy) of necessity condition the exact content of a reasonable standard of health care. The theologian can insist, as a matter of human rights, that there be a reasonable standard. But only an ongoing debate with a host of responsible figures in the human community can determine exactly what this standard should be at a given time in human history and in a given social location. There must always be a desire to raise the reasonable standard higher and higher, and this is why the debate must be ongoing. But our expectations can only encompass what is truly possible at a given time and place.

*A Commitment to the Common Good*

The theme of the common good is one of the most attractive aspects of Catholic social thought. Catholicism views society as organic, participative, and wholistic. There are too many visions of society that promote an "everyone for himself" outlook, an outlook in which success is understood as being rooted in individual gain, satisfaction, and profit. The classic Catholic concept of the common good argues for a deeper vision of society, a creative participative vision that holds that all people must strive for a level of goodness that is larger than any one individual, and indeed larger than the sum total of the goods of all individuals taken separately. In modern Catholic social teaching, Pope John XXIII offered an especially helpful reflection on the common good in the encyclicals *Mater et Magistra* and *Pacem in Terris.*[17]

To apply the theme of the common good to the context of health care, it can be said that if the legitimate health-care needs of all persons are not met, the whole fabric of society suffers. Without a just health-care system, the very stability of a society can be placed at risk, and the goods that we desire as individuals may become less available to everyone. These reflections only become more stark if we move to a global perspective from which one cannot help but wonder whether the lack of justice in health care might emerge as a threat to world peace. The notion of the common good does not answer all of the specific questions about the best economic model for health-care delivery. But if health care is a common good issue, health care can never be understood as a mere commodity that can be supplied on the basis of any economic theory without consideration of the deeper good of both individuals and society.

The theme of the common good is desperately important as we begin the new millennium in the United States. Our society is marked by a sense of rugged individualism. One of the reasons so many people in our culture have difficulty in accepting the fact of death is that death needs to be faced and accepted by a community of persons who are bonded together. If we think of ourselves only as individuals, there is too much likelihood that we will try to run away from death and become a society that expends exorbitant amounts only to prolong the suffering that goes with death. The book *The Good Society* is one important modern attempt to recover a stronger sense of the common good in the United States.[18]

*Social Justice and Care for the Poor*

In the historical unfolding of Catholic thought, "social justice" is a newer term than the classic terms for justice such as "commutative justice," "legal justice," and "distributive justice."[19] Catholic social thought has always been strongly oriented toward an organic view of society, a view that emphasizes the wholeness of the human community and resonates with the contemporary interest in solidarity. To help stress this organic viewpoint, many Catholic scholars in the late nineteenth and early twentieth centuries began to use the term "social justice," understood as synthesizing all three of these themes (distributive justice, positive human rights, and the common good). Pope Pius XI, in the 1931 encyclical *Quadragesimo Anno,* was the first to draw this concept of social justice into official Catholic teaching.[20] Much contemporary Catholic scholarship adds the themes of dynamic development and historical consciousness to the traditional Catholic emphasis on an organic society. But even with this emphasis on historical dynamism, social justice remains a key element in the Catholic approach to human rights and the common good.

In the context of health care, those scholars who focus on the concept of social justice tend to speak of the obligation to furnish health care as an obligation of social justice. I agree strongly with the value of an integrated notion of social justice. Such a notion helps foster a dynamic vision of an integrated society in which we are all responsible, even co-responsible, for one another. Certainly it makes sense to work out of this framework and speak of the obligation to provide reasonable access to health care as an obligation in social justice. But within the broader concept of social justice, the aspect of social justice that most specifically calls for universal access to health care is distributive justice. Thus I continue to highlight this concept when referring to the obligation to provide universal health care. The broader concept of social justice is necessary to help create the larger worldview that will ensure that the issues of distributive justice do in fact get addressed. But the classic category of distributive justice has its own unique importance when considering the delivery of health care.

Closely allied with the themes of social justice and the common good is the concept of the preferential option for the poor,[21] the idea that we have a strong obligation to provide in a special way for those who cannot speak for themselves. In the context of health care, I think the poor persons for whom we are called to have a special love form a very large category, including not only the economically poor, but also such groups as racial minorities, persons with other languages and cultural backgrounds, chemically addicted persons, and persons dealing with mental health issues such as clinical depression.[22] All of these groups may have significant difficulty in finding suitable access to health care, and our special social responsibility extends to them all.

The theme of special love and care for persons who are poor occurs frequently in the scriptures, for instance in Old Testament references to the *anawim* and in Jesus' concern for the little ones.[23] The tradition of the Jubilee year, with its emphasis on reconciliation and forgiveness, is also suggestive of a special social responsibility to care for the poor and the alienated. Many current Catholic documents and theological writers give stress to the preferential option to love and care for the poor. Often such writers refer to the principle that one of the classic tests of the moral worth of any society is the way in which a society treats its weaker members. The Old Testament theme of God's everlasting faithfulness to all people also comes to mind in this context. How can we respect the dignity of all persons unless we are committed to caring for all of God's little ones?

*Additional Elements in the Catholic Theory of Justice*

The reflections on distributive justice, human rights, the common good, and social justice have summarized the major themes in Catholic thinking that apply to the issue of an obligation in justice to provide universal access to health care. But I also want to comment on two follow-up matters. *First,* the theme of distributive justice is often discussed in tandem with the notion of legal justice. If society has the obligation to provide certain basic goods to all people, the citizenry has a legitimate obligation to provide society with the resources it needs to meet its distributive justice obligations. This obligation of the citizenry toward society is called "legal justice." To say it more simply, legal justice means that at the level of principle, taxes are acceptable and people are expected to pay them. This general principle of legal justice does not mean that every specific tax policy is just, nor does it mean that public funding and public systems are the only possible means to accomplish a just distribution of access to health care. The question of public versus private approaches to distributing health care is a matter of economic theory, and we will need to consider the Catholic approach to economic theory. What legal justice does mean is that taxes to help foster the common good are in principle acceptable. Because of the high individualism in U.S. culture, there is a level of popular rhetoric that claims that all taxation is evil. No one with any real sense of social responsibility can seriously hold this position. But the anti-tax attitude is bandied about a lot, and there is a need to keep an open mind as we take up the question of the ways in which tax policy might relate to health-care justice.

The *second* follow-up matter is the question of whether or not health-care rationing could ever be just. By using the term "rationing," I am not referring to efforts to make health-care delivery more efficient. Nor am I referring to decisions to withhold nonbeneficial treatments from patients, for example, a decision to withhold CPR from a patient in a terminal condition. What I mean by *rationing* is withholding a truly beneficial treatment from someone. Can such a course of action ever be just? Obviously great care and caution would need to be present in any rationing decision; rationing could never take place except as a last resort, after all other alternatives have been tried. But can we rule out health-care rationing completely? In the end, I believe that we will have to admit that there are some legitimate examples of such rationing.[24] Probably the classic case has to do with the first team to arrive on the scene of a disaster such as a fire or an earthquake. This team will encounter some patients who are in substantial pain, patients who have broken limbs, and so on. But these patients are not dying even though they are in need medically, and even though the first team has at hand the means to help them. The problem is that, besides these patients, the first team also notices other patients whose injuries are such that the patients will die unless they receive immediate treatment. Since the first team does not have enough resources to care for everyone at the disaster site, its clear task is to care for those whose lives are at stake, even though this means that other patients who truly need medical care will have to wait until more medical help arrives. Without doubt what the first team is doing is rationing its resources so as to use them where they will do the most good.

No one will contest this example of rationing health-care resources. But can the example be transferred to larger contexts? For instance, can we justify cutting down on the money we spend to develop neonatal intensive care units for critically ill babies so that we can have more money to provide basic prenatal and postnatal care to the many mothers who do not have this basic care? In the context of the United States, this question becomes especially troubling if we review statistics that suggest that countries who do emphasize basic prenatal and postnatal care for all mothers frequently see more children make it through the first year of life than do countries such as the United States that have a high neonatal intensive focus but weaker programs of prenatal and postnatal care.[25] These considerations do not rule out the development of neonatal intensive medicine. But there is a question about how many health-care resources should be devoted to high-tech neonatal medicine and how many resources should be devoted to more basic practices. This is a question about rationing.

The discussion about rationing becomes even harder if we focus on the enormous disparity between the standard of care in the world's poorest countries and the standard in some of the richer, more developed countries. How can we not speak of an obligation to improve the health-care standards in these poorest countries, even if it means that there are fewer resources available in the richer countries? Especially when we think about high-end medical technologies that have not yet been developed in the rich countries, there may be a case for setting prudent limits on the development of such technologies in light of the need to do more for the poorer countries. But even complicated technologies that already exist (organ transplants?) may need to be limited if a society or the world at large is unable to meet its more basic health needs.

Great caution is needed when discussing rationing. It helps to recall the foundational Catholic insight that death is a part of the human story, and that our responsibility is to take reasonable steps to prevent death, but that we need not take steps which, all things considered, are not proportionate to the needs of the patient. Can this insight be broadened so that the proportionality to be considered includes the common good of the entire community? In general, the most complete notion of proportionality in health care ought to include the theme of the common good, and some decisions for health-care rationing may be made so as to act in favor of the common good. I have had many experiences of sitting with very sensitive health-care executives as they ponder which services they should try to offer in their communities. The clear implication of these conversations is that some other worthy services may not be offered because the provider does not have the resources to do everything. Perhaps no other provider in the area has the resources either, a situation that may be quite likely in smaller cities and rural areas. I see the executives to whom I refer as being very much value-driven. But it is hard to escape the conclusion that they are making rationing decisions.

In the end, the real question may not be the question of health-care rationing *per se;* the real question may be which approaches to rationing are justifiable and which are not. It is often said that the United States, with its 44 million uninsured citizens, has one of the most highly rationed health-care systems in the world.[26] Almost no other developed country in the world has such a high percentage of persons who lack basic access to health care. The current U.S. system is surely not just, but this does not mean that all rationing methods will be proven to be unjust.

## CATHOLIC SOCIAL TEACHING, ECONOMIC THEORY, AND HEALTH-CARE JUSTICE

The preceding reflections show that there is a clear basis in Catholic thought for construing access to a reasonable standard of health care as an obligation of justice. But how should this right be fulfilled? This is an enormously difficult question, and no one would claim that a religious tradition such as Catholicism could answer such a question all by itself. John Courtney Murray pointed out that complex social issues have about them an aspect of practical feasibility, that is, a level that religious and theological insight is not fully competent to address.[27] This practical feasibility factor helps explain why Catholic thought has always recognized a legitimate autonomy to political and economic questions and to the professional persons who work in politics, economics, science, medicine, and other related fields.

These cautions about autonomy, professional responsibility, and practical feasibility should not obscure the fact that a religious tradition such as Catholicism might be able to offer some very important observations at the level of principle about the complex economic and political questions involved in providing just access to health care. Herein three areas of principled economic observations will be offered on the basis of Catholic teaching. *First,* is either capitalism or socialism to be preferred as the better economic system for providing access to health care? *Second,* what level of government intervention is to be desired or not desired as a means to providing health care? *Third,* can health care be provided equally justly by not-for-profit and for-profit entities, or is one of these types of entities to be preferred?

*Capitalism versus Socialism as a Means of Health-Care Delivery*

One of the most striking aspects of Catholic social thought since the end of the nineteenth century is the way in which Catholicism has consistently refused to endorse any one economic system as the preferred system from the viewpoint of Catholicism. It is true that Pope Leo XIII laid particular emphasis on the right to private property,[28] but in the context of history, it is clear that he was preoccupied with the rise of Marxist socialism and its denial of any right to private property. Other popes began to nuance Leo's position by pointing out that public ownership of some goods and services may be better for people. For example, in his 1931 encyclical *Quadragesimo Anno,* Pope Pius XI argued that property has a social dimension. He also began to make cautious distinctions between Communism and more moderate forms of socialism.[29] In the early 1960s, Pope John XXIII, writing in *Mater et Magistra,* introduced the famous concept of socialization as a way to argue that in an increasingly complex world, social ownership and management of some human services may be a growing necessity.[30]

Pope John Paul II has been especially evenhanded in his treatment of both capitalism and socialism, sometimes subjecting both to equal criticism in the same text. John Paul's balanced approach to capitalism and socialism is particularly noteworthy because of his having spent so many years living under a Marxist socialist economy. It is clear that his concerns about Marxism have not stopped him from sometimes being sharply critical of capitalism, for instance on the issue of international debt, which is a theme of growing significance as we celebrate the new millennium and recall the Jubilee tradition of forgiveness of debt. (John Paul's openness to and criticism of both capitalism and Marxism predates his election to the papacy. Some readers may recall the television interview that John Paul, as Cardinal Wojtyla, gave to the novelist James Michener a few months before he was elected pope. Much that John Paul would later write about economic systems was foreshadowed in that interview.)

In terms of John Paul II's social encyclicals as Holy Father, it is interesting to note that some of these encyclicals, such as *Sollicitudo Rei Socialis,* have about them what might be called a "north-south" focus, whereas others of them, such as *Centesimus Annus,* have an "east-west" focus.[31] John Paul II's north-south texts are often quite critical of capitalism, because of the ways in which the developed capitalist countries, which are frequently in the Northern Hemisphere, can mistreat poorer countries, which are frequently in the Southern Hemisphere. The mistreatment involves issues such as the arms race, international debt, and the tendency of foreign aid programs to prop up repressive and corrupt regimes that do little other than perpetuate the cycle of poverty. On the other hand, the pope's east-west texts are more likely to allude to problems that can be found in socialist countries, problems such as the lack of personal initiative and the tendency toward unproductive economies. John Paul's role as a religious leader calls him to raise critical issues, so it is understandable that many of his comments about both capitalism and socialism are critical comments. But his criticism—and his appreciation—of capitalism and socialism is evenhanded. In papal teaching, there is no one economic system that is the preferred economic system in all respects.

The judgment that the Roman Catholic tradition is evenhanded on economic systems is heightened by studying twentieth-century Catholicism in the United States. Ever since the publication of the famous *Bishops' Program for Social Reconstruction* in 1919,[32] the Catholic Church in the United States has opted for a mixed economic theory that is often described as "social liberalism." Social liberalism is not interested in removing the basic capitalist character of the U.S. economy. But social liberalism is clear that unrestrained capitalism will often treat some people unjustly. Therefore the excesses of capitalism need to be moderated by an ongoing series of socially oriented initiatives, initiatives in which public policy removes certain key issues from private capitalist control and places the management of these issues in public hands. The Social Security system, which virtually no politician in the United States would dare to attack, is perhaps the classic example of the socially liberal policies that the Catholic bishops in the United States supported earlier in the twentieth century.

In our own times there is a clear continuation and even a revival of the tradition of Catholic social liberalism in the United States. The Catholic bishops in the United States are correctly described as conservative on doctrinal issues and personal moral issues. But on issues of social justice, the bishops regularly stand up for the poor and disenfranchised. In 1986, the bishops issued their famous pastoral letter *Economic Justice for All*.[33] The letter stands in marked continuity with the 1919 Bishops' Program and with so much of the mixed economic theory that the bishops stood for in the middle of the twentieth century. But the bishops' commitment to a mixed economic policy and to socially liberal initiatives is not limited to an occasional major statement such as the 1986 pastoral letter. At both the state and national levels, bishops' conferences regularly advocate socially progressive legislation. This hardly means that Catholic bishops are calling for an abandonment of capitalism. Instead the bishops—like Pope John Paul II—recognize both the strengths and weaknesses of capitalism. They are not wedded to any one economic answer to complex social problems. If a private capitalist approach can adequately address a given demand of justice, fine. But if on some issues the demands of true justice can only be met through a government-sponsored program, this is also fine.

But what about Catholic economic theory and the specific question of health-care justice? The openness of Catholic economic theory to a variety of economic systems suggests that there is no one "Catholic" way to justly supply the good of health care. Certainly if a privately managed and funded health-care delivery system, such as a managed-care system, were able to offer a truly just approach to health care, including a reasonable approximation of universal access to health care, such a private system might be said to be a good system. Certainly also, if a publicly owned or at least publicly funded system were able to offer a reasonable approximation of universal access, that system too might possibly be said to be a just system of health-care delivery. I use the term "reasonable approximation" because no system will be able to be completely successful in achieving the goal of universal access. Note also that the issue of universal access is not the only theme to be considered in determining whether a health-care system is just. Issues such as the system's respect for the dignity and freedom of its patients, its respect for the professionalism of its doctors, its treatment of health-care employees, and its attitude toward death and dying also need to be considered. In the end, neither a purely capitalist nor a purely socialist approach to health-care delivery may prove to be the most just approach. Instead, the most just approach may include both private enterprises and publicly owned programs working together to produce a just system of health care. Health-care delivery in the United States already includes a mix of public and private elements, including government programs such as Medicare and Medicaid and private entities such as managed-care companies and traditional fee-for-service insurance plans. In years past, some writers looked at fee-for-service plans as sacrosanct,[34] but if we take a flexible view of health-care economics, fee-for-service is not the only possible option.

I hope that these reflections have shown that the basic Catholic approach to health-care economics is open-minded, flexible, and pragmatic. From the Catholic perspective, the point is not to prejudge any health-care system on the basis of its economic theory. The point rather is to see how well any health-care system meets the goal of true justice and the other values such as respect for human dignity and sensitive acceptance of the meaning of death and dying. In today's context, this means that there is no one Catholic answer to managed care as a system of health-care delivery. Instead the Catholic tradition approaches the burgeoning growth of managed care with a question: Can managed care, as it now exists or may come to exist in our day and age, emerge as a sufficiently just approach to health-care delivery? We will study this question in much more detail, but from the viewpoint of fundamental Catholic economic theory, it is an open question that needs to be tried before the jury of public opinion and assessment.

*Subsidiarity and Socialization*

Besides these general reflections on capitalist and socialist economic systems, is there anything more specific in the tradition of Catholic social thought that may be of help in assessing the pros and cons of possible approaches to a more just health-care system? One theme that deserves mention is the famous distinction between the *principle of subsidiarity* and the *principle of socialization.* The principle of subsidiarity first became prominent in Catholic thought with the 1931 encyclical *Quadragesimo Anno,* written by Pope Pius XI.[35] The central point of the principle of subsidiarity is that whenever a social reform can be justly accomplished by a smaller, simpler agency, this is what should happen. If a state or local government can achieve justice without federal intervention, this is what should happen. If private initiative can accomplish true justice without any government involvement at all, this would be even better. And among private approaches to reform, the simplest approach that can achieve true justice is preferred. Indeed, the very nature of justice calls for less government intervention when less intervention is possible.

In the context of health-care justice, the principle of subsidiarity might be said to suggest that the ideal would be a private physician seeing and billing individual patients and sending them to small, locally owned hospitals. While this ideal may be too much to expect in our complicated times, the principle of subsidiarity would surely suggest that a private, managed-care approach to health-care delivery deserves a serious, fair, and open-minded assessment from the viewpoint of the Roman Catholic social tradition. If such an approach can meet the demands of justice, it would in principle be attractive to the Catholic viewpoint because it would seem to be a simpler approach when compared to a government-owned or -funded health-care system. By avoiding government involvement when such involvement is not needed, such an approach would help reduce any trend toward unjust or even tyrannical forms of government.

The principle of subsidiarity needs to be seen in its correlative relationship with the principle of socialization, which was made famous by Pope John XXIII in his 1961 encyclical *Mater et Magistra.*[36] In introducing the concept of socialization, John XXIII had no interest in denying the principle of subsidiarity. For John XXIII and for Catholic thought as a whole, the burden of proof must still be to show that more socialization and more government interventions are necessary. But John XXIII did want to make this point: By the 1960s the world was becoming vastly more complicated due to scientific advances in fields such as transportation, communication, and medicine, and due to the increasing trend toward a global economic order. Due to this growth in complexity, it was becoming increasingly likely that more subsidiary solutions would not be able to resolve many of the world's more difficult social problems. Instead, for the achievement of justice, it would more frequently be necessary for government—sometimes even higher levels of government—to become involved as an agent and advocate of social justice. It was this growing need for government agency and advocacy that led to John XXIII's concept of socialization.

Not all Catholics were happy with John XXIII's concept. The dissent of William F. Buckley, Jr. *(mater si, magistra no),* is memorable to this day.[37] But recall that John XXIII was not saying that solutions embodying socialization would always be necessary; nor was he saying which specific issues might be best handled through a move toward socialization. All he was saying was that the need for socialization was in principle more likely in his times. His comment applies to our times as well.

In the context of health care, the principle of socialization calls on us to ask questions such as these: In a complex time such as ours, with 44 million citizens lacking health insurance, can a privately financed and operated system such as managed care really bring about justice in the delivery of health care? Can a private realignment of health-care services be an adequate means to social justice in the delivery of health care? Can the decrease of government support for health care, as reflected in the Balanced Budget Act, be seen as an acceptable step toward a more just health-care system? The principle of socialization does not give us simple answers to these questions. But the principles of socialization and subsidiarity clearly insist that we be willing to ask these sorts of questions.

The great beauty of the principles of subsidiarity and socialization is the way in which the two principles work in tandem. It is hard to see how we can look at any complex social question without invoking both principles. Social ethical questions have about them a very high degree of intractability. There are no simple answers. It would be wrong to prejudge any program, private or public, that sets out to deliver health care. But in the end we do need to make a judgment about health-care programs, and by seeing the principles of subsidiarity and socialization as a unified whole, I believe that the right questions can at least be brought to the surface.

*For-Profit vis-à-vis Not-for-Profit Health Care*

One more question arises in the discussion of Catholic economic theory and health-care justice. From the viewpoint of Catholic teaching, is there any preference to be given to either for-profit or not-for-profit methods of delivering health care? Certainly there is much less specific content in Catholic thought about this subject than there is about the comparison of capitalism and socialism or about the relationship of subsidiarity and socialization. Catholic thought could not give an unequivocal answer as to whether the earning of a profit is always justifiable or unjustifiable in the delivery of health care. Health-care delivery occurs in many different contexts. These multiple contexts make it impossible for anyone to offer an unequivocal answer about profits in health care. For instance, some small profit-making entities (such as a small physicians' group that works on a fee-for-service basis) are surely justifiable, even if there is substantial doubt about whether some of the other, much larger profit-making entities can be justifiable.

The difficulty in offering a global reflection on health care and profit-making only increases when we consider that, in actual operation, for-profit and not-for-profit health-care ventures are often very much alike. In both for-profit and not-for-profit health-care entities, there is a strong concern about prudent fiscal management. In both, the financial bottom line is always an important issue. Even not-for-profit entities with a strong commitment to care for the poor need to keep reminding themselves that without a profit margin, they may not accomplish their mission of caring for the poor. But this does not mean that there is a complete lack of difference between for-profit and not-for-profit approaches to health care. There is the key fact that for-profit health corporations must be concerned about paying dividends to their stockholders. But there are strong similarities between the for-profits and the not-for profits that complicate the process of ethical reflection.

An analysis of current ethical literature on the for-profit versus not-for-profit approaches to health care shows a fair degree of ambivalence. Some authors, relying on the similarities between for-profit and not-for-profit approaches, argue that there is little or no moral difference between these two approaches.[38] These authors tend to point to factors that argue in favor of an ethical tone in for-profit health care, factors such as the enhancement of individual initiative, a focus on quality, and fiscal efficiency to reduce the cost of health care. But other authors[39] argue that the for-profit motive is always a severe compromise in terms of the mission of health care to care for the poor, a compromise that is very likely to continue the current context in which so many persons lack access to health care. Only very rarely do not-for-profit health providers enter major new ventures with large for-profit health-care providers. At least implicitly, the reluctance of not-for-profit providers to partner with for-profit entities suggests significant cultural and moral differences between the two approaches, as well as major differences in purpose and accountability.[40]

But how to put all of this together from the viewpoint of Roman Catholic moral theology? *First,* even granting that Catholic hospitals themselves should always be not-for-profit entities, there is no clear-cut answer to the question of whether not-for-profit health care is always better than for-profit health care. Each individual case needs to be evaluated on its own merits in terms of how well a given health-care provider meets the demand for health-care justice. *Second,* in view of the strong Catholic commitment to a preferential option to care for the poor, there would seem to be a Catholic presumption in favor of not-for-profit approaches to health care.[41] The long and honorable history of the Catholic Church as a not-for-profit provider of health care is a key element in the background of this presumption. This presumption does not rule out the possibility of for-profit health-care entities. It does, however, place the burden of proof on for-profit health-care providers. The burden is to show that the for-profits are in fact contributing to the achievement of true justice in the delivery of health care rather than serving to perpetuate the very troubled health-care system that exists in the United States today.

## CATHOLIC TEACHING AND THE JUST TREATMENT OF HEALTH-CARE EMPLOYEES

No presentation of the Catholic principles of health-care justice would be complete if it did not reflect on the Catholic commitment to the just treatment of employees. In the United States there are millions of persons employed in health care. In these days of the Balanced Budget Act, when billions of dollars of public funding are being withdrawn from health care each year, health-care providers can be sorely tempted to make ends meet through strategies such as the reduction or elimination of cost-of-living increases for employees. But how can a health-care system be just if it does not treat its employees justly? And how could Catholic thought, with its historic commitment to working people, not see justice to employees as an essential component of just health care?

To summarize Catholic thinking on justice for health-care employees, five issues will be reviewed: (1) the right of working people to just earnings and benefits, (2) the right of working people to a genuine experience of participation in their work and to ongoing development of their abilities, (3) the responsibility of working people to share in the mission of their work, particularly in the special mission of health care, (4) the right to non-discrimination, and (5) the right to unionize.

*Just Earnings and Benefits*

The main beginning point of modern Catholic social teaching in the 1890s was the idea that working people had a right to be paid a living wage, that is, an earning level that enabled them to live in a reasonable and frugal comfort.[42] Certainly, those who work in health care deserve to earn enough to live in the reasonable comfort and security envisioned by Catholic teaching. Any pressure to respond to the financial burdens of health care today by underpaying health-care employees must be strictly resisted. Especially when we consider that health-care executives earn very large incomes, the injustice of underpaying employees becomes very clear. The minimum wage provided for in U.S. legislation does not deserve to be considered a living wage. At current price levels, how can anyone be expected to live in reasonable and frugal comfort (with adequate food, clothing, shelter, and health care) for only about $10,000 per year?

Three issues can be raised in order to fill out the context of the right of health-care employees to a just wage. *First,* the exact specifics of what constitutes a living wage may vary in different economic times and settings. To show how much the level of a just wage can shift in changing economic times, we need only recall that some of the first serious scholarship on the living wage proposed that in the early 1900s a family in the United States needed to earn $600 annually in order to be said to have a living income.[43] While no one would dream of this figure today, economic factors influencing the cost of living can change rapidly, meaning that health-care leaders need to maintain an ongoing vigilance to be sure that they are paying just wages.

*Second,* just benefits are an intrinsic part of the concept of a living wage. The major elements in a just benefits package are retirement security and health-care coverage. On the topic of health-care benefits, there is a special obligation on health-care providers to construct truly just packages of health-care benefits for health-care employees. I am not implying that every conceivable service need be offered (for example, merely cosmetic plastic surgeries). But the package of benefits must be just, based on criteria that both employers and employees can accept. If a health-care provider offers a great many extra health benefits to its higher level employees, or if the higher level employees who can afford it very frequently seek treatments beyond the basic package, there may be significant questions about the justice of the basic package of health-care benefits. Also, there is a need for special care in the administering of health-care benefits for health-care employees. Health-care employees are likely to seek care from the health-care provider for whom they work. Hence there are important obligations to make sure that the confidentiality of employee-patients is properly protected and to make sure that employees with complicated health issues suffer no prejudice in the workplace because of their illness. There are also special considerations needed on the theme of employee health and the safe treatment of patients.

*Third*, in the earlier history of just wage theory, there was often a tendency to focus on the need to pay a just wage to heads of families, who were usually men.[44] Perhaps this approach was understandable in a former time, when relatively few women, especially married women, worked outside the home, and when it seemed a reasonable social objective to ensure that each family had enough income to live comfortably. But this earlier approach had the undeniable side effect that persons—very often women—who were not heads of households frequently earned significantly less than heads of households. Partly due to the two world wars of the twentieth century, the world is very different today, and in many cases it is an economic necessity for married women to work. There has been some progress in recent decades in moving to pay all employees—including women—equally and justly when they perform tasks of equal worth to those performed by men. But the issue has not gone away completely, and women remain statistically likely to be paid less than men for work of equal value. These considerations are especially important in a field like health care, which employs many women. Wages cannot be just unless they are gender just.

*Genuine Participation and Ongoing Development of Employees*

For many people, Catholic thought on employees is almost synonymous with the idea of just compensation. But Catholic thought on employees goes far beyond the topic of financial compensation. The employee is far more than a mere commodity whose function is to get some specific task accomplished. The employee is a human person with all the rights and dignity inherent in human personhood. For this reason, Catholic thought understands human work as a noble action. When a human person works, she or he adds an element of transcendence to the task, an element that cannot be described in quantifiable terms. As a specifically human activity, work is endowed with a human dignity and worth that goes far beyond economic or utilitarian values. The human working person must therefore be honored and respected in the workplace. What she or he thinks about the work should be attended to carefully by employers, and if employee suggestions about the work or the workplace are feasible, they should be implemented.

A term that helps express all this is "participation." Employees ought to have a genuine sense of participation in their work.[45] With a genuine sense of participation, the employee will feel heard, honored, and respected in the workplace, even if the work itself is difficult and demanding, as is often the case with work in health care. In September 1999, the Domestic Policy Committee of the United States Catholic Conference issued an important statement on justice for workers in Catholic health care. Participation emerged as a very important theme in that statement.[46]

It would be wrong to understate the classic Catholic commitment to just wages and benefits. Still, there are ways in which genuine participation in one's work may be even more important than wages and benefits. People need to be paid enough money. But we should ask why employees become especially loyal to their work, or why it is that sometimes employees stay with the same work situation for many years, even in the face of other, perhaps financially more attractive options. This kind of loyalty is generated more through participation than through financial incentives. And this kind of loyalty can be pricelessly important in a field such as health care.

A climate of true participation ought to include opportunities for both human and professional development. If there is true participation, there will be natural opportunities for the building of meaningful human relationships and for the ongoing human development of both employers and employees. Some critics argue that many people today have almost too much of their human development based in the workplace. This happens because the pace of modern life can restrict time for the building up of family relationships. Family life should retain its traditional importance. But this does not take away the importance of human development in the workplace. Development in the workplace needs to include the creation of opportunities for employees to move ahead in their work. Opportunities to learn new skills and take on new responsibilities are highly important, both humanly and professionally. People in the workplace will not all possess the same potential for professional growth and career advancement. But a climate of opportunity needs to be present, especially for employees at lower levels.

### The Mission Responsibility of Health-Care Workers

One of the main cautions in Catholic thinking about human rights is that rights can never be an occasion for an attitude of "I demand my rights," with its implication that no one else's rights matter. Instead the Catholic vision is that rights always involve correlative responsibilities. In the context of employment, the correlative responsibility is that employees are to do the work for which they are employed to the best of their ability. Without this commitment and effort on the part of the employees, work loses its nobility and human meaning. The responsibility of employers to furnish compensation, participation, and development becomes empty and meaningless.

These comments about the responsibility of employees have their force in any employment situation. But the notion of employee responsibility takes on a unique dimension in the health-care context. Shortly we will discuss the point that dying stands as perhaps the most basic existential challenge of human living and that therefore one of the most basic of all human responsibilities is the responsibility we humans have to stand by one another as we confront serious illness and the journey toward death. While every human person shares in this responsibility, those who work in health care share in it in a very special way. This is true not only for nurses and doctors but also for those whose work in health care requires lesser training or is removed from the locus of the patient, for example, persons who clean rooms, wash linens, fix meals, or work as accountants or computer programmers. Even these health-care workers have a special connection with the human mystery involved in serious illness and dying.

In this context, everyone who works in health care is called upon to have a special sense of *mission,* of commitment to stand by the sick and the dying, so as to make the experience of serious illness and dying as human an experience as possible. The environment of the health-care workplace should be palpably different because of this sense of mission. While many themes can be stipulated as part of this sense of mission, it might help to highlight the quality of presence that health-care workers are called to have to patients and families and to one another. In the end, health care is about caring, and gestures such as a welcoming presence and a genuine compassion and respect for all, especially the sick, serve to put flesh and blood on the mission of caring. Yes, employers are to treat health-care workers well, but the workers in their turn have a clear mission responsibility.

The issue of mission is a two-way street. Because a sense of mission is pivotally important for the successful provision of health-care services, I have argued that employees in health care are obligated to develop a sense of mission. But also because of the importance of mission, employers have an added responsibility to meet all the demands of employee justice (compensation, participation, and so on). If the employers fail to meet these needs, how will employees be able to develop a sense of mission, and how in the end will health care be able to be truly successful in reaching out to patients and families?

*Health-Care Workers and Non-Discrimination*

For the student of Catholic social teaching, Vatican II's *Pastoral Constitution on the Church in the Modern World (Gaudium et Spes)* contains many important highlights. One of these highlights is No. 29's forceful assertion that discrimination in any form—whether on the basis of sex, race, color, social condition, language, or religion—is to be rejected as contrary to the will of God.[47] To help buttress *Gaudium et Spes*'s position, many authors quote Galatians 3:28: "There is neither Jew nor Greek, there is neither slave nor free person, there is not male and female; for you are all one in Christ Jesus."[48] Vatican II's words against discrimination were written in the mid-1960s, against the backdrop of worldwide concern about racial justice. But the words remain remarkable today. What seems especially refreshing and inspired about the words is that they are not limited to any one form of discrimination. Instead the words reject *all* discrimination.

In the context of health care, the obligation to avoid discrimination touches all the usual issues. There should be no discrimination based on race, gender, or other circumstances in hiring, pay scales, health and retirement benefits, promotion, recognition, opportunities for additional learning, termination, and support for those who are being terminated. Health-care providers are expected to put into place personnel systems that protect the rights of all employees (and also all patients) on any matters related to discrimination. It should also be added that, because of health care's special focus on human frailty and human illness, health-care providers have a unique obligation not to discriminate against employees because of developmental disabilities or problems of physical or mental health. I am not implying that health-care employers are obligated to retain employees who simply cannot do their work. But frequently the employees I have just mentioned can do their work, perhaps with some adjustments. Or they can be shifted to some other tasks that they are able to manage.

In raising these issues about discrimination, I want to note that I have personally seen many strong anti-discriminatory stances taken by hospitals and other health providers. In these complicated times for health care, it is not unusual for a health provider to need to reduce its work force. I have seen such work force reductions accomplished with a great deal of care for those involved, and with a real effort to help those who lose their jobs prepare for and find meaningful work elsewhere. I have also seen health-care providers implement highly effective policies for the hiring of special people. But discrimination can have a pernicious way of creeping in if we fail to be vigilant. The challenge for health care is to maintain a constant watchfulness, so that the richness of the mission of health care is not tainted by any discrimination.

### The Right of Health-Care Employees to Join Labor Unions

Both the *Ethical and Religious Directives for Catholic Health Care Services (ERD)* and the United States Catholic Conference's September 1999 statement are clear in their insistence on the right of health-care workers to form and join unions. The *ERD* in No. 7 affirms "the rights of employees to organize and bargain collectively without prejudice to the common good."[49] The September 1999 statement, entitled *A Fair and Just Workplace: Principles and Practices for Catholic Health Care,* says that "workers have the right to organize themselves for collective bargaining and to be recognized by management for such purposes."[50] The directness of these two statements leaves no doubt about the Catholic openness toward unions as a matter of basic principle. But these two statements do not answer all of the practical follow-up questions about whether a union is appropriate in a given situation or whether, and under what conditions, strikes might be justifiable in the health-care context.

Some historical background may help explain the nature and depth of the Catholic commitment to unions, especially in the United States. In the late nineteenth century, the combination of *laissez-faire* economics and the Industrial Revolution left many workers, both in Europe and in the United States, in a very difficult position. In response, workers in a number of places sought to form labor unions as a means of improving their lot. The original attitude of the Vatican was to oppose labor unions, which were understood, in the context of the growth of Marxism, as secret societies with an anti-religious, even atheistic outlook. Some of the early union leaders in the United States were Catholics who were concerned about the situation of coal miners in states such as Pennsylvania. Cardinal James Gibbons of Baltimore had the opportunity to meet with these early Catholic union leaders, especially with leaders of the union known as the Knights of Labor. Cardinal Gibbons became convinced of the justice of the Knights' cause, and the rest is history.

In the 1880s, Gibbons made his famous trip to the Vatican during which he succeeded in getting the Vatican to drop its opposition to unions.[51] The results of Gibbons's trip were very significant both for working Catholics in the United States and for the Catholic Church in the United States. Many of the millions of Catholics then migrating to the United States became part of union families, and their earnings helped send their sons and daughters to college. Catholics became an upwardly mobile group in the United States. This upward movement was due in part to the success of the labor movement. By the mid- and late twentieth century, Catholics were able to assume many prominent positions in the social, economic, and political structures of U.S. society.

If the results of the Catholic commitment to unions were notable for Catholics in the workplace, the results were also very significant for the church itself. In Europe, after the Industrial Revolution, vast numbers of Catholics stopped practicing their faith, and they have never really returned to the practice of the faith. But working Catholics in the United States did not leave the church in great numbers. They stayed, and became the basis for the church's twentieth-century expansion that saw the establishment and/or development of many parishes, schools, hospitals, and colleges and universities. Commitment to unions became part and parcel of the Catholic tradition of social liberalism that I described earlier. Indeed, virtually every stage of the Catholic tradition of social liberalism included support for trade unions. For someone who understands this tradition, there can be no surprise that the *Ethical and Religious Directives* say what they say about unions.

But what does Catholicism's strong historical support for unions have to say about health-care providers and the unions of today? While the church's support for unions at the level of principle is unquestionable, what about unions in practice? Surely it is wrong for any health-care provider to reject unions as a matter of principle. A health-care employer cannot simply forbid employees to form or join unions. Nor should an employer create a climate of undue duress around the union question. Similarly, a health-care employer could not be said to be acting with justice if the employer refuses to bargain in good faith with legitimately recognized unions.

But are unions always the best answer from the viewpoint of the employee? Not necessarily, especially in our times, which have seen changes in labor legislation as well as other factors that are quite different from the original context in which Cardinal Gibbons elicited Catholic support for unions. The real bottom line for employees is that the employer meet all the issues of justice that have been outlined in the past few sections: compensation, participation, development, and non-discrimination. If a given health-care employer is truly just in addressing all of these issues, so that the employees do not experience a need to unionize, all well and good. If the issues of employee justice are not met, the case for unionization becomes all the more compelling.

Geography is a large factor in assessing how necessary unions are as agents of justice for health-care employees. In some locales, unions have played a strong historical role in health care, and they will surely continue to do so. In other geographical areas, there may be a stronger custom of health-care employers and employees working out true employee justice with lesser or even no union involvement. Because of these geographical factors, it is wrong for large national health-care systems to agree to national union contracts for all their employees in a given field. Instead, these systems should work out suitable approaches to the union question that are tailored to the diverse local areas in which these national systems are present. What seems crucial is that in all geographical areas health-care providers maintain an attitude of genuinely open dialogue on the union question. I understand this commitment to true dialogue to be a key element in the *Fair and Just Workplace* statement. If the dialogue is present, and if the result is true employee justice, the objectives of the church's principled stance on unions will be met in the health-care context, regardless of the specific decisions made about unions in the many various and diverse health-care settings.

## DOCTORS, NURSES, AND HEALTH CARE AS A PROFESSION

In addition to the comments on health-care employees in general, there is a need to focus on the specific question of health-care professionals. This focus must address the responsibilities of these professionals to their patients and to the health-care systems in which they serve. This focus must also address the legitimate expectations of professionals, expectations of the systems in which they serve, and expectations of the patients and families for whom they care. Many critics feel that the role of the professional is under severe threat in today's health-care context, so it is important to review the traditional thinking about professionals in both Catholic and related sources.

When we use the term "professionals" in the health-care context, we most often think about doctors. While doctors surely are professionals, modern health care embraces many other professionals as well. Nurses, physical therapists, social workers, pastoral counselors, health-care administrators, and several other groups can be legitimately described as health-care professionals. Here there will be a special emphasis on the doctor as a professional, because of the unique character of the doctor-patient relationship. But this emphasis should not obscure the clear professional role of others who are involved in the provision of health-care services.

There is an intersection but not a complete overlap between health-care employees and health-care professionals. Some health-care professionals are employees, and some are self-employed. Historically, a great many doctors owned their own medical practices and were given privileges to practice medicine at one or several hospitals. While this still happens in some cases, large numbers of physicians today work for medical practices that are owned by hospitals or by managed-care organizations. So today's physicians are often employees instead of being self-employed. But whether they are employees or independent, the standards of professionalism apply to all physicians, as well as to other health-care professionals.

Several themes in classic Catholic social and moral teaching help shape the concept of the professional person, whether in medicine or in other fields such as law, public service, science, or engineering. The very word *professional* has important roots in medieval Catholic thought. The theme of professional confidentiality has roots in the ancient world, for instance in the oath of Hippocrates. A basic theme in traditional Catholic thought is the idea that the secular realm is autonomous in its own sphere.[52] The implication of this notion of autonomy is clear: even though the church expects that Catholics who are professionals will be committed to Catholic teaching and values, the church recognizes that the professional has a legitimate autonomy. He or she has a specific and proper knowledge that is best challenged on the basis of a competent professional assessment of the issues which are at stake. Religious authorities should maintain a stance of respect for the place of professional competence.

Closely related to this theme of autonomy is the Catholic position that qualified[53] lay persons, clearly including professionals, possess a lawful freedom to inquire into the specific areas in which they are competent.[54] Such a freedom to inquire surely implies a place for legitimate professional judgment. The new *Code of Canon Law* reasserts these traditional themes about the secular order and about those who exercise secular professions. The new code also makes the notable statement that lay persons who are qualified are expected to make their views known, not only to church leaders, but also to others who need to hear what the qualified person has to say.[55]

These Catholic themes rather clearly set forth a foundation for a theology of the professions. Other traditional sources can be conjoined to these themes so as to articulate a more developed concept of the professions. In the context of medicine, probably the most important ancient source is the oath of Hippocrates, with its insistence that the doctor never harm the patient, that the doctor always act for the patient's benefit, and that the doctor always maintain confidentiality about anything he or she learns while caring for the patient.[56] It is no surprise that from very early days, Christianity, with its incipient concept of professionalism, felt a strong compatibility with the Hippocratic oath. Almost at the beginning of the Christian era, there were Christianized versions of the Hippocratic oath in which the oath was taken in the name of the Father, Son, and Holy Spirit instead of in the names of the Greek gods.[57]

In today's health-care context, three key questions concerning the role of the doctor as a health-care professional come to the surface. *First,* what about the legitimate autonomy of the doctor as a professional to arrive at her or his own best medical judgment about the proper course of treatment for a given patient? Obviously no doctor (or other professional) is so totally autonomous as to be completely free of external accountability. But physician autonomy does seem to be under particular stress in our times, and we will need to inquire as to whether the solid tradition of professional medical autonomy is sufficiently protected in the current climate. *Second,* what about the long-standing tradition of the doctor, as a professional, having a strong obligation to speak her mind to those who have a right to hear her judgment? Do doctors have sufficient freedom to do this today? *Third,* what about the doctor's basic obligation to avoid all harm to her or his patient and only to act in the patient's best interest? Is there sufficient protection of this physician responsibility in today's health-care world? Or are there too many financial incentives that may undermine the physician's professional judgment?

The point about the obligation to act in the best interest of the patient opens up the more explicitly Christian theme of the covenantal loyalty. There are several possible images out of which a doctor might understand herself: as the advancer of scientific knowledge, the fighter against disease, the conqueror of death, and so on. In light of the tradition of professionalism, the doctor is best understood as the person who is radically committed to caring for the patient and doing only

what is good for the patient. This radical commitment suggests that the doctor owes the patient a special loyalty, a loyalty sometimes described as a "covenantal loyalty." William F.
May very helpfully develops this theme of covenantal loyalty in
his book *The Physician's Covenant,* but the term also has echoes
in the work of the late Paul Ramsey, who did so much to help
shape the entry of Protestant thought into a disciplined
approach to medical ethics.[58]

The richness of the term "covenantal loyalty" opens up a
very profound question. Granted the long historical rooting of
the concept of the doctor as a professional, does the theme of
professionalism ultimately go far enough in identifying who
the doctor is? Once we grant the special covenant of trust that
ought to exist between doctors and patients, and as we begin
to explore the powerful existential meaning of serious illness
and dying, I believe it can be said that the doctor's committed
presence to the seriously ill and the dying has about it an even
deeper meaning, so that the practice of medicine should be
described as a vocation. This theme of medicine as vocation
does not take away professionalism and professional standards, but it does suggest that the doctor—and some of the
other health-care professionals as well—has an even more profound vocational identity. If this is true, the questions about
today's threats to the identity of the physician become all the
more serious.

## DEATH AND DYING AS A PART OF THE HUMAN STORY

What about Catholicism's contribution to the ethical standards that apply to care for the dying? It is to the great credit
of Roman Catholicism that it has been dealing with the ethics
of care for the dying for almost 500 years, far longer than
almost any other large organization in the modern world.[59]
Beginning in the 1530s, Catholic scholarship began to discuss
issues such as the force feeding of old people who were facing
death, and the applicability of the vow of religious obedience
to the question of life-sustaining treatments. Catholicism's
prompt conclusions were that there was no obligation to force

feed persons whose death was at hand, and that the vow of obedience should not be used to compel a dying religious subject to undergo life-sustaining treatment.[60]

From these simple beginnings, Catholic thought—even before the end of the sixteenth century—developed the famous and now classic distinction between ordinary and extraordinary means of preserving human life.[61] The point of the distinction was that human persons are obligated to use ordinary means of prolonging their lives, but that human persons need not use extraordinary means to prolong their lives. This distinction and its subsequent developments have guided Catholic thought ever since. It would take us too far afield to explain all the history and nuances of the ordinary/extraordinary distinction. It should be noted, however, that today Catholic thought is increasingly unlikely to rely exclusively on the classic terms "ordinary" and "extraordinary" means.[62] Instead, even in statements from the Vatican and the bishops,[63] Catholicism tends to speak of the obligation to render care that is proportionate to the circumstances of the patient, or of the obligation to offer treatment that brings the patient true benefit without at the same time imposing undue burden.

The bottom line is that Catholicism, for all its commitment to the sacredness of human life, understands very deeply that death is a part of the human story. While we ought to do the reasonable things to prevent dying, there is a limit to how much we, as mortal beings, ought to do to prolong the lives of those who are in the process of dying. I believe that our world, which has such a tendency to deny the reality of death and even a tendency to promote death without admitting it, very much needs to hear this message. At its core, John Paul II's encyclical *Evangelium Vitae* is both challenging and refreshing because of the way in which it deals with contemporary attitudes toward death.[64]

But what does this historic Catholic stance on care for the dying mean in terms of specific implications for a better approach to the broader question of achieving justice in the delivery of health care? The Catholic stance helps us to a better focus in three areas: (1) wisdom about the prudent use of health-care resources, (2) a deeper sense of the true goals and purposes of medical care, and (3) an understanding of dying as a personal-spiritual process rather than as a merely physiological process.

On the question about resources, once we accept the theme that dying is a part of living, and that there are limits on how much we ought to do to prolong the dying process, the question about the wise use of health-care resources becomes a very coherent and even a patient-centered question. When it is the patient's judgment (or the judgment of the person who speaks for the patient) that the use of resources is not for the patient's good, it is better not to use the resources, for the sakes both of the patient at hand and of other patients who might need the resources and who may not get them if they are inappropriately used.[65] It is fascinating to note that the traditional Catholic moral manuals of the pre–Vatican II era regularly mentioned high cost as a factor that could render a medical treatment extraordinary and non-obligatory. One manual revised shortly before the beginning of Vatican II stipulated $2,000 as the dollar figure that defined the borderline between low-cost (and therefore ordinary) treatments and higher-cost (and therefore extraordinary) treatments.[66] Obviously no one would advocate that figure today. But even in earlier times, the Catholic tradition, with its understanding of the meaning of our dying, realized that economic prudence is an important factor in some health-care decisions. At the level of principle, the contemporary concern about stewardship of health-care resources is a concern supported by the Catholic tradition, even if there are questions about specific decisions on the use of resources.

On the theme of the goals or purposes of medicine, the Catholic understanding of the place of death in human life helps us realize that very often caring for the patient and keeping company with the patient may be even more important than curing the patient.[67] In the end, our efforts to cure will fail in the case of every one of us, and no one will escape the reality of dying. So what is medicine really all about and what is medicine supposed to do? In many quarters today, the model of scientific progress to cure disease dominates our thinking about the purposes or ends of medicine. Surely the cure of disease is a worthy purpose for medicine. But is it the only purpose, or even the primary purpose? When we consider the Catholic tradition's acceptance of dying as a part of living, I think we can argue that efforts to give true care to the dying are as central to medicine as are the efforts to cure. There is a wonderful old French proverb about health care that is prominently associated with Dr. E. L. Trudeau and the tuberculosis sanitarium at Saranac Lake, New York. The proverb states, *"Guérir quelquefois, soulager souvent, consoler toujours"* ("Sometimes to cure, often to assuage pain, always to bring consolation").[68] I think this proverb offers a magnificent vision of the meaning of health care, a vision that ties in with what Catholicism has been saying since the sixteenth century.

One of the most significant developments in biomedical ethical scholarship in recent years has been the goals of medicine project, headed especially by Daniel Callahan.[69] This project gathered a group of experts from all over the world to revisit the question of what medicine is all about. The group's underlying conviction was that true health reform and true health-care justice will not be possible unless we can come to a clearer understanding of the purposes of medicine in the first place. The project articulated four major goals for medicine: (1) the prevention of disease and injury and the promotion and maintenance of health, (2) the relief of pain and suffering caused by maladies, (3) the care and cure of those with a malady and the care of those who cannot be cured, and (4) the avoidance of premature death and the pursuit of a peaceful death. The results of the goals project were excellent and fully coherent with the instincts that have been found in traditional Roman Catholic ethics. In the end, we will all be much clearer on what we should be trying to do with modern health-care technologies if we focus the purposes of medicine through the lens of our common mortality. Both Catholic thought and modern scholarship help us do just that.

The Catholic tradition on death and dying also makes it very clear that dying is a personal-spiritual process, and hence much more than a mere physiological event. Once we begin to construe dying as a personal-spiritual event, certain support services, such as pastoral care and social work, immediately become an essential part of genuinely just care for the dying. These services are part of the radical call to keep company with the dying and to bring them consolation always. Sometimes the desire to save money can tempt health-care providers to cut back on these kinds of services. But if we know from the human perspective what dying is all about, such services are an inherent part of what the best health care should offer. In the end, good pastoral, spiritual, psychological, and social care may actually save health-care providers money, by causing patients and families to cooperate better with the wisest course of treatment. The standard is clear: Justice from the Catholic perspective calls for spiritual and social care for the seriously ill and dying.

## A NOTE ON THE ETHICAL AND RELIGIOUS DIRECTIVES

This chapter has described five major aspects of traditional Catholic thought that can help shape today's debate about health care: (1) an understanding of justice and care for the poor, (2) a theory of economics, (3) an emphasis on proper treatment of employees, (4) a reflection on professional responsibility, and (5) a grasp of the mystery of life and death. To end the chapter, I want to highlight one of the most important publishing events in Catholic health care in the past few years: the issuance of the third edition of the *Ethical and Religious Directives for Catholic Health Care Services* in 1995.[70] I end with the *ERD* because in so many ways they very helpfully articulate the five themes I have described. The first section is excellent in its focus on care for the poor and the marginalized as well as on the rights of employees. The second section very clearly presents serious illness as a personal-spiritual issue. The third section offers much useful input on the rights and responsibilities of health-care providers. The fourth section highlights the sacredness of human life, especially in its beginnings; and the fifth section contains a wonderful articulation of the Catholic tradition of caring for the sick and dying. The sixth section sounds a real note of hope about the future of Catholic health care in these complex and changing times. If anyone wants to get at the spirit behind the issues raised in this chapter, the *ERD* can serve as an excellent vehicle. This becomes true all the more if one reads the *ERD* and then reads John Paul II's encyclical *Evangelium Vitae*.[71]

To say that the *ERD* is very helpful in setting forth basic Catholic perspectives does not mean that the *ERD* resolves every question or closes every discussion about Catholic health-care ethics. It would not be germane to the purposes of this book to present a complete and critically reflective analysis of the *ERD*, even though such an analysis would be a worthwhile project in and of itself. But it should at least be noted that the *ERD* themselves state that while they set forth fundamental Catholic principles, they do not provide every application of these principles.[72] For instance, the exact details of the treatment of women who are victims of sexual assault are not described fully in the *ERD*, and these details may even change with developments in medical science. Similarly, the precise cases in which labor may be induced in pregnant women are not fully clear, and these cases also may be subject to change as medical science progresses. Likewise, there are many questions about the precise applications of the *ERD*'s basic stance in favor of the right of health-care employees to join unions. So the *ERD* does not answer all the questions or resolve all the issues. But this fact in no way undercuts its basic value in articulating the principled context that has been the focal point of this chapter.

The purpose of this first chapter has been simple: to set forth a description of major Catholic themes that can guide us on the journey toward a more just health-care system. Catholicism does not have all the answers, nor is it the only source to be considered in the quest for just health care. True dialogue is needed. But Catholicism does have much to bring to the table. We are now ready to assess some of today's key health-care issues, especially in light of the Catholic values outlined in this chapter.

# Chapter 2
# MANAGED CARE: DEFINITION, HISTORY, AND MORAL SUCCESSES

The goal of this chapter is to describe the moral or ethical successes of managed care. These successes are significant; they should not be forgotten because of the criticisms of managed care that are so prominent today. Before turning to the successes of managed care, we will take two preliminary steps. *First,* we will present a definition of managed care and of several related terms. *Second,* we will review and assess the history of managed care in the United States. At the level of theological method, we can understand something much better if we know its history.

## TOWARD A DEFINITION OF MANAGED CARE

### Overall Description of Managed Care

In a general sense, managed care can be described as any system of health delivery that focuses on four themes: (1) prepayment for health care instead of payment for each individual service used (fee-for-service), (2) efforts to control health-care costs by limiting utilization of health-care services to those services that are truly beneficial, (3) efforts to compare approaches to care so as to determine which services are genuinely effective (that is, which services offer quality medical care), and (4) an emphasis on preventive health-care measures so that persons are less likely to need critical health-care services in the first place.[1] These four elements do not have equal weight. Probably the shift away from fee-for-service payment for health care to prepayment for all of a person's health-care needs is the most central element in the definition. The effort to reduce cost through the control of the utilization of services stands as a close second.

To clarify the definition of managed care, several matters are deserving of note. "Managed care" is a rather new term. The key early managed-care plans, such as Kaiser Permanente and Group Health, were described as prepaid group practice."[2] These plans originated in the 1940s. If we look at more recent history and consider the support that managed care received from the Nixon administration in the 1970s, we encounter the term "health maintenance organization" (HMO). This term was first used in 1970 by Dr. Paul Ellwood of Minneapolis.[3] The existence of these two earlier terms, prepaid group practice and health maintenance organization, shows that many of the concepts underlying managed care can be found in earlier times. But the term "managed care" was practically nonexistent until recently. Paul Starr's Pulitzer Prize-winning book *The Social Transformation of American Medicine,* published in 1982, makes frequent use of the term "HMO," but has almost no mention of the term "managed care."[4]

The now common term "HMO" ordinarily has a narrower range of connotation than does "managed care." When people say, "HMO," the reference is often to the classic staff model of prepaid group practice in which the doctors are actually the employees of the HMO. Or the reference is to a closed prepaid group of doctors, who, while not employees of the HMO, receive an annual per-patient payment from the HMO to care for the patient. The staff model HMO has ties to the early structure of Group Health, and the closed prepaid group model HMO has ties to some aspects of the early history of Kaiser Permanente. Granting the importance of these two models, recent years have seen the emergence of a whole range of health-care plans that use strategies such as prepayment, review of decisions about individual medical cases, efforts to define quality medical care, and cost control measures. "Managed care" has become the popular term for describing this wide variety of plans, and the HMO is understood today as only one variety of managed care.

*Types of Managed-Care Plans*

It will not be possible to describe every type of managed-care plan here. We will outline five of the most popular models of managed care: (1) the staff model HMO, (2) the Independent Practice Association (IPA), (3) the Preferred Provider Organization (PPO), (4) the Point-of-Service Plan (POS), and (5) the Physician Hospital Organization (PHO).

The *staff model HMO* refers to the classic design in which the HMO not only collects the monies and oversees the utilization of services, but also employs the physicians and pays them a salary for their services to the patients. Such an HMO may own its own hospitals, or it may have contractual arrangements with other hospitals where the HMO's doctors care for their patients. Historically, this sort of HMO tended to let its staff doctors make the care decisions. There was a fairly strong emphasis on quality control, and there were only limited financial incentives for doctors to encourage them to save money. Today's staff model HMOs may operate in many different ways. Of the models we will consider, the staff model HMO places the greatest restrictions on the patient's choice of a physician. This does not always mean an absence of strong doctor-patient relationships.

In the *Independent Practice Association* (IPA), the HMO is a financial entity and utilization review organization, which may or may not own its own hospitals. The HMO enters into contracts with groups of doctors, with the doctors' groups being called Independent Practice Associations. Sometimes the HMO will pay the IPA doctors on a fee-for-service basis, but it is quite common today for the IPA to receive a fixed annual sum (a capitation fee) for each patient to whom it is responsible for providing care. Often these individual patients are described as "covered lives."[5] The capitation approach places the income of the IPA at risk, since the IPA doctors know that they will only receive a set amount for each patient, no matter how much or little care they offer. Some IPA doctors are relatively in control of the care decisions that they make, but there is likely to be an external review process managed by the company that holds the contract with the IPA.

There are a great many subtle variations in the exact structure of IPAs; these same variations are present in the other major forms of managed care.

In the *Preferred Provider Organization* (PPO), the financial-utilization organization that covers the patients enters into a relationship with a large number of doctors or groups of doctors who agree to meet the financial and utilization requirements of the parent organization that pays for the patients' care. Since these doctors, who may be organized into IPAs, agree to the insurer's requirements, they are listed as Preferred Providers. The preferred providers may be paid on a discounted fee-for-service basis, although this is not always the case. Typically the patients will get significantly better benefits by using the PPO doctors. The patients remain free to go to other doctors. Their costs when they seek care from a non-PPO doctor will be eligible for coverage, but there will usually be a higher copayment required from the patient who sees a doctor outside the PPO. The PPO model thus differs from plans that offer no coverage for services rendered by non-HMO or non-IPA doctors. The patient has greater flexibility, if she is willing to pay for it.

The *Point-of-Service* (POS) model is similar to the PPO in that patients covered by a point-of-service plan are able to receive services from both participating and nonparticipating providers of health-care services. A variety of mechanisms may be used to enable patients to receive services outside the plan. The services covered outside of the plan may have certain limits set on them. A supplemental insurance policy may be used to cover the costs of services outside the plan. These and related steps may be combined in different ways. Point-of-service plans will often provide for emergency care and for access to specialists outside of the system.

In the *Physician Hospital Organization* (PHO), a hospital and one or several physician groups form a joint entity that enters into contracts with managed-care providers. A few years ago, it was very common for hospitals to purchase physicians' practices in order to form PHOs. Today there is more hesitancy about hospitals purchasing physicians' practices. It is more common for PHOs to be created through operating agreements between hospitals and physicians' groups. One advantage of the PHO is that the combination of doctors and hospitals is in a strong position to attract business from the companies that finance managed care. A second advantage is that the PHO is often able to negotiate for fees and services to be covered in a way that neither doctors nor hospitals might be able to accomplish on their own.[6]

### Managed Care as a Blanket Term and a Work in Progress

Even a cursory review of these five models of managed care shows us that none of the five models is completely distinct. Frequently an overall managed-care plan may involve several of these elements combined into a variety of individual health-care plans. The most important point to be noted is that *managed care* does not mean just one thing. In the past there was a tendency to think of *managed care* as a univocal term that described one common plan, most likely a classic HMO. But in the present context, it is best to understand managed care as a blanket term, an umbrella under which are gathered a number of related but still distinct approaches to the delivery of health care. The various plans under the umbrella keep changing, so that managed care should be understood as a work in progress, rather than a reality with a permanent definition. The theme of managed care as a work in progress has been especially well articulated by Drs. Paul Ellwood, who coined the term "HMO," and George Lundberg, the former editor of the *Journal of the American Medical Association (JAMA).*[7] The ongoing development of managed care makes it important for employers and patients to study individual managed-care plans carefully, so as to be sure they know what they are buying. Not all managed-care plans are the same, and they may not be the same this year as they were last year.

### Definitions of Some Related Terms

There are several related terms that should be defined to help us throughout this book. Ten such terms will be defined here: (1) managed competition, (2) the physician as gatekeeper,

(3) medical loss ratio, (4) stop-loss insurance, (5) utilization review, (6) quality assurance, (7) copayment, (8) capitation, (9) cost shifting, and (10) the single-payer system.

"Managed competition" describes an approach in which several companies in an area compete to offer health-care services on the basis of cost, quality, and other issues. Through governmental regulation, the performances of the managed competitors are assessed and publicly documented.[8] Employers and patients may use this documentation to choose health-care plans. The goal is to generate quality health care at a reasonable cost through the establishment of cost and quality targets and through employer-patient choice. Like prepaid group practice, the managed competition model of health care has significant roots in the World War II period. The term "managed cost" is often used in conjunction with managed competition. This term refers to the efforts to attract patients by offering more cost-effective health services. It is a sub-element of managed competition that seeks to compete based on both the quality and the cost of the services offered.

The theme of the "physician as gatekeeper" draws much negative attention today. The fundamental notion of gatekeeper is that, in some managed-care plans, access to medical specialists is controlled by primary-care physicians, so that a patient cannot see a specialist without a referral from a primary-care physician. Many persons, including a sizable number of physicians, believe that the gatekeeper role creates a conflict of interest for the physician.[9] The conflict exists especially if the physician has a strong financial incentive not to refer the patient. In this case, does the gatekeeper role conflict with the physician's responsibility to act always in the best interest of the patient? There may be a tendency for some patients to be too ready to go to specialists, and the related (but now reversing) decline in the number of primary-care physicians is surely not for the common good. So despite the criticisms, there may be value in the gatekeeper model if it helps restore a more suitable balance of primary-care doctors and specialists.

The term "medical loss ratio" describes the percentage of a managed-care company's total income that is spent on the actual care of patients. In traditional not-for-profit managed-care plans, the medical loss ratio has tended to be quite high, with sometimes as much as 90 percent of a health-care plan's income spent on actual patient care. In for-profit plans, the medical loss ratio can be significantly lower, with cases in which only 60–70 percent of the plan's income is spent on patient care.[10] Advocates of the for-profit plans point out that in many cases the medical loss ratios of the for-profits and the not-for-profits are much closer, and they also argue that the greater efficiency of the for-profit plans means that the patient actually receives quality care at a better price, even granting that some of the income of the for-profit plans goes to the shareholders. The very phrase *medical loss ratio* is troubling to many critics of contemporary health-care delivery systems. The fact that patient care, the central mission of health-care providers, is described as a loss raises questions about the overall purpose of health-care plans that use such a term. What is health care all about? To care for the patients, or to avoid losses so that there is more income for the provider and its stockholders?

The term "stop-loss insurance" relates to the fact that in many health-care settings today, a significant part of a doctor's income depends on his financial performance. If the doctor meets certain financial targets through efforts to reduce the use of medical services, the doctor is eligible for some sort of bonus, perhaps a very significant bonus. If a doctor is part of a small practice group, one or two unexpected cases may significantly raise the group's annual costs, thereby removing the possibility of any bonus. This is where stop-loss insurance comes into play. It restores to the doctor or to the practice a very substantial portion of any financial loss that is incurred because of the necessary and perhaps quite expensive care decisions that the doctor or group of doctors have to make. As much as 90 percent of lost financial incentive income can be restored through stop-loss insurance. Critics argue that even with stop-loss insurance, the environment created by financial incentives is still very coercive for physicians. It is surely clear that, without stop-loss insurance, some financial incentives would place an intolerable burden on physicians in terms of their call to act always in the best interest of their patients.[11]

The term "utilization review" refers to the process of assessing the specific medical recommendations of a doctor about a given case, to see whether her recommendations seem to be medically justified. Utilization review can be either retrospective (occurring after the course of treatment has been undertaken) or prospective (occurring before the treatment has begun). Utilization review can occur in a number of different ways. Many hospitals have utilization review practices. In the context of managed care, utilization review has become more controversial, since it refers to the prospective approval or disapproval process that many managed-care companies require before they will fund a procedure that the patient's doctor recommends. Some scholars even state that if a managed-care company does not own hospitals or employ physicians, it is essentially a utilization review organization, focusing on utilization as a means of financial control.[12] There are both pros and cons to the utilization review process. While it can limit the freedom of doctors, it can also challenge doctors to follow better medical practices.

The term "quality assurance" relates to utilization review, but it involves a broader and more positive context. Quality assurance refers to the ongoing process of seeking to find and implement the very best medical practices. Quality assurance has historical roots in some of the earliest history of managed-care organizations. It also has roots in the work of major twentieth-century industrial philosophers such as W. Edwards Deming, who had so much influence in Japan and in the remarkable success of the Japanese automobile industry.[13] There is some debate about whether or not managed-care systems improve the quality of care, and about whether medicine as a whole is succeeding in offering a high enough quality of care.[14]

The term "copayment" refers to a health-care plan's requirement that the patient pay some fixed amount in addition to what the health insurance provides. Because copayments make us stop and think about whether or not we really need a given medical service, many persons feel that the requirement of modest copayments, except for the poor, is a socially responsible policy. A number of managed-care plans require a higher copayment to help cover the cost of seeing a specialist who is not part of the plan. Copayments are distinguished from *co-insurance*, with copayments referring to a specific dollar amount required of the patient, while co-insurance requires the patient (or perhaps a supplemental insurance policy) to pay a percentage of the actual cost of the health-care service. A common example of co-insurance can be found in the plans of many senior citizens. These plans often pay a percentage of the senior citizen's post-Medicare expenses.[15]

"Capitation" is the term most commonly used to describe health plans that pay doctors or hospitals a fixed amount for caring for a given group of patients over a set period of time, frequently a budget year. Such an approach places the doctor or hospital at risk financially, in that whatever care is needed for a set of patients, no more than a set amount of funding will be available to cover that care. Stop-loss insurance can serve to offset the effects of capitation, and contractual negotiations for the next budget year can take into account the history of current and preceding years, but the reality of the capitation approach remains, as does its potential influence on the decision-making process. The larger the number of patients who are covered under a specific capitation agreement, the less likely it is that decisions about an individual patient will be affected. A large capitation agreement, if well designed, ought to have enough total funding to provide necessary care to those capitated patients who do need unusual and expensive care. Capitation changes the tone of health care and health-care decision making, but it does not automatically imply that there will be unjust decisions about individual cases.

"Cost shifting" was a frequently used term in past health-care settings. There were always patients who were unable to pay for truly necessary health care. Past health insurance structures were such that doctors and especially hospitals knew that they could charge enough for their paying patients so that they would have enough left over to cover those patients who could not pay. The pressures against cost shifting began during the presidency of Ronald Reagan. Before the Reagan era, Medicare essentially permitted hospitals to set charges for their services. The Reagan administration moved to the use of Diagnosis Related Groups (DRGs), a system that established payment rates for about 750 different disease situations, so that the hospital caring for a patient could only recover the set DRG amount.[16] Modern managed-care plans, through capitation and other mechanisms, have pushed this trend further, so that doctors and hospitals are much less likely today to be able to recover more money from any case than what that case actually costs. The tradition of cost shifting is much harder to accomplish in the current climate.

In fairness to the Reagan administration, there was a great deal of waste in health care and a sense on the part of providers that they could simply charge more whenever they felt they needed to do so. There was little incentive to reduce waste and to look for more cost-effective ways of delivering health care. In the first years of the DRG system, many hospitals found ways to manage themselves more effectively and save substantial amounts of money. But as the years have passed, the climate created by DRGs and by recent managed-care utilization strategies has made it harder and harder for hospitals to locate sources of funding so that they can care for the poor. The simple cost-shifting mechanisms of the past are no longer available.

This does not mean that all charity care has ceased. Very substantial levels of charity care and uncompensated care still exist. For the U.S. health-care system as a whole, the worth of these services amounts to billions of dollars annually.[17] Charity care is harder to accomplish in these times, but it has not stopped. It will be important to inquire as to whether there are differences in the approach to charity care of for-profit health-care providers in comparison with not-for-profit providers.

The term "single-payer system" refers to a health-care system in which there is a unified national insurance plan, with the government acting as the only payer of all health insurance claims. The funds used to support a single-payer system may come from one general tax or from several separate taxes, for example, a tax on the income of those who are employed, a Social Security tax for the retired, and an allocation of general tax revenues to care for the poor. In a single-payer system, the government does not ordinarily own hospitals or employ physicians. Doctors and hospitals continue to be private. But the government acts as the one insurer who pays the doctors and hospitals for the cost of the care they provide. In places where a single-payer system is in use, governments often contract with private insurance companies who oversee the disbursement of the funds to the health-care providers. This is what happens with Medicare. So it is not accurate to say that a single-payer system simply destroys the private health insurance industry. Probably the best known example of a single-payer system is the Canadian health insurance system.[18] Technically, "single payer" is not a term that is relevant to today's context of a multiplicity of privately operated managed-care companies. But the term is important in the managed-care context. If the managed-care industry breaks down in the United States, many persons will push for the single-payer system as the best alternative.[19]

## THE HISTORY OF MANAGED CARE
## IN THE UNITED STATES

Before we begin our moral assessment of managed care, it will help to review the history of managed care in the United States, at least briefly. Managed care in the United States has a pre-history that reaches as far back as the eighteenth century. One thinks of prepaid group health plans, such as the Boston Dispensary, which assisted veterans of the American Revolution. In the nineteenth century some of the early industries in the United States, such as the railroads (notably the Southern Pacific), turned to health-care antecedents of managed care. The Mayo Clinic, founded in Rochester, Minnesota, in the 1880s, the Guthrie Clinic, founded in Sayre, Pennsylvania, in 1910, and the Menninger Clinic, founded in Topeka, Kansas, in 1914, used the fee-for-service model, but they all established the precedent for group practice instead of the earlier tradition of individual physicians with no partners.[20]

The more recent historical roots of managed care in the United States go back to the 1930s and 1940s. These roots are found in a number of places, especially in the west coast states. Our comments on this more recent history will be divided into five sections: (1) the background and early history of Kaiser

Permanente, (2) the founding and development of the Group Health Cooperative of Puget Sound, (3) related developments in places such as California, New York, and Washington, D.C., (4) developments in managed care in the 1960s and 1970s, and (5) the roots of managed competition in the World War II period.

*The Background and Early Development of Kaiser Permanente*

In 1938, the industrialist Henry Kaiser and his son Edgar became involved in one of the great public works projects of that or any era: the building of the Grand Coulee Dam on the Columbia River in Eastern Washington. One aspect of the project that was of great concern to Henry and Edgar Kaiser was the provision of health care to the thousands of workers and family members who came to the dam site for the years of construction. Because of the remoteness of the area, all sorts of services had to be provided near the site (schools, roads, stores, and so on). In terms of health care, it seemed completely impractical to recruit traditional fee-for-service doctors and ask them to establish medical practices near the dam. Instead, the Kaisers recruited Dr. Sidney Garfield to oversee the health care aspects of the Grand Coulee project.[21]

By 1938, Dr. Sidney Garfield, a thirty-two-year-old son of Russian immigrants, had spent six years in the Mojave Desert of Southern California providing health care to the workers who were building the aqueduct from the Colorado River to Los Angeles as well as the Parker and Imperial dams. Dr. Garfield had built three hospitals in the Mojave and had gone to Los Angeles and recruited a group of physicians who were paid a fixed annual sum to care for all of the construction workers and their families. At first Garfield and his medical team were paid 50¢ per month for each worker and 25¢ per month for each wife and child. Using the principles of capitation and prepaid group practice, Dr. Garfield and his colleagues established a very successful health-care system. They became known to history as "the desert doctors."

Henry Kaiser was a contractor on the Parker and Imperial dams, so he knew of Dr. Garfield's work in the Mojave. But their first personal meeting and lifelong association began in 1938 with the Grand Coulee. Garfield again recruited a group of physicians, this time from Stanford University and other places, and he established a hospital and a prepaid group practice to care for the 5,000 dam workers and their families. Dr. Garfield's group developed several approaches that have been central to the better managed-care systems ever since. They placed strong emphasis on preventive health care and on the education of their patients into good health habits. They paid close attention to the outcomes of their treatments, comparing outcomes so as to determine which course of treatment was the best medical practice to follow. They developed a sense of colleagueship, seeing themselves as a team for all of the patients instead of as competitors for the patients. Whatever one thinks of some of the problems associated with managed care today, it is hard to read about Garfield, his fellow doctors, and even their wives (who were often nurses) and not be filled with a sense that theirs was an approach to medical practice genuinely committed to a deep sense of caring. From the theologian's viewpoint, such caring is the very essence of what medicine is all about.

History moved rapidly in those days. Henry Kaiser quickly found himself involved in major projects to support the United States' efforts in World War II, projects such as steel production and the building of PT boats and aircraft carriers. These projects were centered especially in the San Francisco Bay Area and in Vancouver, Washington–Portland, Oregon. As he geared up for the war effort, Kaiser remembered the successful health-care program connected with the Grand Coulee, and he wanted to provide something similar to his rapidly increasing work force in the Bay Area and in Vancouver–Portland. Sidney Garfield was already an Army medical officer preparing to go overseas when a letter arrived from Franklin Roosevelt releasing him from the military so that he could establish a health-care service for the vast number of Kaiser defense workers. Amadeo Giannini, the founder of the Bank of America and a hero of the San Francisco earthquake, had already given Henry Kaiser the largest loan ever made in the United States up to that time. After meeting Sidney Garfield, Giannini put up an additional loan to support the building of health-care facilities for Kaiser's workers.[22]

So it was that in 1942 Henry Kaiser established two Kaiser Permanente foundations as prepaid group practices for his workers. From the beginning, Kaiser Permanente was (and still is) a nonprofit, foundation-sponsored enterprise. From the beginning it contracted with groups of physicians rather than employing them. Although the term "HMO" is anachronistic for 1942, the *Encyclopaedia Britannica* describes Kaiser as the first HMO.[23] It is true that Garfield and his colleagues did speak about the maintenance of health without actually using the term "HMO."

Kaiser only intended the plan for the duration of the war, and the assumption was that Kaiser Permanente would end when the war ended. It nearly closed in 1945, but the obvious values of the plan led to the decision to keep the Kaiser plan and open it to the public. With the passage of the years, Kaiser Permanente developed a strong following in the West and in Hawaii. I recall how widely accepted the Kaiser plan was in Hawaii when I lived there many years ago. There was none of the strong negative criticism that we find against some managed-care plans today.

Here I want to add one of my favorite pieces of health-care trivia. During the years when the Kaiser plan was being founded, Henry Kaiser and his wife Bess were very fond of a stream located in the Los Altos Hills in Santa Clara County, south of San Francisco. Kaiser had established a cement plant near the stream in the early 1930s, and he and his wife frequently visited the area for rest and meditation. The stream was beautiful, and it had one very special feature. Unlike so many streams in that part of the United States, it never ran dry. Hence it was called the Permanente Creek. The lasting character of the flowing water seemed especially meaningful in the context of health. So it was that the health-care plan that the Kaisers founded became not Kaiser, but Kaiser Permanente.[24]

More important than the story of its name is the story of the success Kaiser Permanente has had over the years. Some argue that in recent times, Kaiser has capitulated to the pressures of the newer for-profit managed-care companies, so that it is not as socially responsible as it once was. But even today, Kaiser retains a strong reputation as a socially and morally responsible health plan. In the fall of 1999, *Newsweek* published a rating of 100 managed-care providers in the United States. Nine of the descendants of Kaiser Permanente ranked in the upper third of the 100 plans, and one Kaiser plan fell only slightly below this level.[25] There should be no doubt that Kaiser has a long and generally highly responsible history as a provider of health care.

### The Group Health Cooperative of Puget Sound

Many factors came together to make the Puget Sound area fertile ground for the early development of a managed-care approach to health delivery. Almost from its establishment as a state in 1889, Washington had a notable populist tradition. Trade unions were strong, as were the farmers, and especially the Grange. The Grange and other groups were very interested in cooperative ownership of public utilities. By the 1930s, the leaders of the cooperative movement included the attorney Jack Cluck and the Rev. Fred Shorter, who founded the Church of the People near the University of Washington.

In the 1930s, true cooperatives, owned by the people, were founded in the Seattle area in fields such as grocery stores, dairies, student housing, and mortuaries. This took place especially through the organizational skills of Addison Shoudy. The nationally prominent camping and wilderness gear supplier, Recreational Equipment Incorporated, was founded as a cooperative in Seattle in the 1930s. Its original purpose was to make camping gear available to ordinary people at an economical price.

Many of the leaders of this populist cooperative movement were among those who established the Washington Commonwealth Federation (WCF) in 1935. The WCF helped engender the careers of many socially progressive politicians, with long-time U.S. Senator Warren Magnusen being perhaps the most prominent example. Washington's politics were so progressive in this era that there is a famous story of Postmaster General James Farley once having referred to the forty-seven states and the Soviet of Washington.

From this background, it is no surprise that a cooperative approach to health-care delivery, in which the patients owned or at least controlled their own health-care system, became a high priority for many ordinary citizens in western Washington. Add to this the fact that the Grand Coulee Dam project had occurred nearby. By the end of World War II, the Seattle area was ready for a unique and clearly populist approach to health care. At the end of the war, there was great interest in Seattle in the work of Dr. Michael Shadid, a Lebanese immigrant, who had founded the United States' first cooperatively owned hospital in a small town in Oklahoma in the 1920s. Dr. Shadid was on hand in Seattle regularly during the years that led up to the founding of Group Health. There was also Dr. Sandy MacColl, a Boston-educated World War II veteran whose war experiences had left him deeply committed to health-care reform and to care for the poor. MacColl was the leader of a small prepaid group practice in Seattle. His group practice, known as the Medical Security Clinic, provided the nucleus of Group Health's first patients. Walt Crowley, in his moving book, *To Serve the Greatest Number,* states that a post-war meeting between health cooperative proponent Jack Cluck and Dr. MacColl provided the final spark that led to the creation of Group Health.[26] The title of Crowley's book is taken from Group Health's Preamble.

When Group Health officially began to care for patients at the beginning of 1947, it was not a true cooperative in the sense that the members actually owned shares in Group Health. Instead, the members elected a board of trustees who controlled Group Health. There were also many patients who were not members of Group Health, but who were cared for in Group Health as enrollee-patients. From the outset, Group Health employed its own physicians and owned its own hospitals. This arrangement made Group Health a staff model managed-care organization, unlike Kaiser, which entered into contractual relationships with independent physician groups. The long-term members of Group Health considered their approach to be a purer approach to managed care. All the elements—members, other patients, doctors, trustees, and administrators—were seen to be part of a common venture. The location of Group Health in only one geographic area may have helped make its staff model more feasible than was the case for Kaiser.

Group Health began small, with fewer than 5,000 patients. The early growth was slow, with occasional ups and downs and occasional controversies, but with a general trend of upward progress. One controversy that broke out in the 1970s was a dispute about whether Group Health was sufficiently attuned to the health-care needs of women. Adjustments were made to make Group Health more responsive. In more recent times, Group Health's growth became quite rapid, with more than 650,000 patients enrolled by the mid-1990s.[27] Group Health began with strong opposition. In the early years, the King County Medical Society blacklisted the physicians of Group Health as unethical, simply because they were compensated through prepayment instead of through a fee-for-service method. There were incidents of the Medical Society's barring Group Health's physicians from admitting patients to non–Group Health Hospitals, even in emergency cases. It took a unanimous 1951 ruling by the Washington State Supreme Court to put an end to the King County Medical Society's anti–Group Health tactics.[28]

In 1997, after fifty years of independence, Group Health became the western Washington subsidiary of Kaiser Permanente. Because of the historic rivalry between these two plans, some of the older Group Health members must have seen this as the ultimate sell-out. But times are changing, and the trend is clearly toward larger health systems. The same thing occurs when smaller Catholic health systems join to form larger systems. Here the point is simply to recall the historical importance and patient-centered values that led to the establishment of the Group Health Cooperative of Puget Sound.

*Other Forerunners of Managed Care in the 1930s and 1940s*

The prominent histories of Kaiser and Group Health should not obscure the fact that there were other significant health-care developments in the same time period, developments that form part of the background for today's managed-care endeavors. Three such developments will be noted here. *First,* in 1937, in Washington, D.C., the interest in the cooperative movement led to the formation of the Group Health Association of Washington, D.C. Group Health of Washington's physicians were salaried employees of Group Health, and its patients were exclusively U.S. government employees. The American Medical Association struggled mightily against the Group Health Association and against other externally controlled prepaid health plans in Chicago and Milwaukee. Ultimately, the AMA was indicted on the basis that its actions against the Group Health Association were a violation of free trade and therefore illegal under the Sherman Antitrust Act. In 1943 the U.S. Supreme Court upheld the conviction of the AMA.[29]

*Second,* during the Depression era, most state medical societies continued to oppose prepayment plans for medical care. But the pressures of the Depression raised the stark reality that many patients might not be able to pay and that some hospitals might have to close. Gradually, the state medical societies began to make some exceptions and to support those medical prepayment plans that were controlled by doctors or hospitals. In 1929, Baylor University Hospital in Dallas agreed to provide twenty-one annual days of hospital care to 1,500 Dallas school teachers for a fee of $6 per year. This incident is usually understood as the beginning of Blue Cross and Blue Shield, which were physician- and provider-controlled health plans. By the late 1930s, the state medical societies in California and Michigan began to support larger medical society-sponsored prepayment plans. The California Physicians Service, which covered home and office visits as well as hospitalization, went into operation in 1939, at a time when 90 percent of Californians earned less than $3,000 per year and very much needed the coverage. Medical societies in other large states such as New York and Pennsylvania also began to support physician- and

provider-controlled prepayment plans. All of these developments led to the establishment of Blue Cross and Blue Shield,
an event that Paul Starr charmingly describes as "the birth of
the blues."[30] The Blues did not move in the direction of salaried
physicians or prepaid group practices, instead retaining the
fee-for-service tradition. But the Blues solidly established the
concept of patient prepayment for services.

*Third,* during the war years in New York City, Mayor Fiorello
LaGuardia developed a great concern about the health-care
needs of the city's employees. In 1943 he created a committee
to work out a new approach to health care for New York City
employees. LaGuardia's committee struggled to find consensus, and he eventually established a second committee that
focused on prepaid group practice. All this led to the founding of the Health Insurance Plan of New York in 1947. The
Health Insurance Plan (HIP) began with twenty-two prepaid
group practices and more than 400 physicians. Due to the
restrictions of state law, HIP covered medical care but not hospitalization. By the mid-1950s, HIP had more than 500,000
members. The members had a separate policy with Blue Cross
to cover their hospitalization, and the city paid half of each
member's total cost for enrolling in HIP and Blue Cross.[31]

On an international historical note, it was also during 1943
that Winston Churchill addressed the British Parliament in London on the one major domestic issue he supported during the
war years: the creation of a new health service for Great Britain.
Churchill was out of office during the immediate postwar years,
but 1948 did see the establishment of the British National
Health Service, which he had started promoting at the same
time that LaGuardia's efforts began in New York.[32]

Other developments from this same time period can be
pointed out or studied in standard reference sources. What is
clear is that Kaiser and Group Health of Puget Sound were not
isolated incidents but part of a nationwide pattern. The key
historical fact is that today's efforts to reform and reorganize
the delivery of health care have very significant roots in the
World War II period.

*Transitions during the 1960s and 1970s*

When we think about health care in the United States in the 1960s and 1970s, the most obvious topic is the passage of Medicare and Medicaid in 1965. In general, Medicare has shown itself to be a quite effective health-care system. It is under substantial stress today because of the combined pressures of budget cutbacks, increasing numbers of senior citizens, and the escalating costs of health care in general. At its creation, Medicaid was much less well thought out than Medicare, and its performance over the intervening years has been somewhat, but certainly less effective than Medicare. A detailed history of Medicare's efforts to care for seniors and Medicaid's efforts to care for the poor would be very interesting, but it is beyond the scope of this book.[33]

The '60s and '70s saw another development that had an even greater impact than Medicare on the current growth of managed care. I refer to the national legislation on HMOs that was enacted during the early 1970s with the active support of the administration of Richard Nixon. Nixon understood that the passage of Medicare was changing the face of health-care delivery in the United States. He knew that the cost of health care was going to become a major issue in the United States, and he sought to do something about it. Nixon raised the need for decisive action on health care within six months of becoming president, and in February 1971, he called for a new national health-care strategy. At the same time, he introduced the American public to the then-new term "health maintenance organization." Nixon's actions led to the passage of the HMO Assistance Act in 1973. Nixon hoped to foster the creation of 1,700 new HMOs, but the total in the early years after the HMO act was only slightly more than 200.[34]

It is fascinating to look at the tone of the debate about HMOs during the Nixon period. The whole tone of the legislative discussion was focused on finding ways to free HMOs of restrictions so that they could function effectively as cost-efficient providers of health care. The support of the HMOs was seen as strongly socially progressive. There was no sense of a need to rein in HMOs and keep them under control, as there is in today's debates. Nixon's interest in the reform of health-care delivery was much broader than the HMO question. His ideas had some clear continuity with earlier approaches to national health reform that had surfaced during the Roosevelt and Truman administrations. He consulted with leaders of both parties on health care, notably including Senator Edward Kennedy. He was aware that in these same years Canada was in the process of adopting and implementing its nationally unified single-payer system as a means of financing health care. Had Nixon's presidency not ended when it did, there is at least the possibility that more far-reaching health reforms would have occurred in the United States and that our situation today might be very different. In future ages historians may well say that the late twentieth century produced two presidents who were greatly interested in health-care reform, but who did not succeed as much as they might have, due in part to issues of character.

There is an ironic fact about Nixon and health-care reform. Nixon began his political life by defeating the popular Congressman Jerry Vorhis in the 1946 congressional election. After his defeat, Vorhis spent the next twenty years as the head of the Cooperative League USA, where he worked on issues such as health-care reform and the support of HMOs. In the end, Nixon's own approach to health care embraced a fair amount of the agenda of the man he had defeated to get his start in politics.[35]

After the passage of the HMO Assistance Act of 1973, a number of important new HMOs began operations, even though the total number of new HMOs was not what Nixon had anticipated. The Harvard Community Health Plan had actually begun service in 1969. Two other major New England HMOs opened in the early years after 1973. These were the Tufts Health Plan, which opened in 1979, and Pilgrim Health Care, which opened in 1981.[36] These plans were all not-for-profit entities, and the not-for-profit HMOs continued to dominate the HMO scene until the mid-1990s, when the for-profit HMOs reached the point of enrolling the majority of all HMO patients. In addition to expecting a larger growth of HMOs because of the 1973 legislation, Richard Nixon had expected the for-profit segment of the HMO industry to become stronger more rapidly. He was off by twenty years in his judgment on this point. The Harvard Plan combined with Pilgrim in the mid-1990s. Both Harvard Pilgrim and the Tufts plan became enormously respected not-for-profit HMOs. In *Newsweek's* survey of 100 HMOs, these two plans took two of the top four positions.[37]

### The Historical Roots of Managed Competition

Up to this point our historical review of managed care has focused on the development of plans whose aim was to find alternative methods of providing quality health care to large numbers of poor and middle-income people at a reasonable price. Cost management and control were issues even in past times, but questions of cost management and organized competition between HMOs reached a new level of intensity in the 1990s. New terms have found their way into the popular discussion about HMOs, especially the terms "managed competition" and "managed cost." These terms, which have so much significance in today's HMO debates, also have roots in the World War II period.

As the 1940s began, Franklin Roosevelt faced the awesome task of preparing the United States for war. Roosevelt felt that it was crucial for the approach to the coming war to be handled on a bipartisan basis, so he decided to bring some very senior Republicans into his cabinet. In particular he asked the elder statesman Henry L. Stimson, who had served in the cabinets of two earlier presidents, to return as Secretary of War, a post Stimson had first held under Theodore Roosevelt. One of Stimson's most daunting responsibilities was to put the United States on a war footing, that is, to prepare for the production of the incredible amounts of war matériel that would be needed. To oversee the production of the war matériel, Stimson brought Robert Lovett to the War Department. Lovett very successfully led a prodigious war production effort and became a postwar Secretary of Defense, after the War and Navy Departments were finally united.

To help manage the war production effort, Lovett did not recruit a group of experts in the weaponry of that era. Instead he contacted the major universities and recruited a group of the most brilliant young economists he could find. These economists, known to history as the "whiz kids," organized the United States' war production efforts. Using practices originally developed at DuPont and General Motors, the whiz kids very successfully employed a series of concepts such as financial control, statistical control, and management control. After the war, the whiz kids were hired en masse by the Ford Motor Company, where their system, whatever problems were later seen in it, probably helped save Ford. The most famous of the whiz kids was Robert MacNamara, who eventually became president of Ford and then Secretary of Defense, and who applied the themes of the whiz kids to the production of weapons in the 1960s. By MacNamara's time in the Pentagon, people were calling the whiz kids' system "managed competition."[38]

As Secretary of Defense, MacNamara followed the precedent of his own past and hired a new group of whiz kids to work for him in the Pentagon. Under the aegis of these second-generation whiz kids, the concept of managed competition was very clearly present in the United States' approach to the Vietnam conflict. Much of the contemporary thinking about health-care economics has its roots in the economic planning models used by the War and Defense Department. One very direct link can be seen in the career of the brilliant economist Alain Enthoven, who served as a key advisor to MacNamara during the Vietnam War, and who in the 1980s and 1990s emerged as an eloquent spokesperson for a managed competition approach to health-care reform.[39]

At one level there are strong parallels between the provision of armaments and the provision of health-care services in the United States. Both are enormous economic realities, the two biggest economic activities to occur in our lifetimes. Both are in need of some national organization and integration. In both cases it is also very desirable to give the individual providers a strong degree of autonomy. From these perspectives one can see why managed competition is an attractive option for health-care planning. Some would even argue that health-care costs are in fact beginning to come under control and that managed competition has helped bring about this control.

But there are also important differences between the production of armaments and the provision of health-care services. When economic planners shape arms production, we will likely get some wonderful products like airplanes, but we may also get the occasional unsatisfactory airplane, such as the TFX. While such airplanes are regrettable, they may be written off as a necessary side effect of an efficient production planning system. But if economic planning by nonmedical personnel leads to the occasional poor health-care decision, the result may be disastrous and even fatal for the patient. Is the unique relationship of health to the meaning of human life such that otherwise useful economic models can be applied to health care? This question becomes even more complicated when we consider that managed competition would seem to have its highest level of effectiveness in a for-profit context, a context whose applicability to health care is a matter of debate.

Our comments have begun to move from the history of managed competition to some reflection on the ethical viability of managed competition as a means of facilitating health-care delivery. Hopefully the historical survey will aid us in our critical ethical assessment of managed care.

## THE MORAL SUCCESSES OF MANAGED CARE

The word *success* can mean a number of different things in the context of managed care. Managed-care plans have enrolled vast numbers of patients in recent years, so that these plans (if all the forms of managed care are included) now enroll about 87 percent of all those persons in the United States who have health-care coverage.[40] So how can we say that managed care is not a success? But our project is not to look for statistical or fiscal success. Our goal is to reflect on the moral successes of managed care, especially its successes in terms of Catholic moral values. There are five moral successes of managed care to be highlighted. These are (1) managed care's concern to offer health care to ordinary working people, (2) managed care's vision of solidarity between health-care providers and between the providers and the patients, (3) managed care's commitment to quality care that enhances both the professionalism of the provider and the dignity of the patient, (4) managed care's interest in health as a wholistic reality that involves much more than the curing of disease, and (5) managed care's commitment to accomplish all of these goals in a fiscally responsible manner. Not every managed-care organization embodies all of these successes. But these successes are inherent in the meaning of managed care, at least as that meaning developed historically.

### Health Care for Ordinary People

In reading about the past history of managed care, it is hard not to be struck by the genuine commitment of the early managed-care plans to provide good care to those who truly needed it, to groups such as working people, families, and even the poor.[41] If we accept the fundamental notion that access to a reasonable standard of care is a human right, managed care's past history has embodied that basic right. In the past, managed care has provided for health care in difficult circumstances, including the circumstances of groups such as teachers, construction and shipyard workers, and big city employees. Even the current surge of interest in managed care came at a time when health-care costs were skyrocketing out of control, so that everyone's access to health care was under threat. The very stability of the U.S. economy was at stake. The mid- and late 1990s saw great improvement in the U.S. economy, and the shifts in the means of delivery of health care may be part of the reason for the improvement. This does not mean that every specific strategy of contemporary managed-care providers is to be endorsed. Especially, there is no endorsement of the fact that the United States has 44 million people who lack access to health care. But in principle, managed care's desire to offer broad access to care for great numbers of

people is deserving of praise. This desire connects with fundamental principles of justice.

Two comments can be added to these observations about
managed care's desire to supply good care to ordinary people
who need it. *First,* the historical connection of managed care
to the common people was very often a connection to working
people and even to labor groups such as the Grange or trade
unions. Catholicism has a long-standing commitment to working people, including a commitment to the right of workers to
belong to unions. Not everything about unions is the same
today as it was in the past, but it can still be argued that managed-care systems help support the traditional Catholic concern about working people. Pope John Paul II especially
stressed the right of workers to cheap or free health care.[42] If
managed care can help bring care to workers, this must be
seen as a good.

*Second,* Catholicism is open to a variety of approaches to economics. For so much of its history in the United States, health-
care delivery has been strictly wedded to only one economic
model: the model of fee-for-service. Recall the early history of
managed care. It created enormous opposition, and there was
the need for court decisions to prevent the harassment of managed-care doctors. But there is no one uniquely just way to
finance the delivery of health care, and Catholic ethics stresses
the need for openness to new and perhaps better delivery models, models that will help to serve the greatest number of
people. If managed care has helped us all to stretch our imagi-
nations and find new ways to furnish health care, it deserves our
respect for this reason. The early health-care strategies of Henry
Kaiser and Group Health can be seen as acts of creative imagination. Even if managed care (in its current from) does not
endure, it will deserve credit for having stimulated our thinking
about different economic settings for health care.

*Solidarity of Providers and Patients*

One key theme from the early history of managed care is
the way in which the early managed-care physicians seemed to

have a strong sense of working together as colleagues. Often when we think about professionalism in the practice of medicine, our focus is on the physician's autonomy. Autonomy is important, especially in terms of the physician's freedom to exercise her best medical judgment. But in the contemporary world, with its strong emphasis on individualism, the concern for autonomy can sometimes be too much of a good thing. Even in medicine, today's climate can place too high a priority on competition against other doctors so as to get the most or the best patients. The idea of doctors as autonomous can also tend to bring about the image of the doctor as untouchable, as beyond all criticism, even by his peers. So without unduly criticizing the concern for autonomy, another vision of medical practice can be cited, a vision more focused on collegial efforts, so that everyone is working together to seek the patient's good. An attractive feature of the medieval guilds was that the guilds had a strong communal sense. If we look at managed care we can sometimes see this same sense of community. The desert doctors clearly saw themselves as united in a common venture with and for the patients. This communal sense is an element of true professionalism, albeit a different element than the stress on the autonomy of the individual professional and on the freedom from lay interference that is owed to the professional's judgment.

In contemporary bioethics literature there are many instances of appeals to medicine as a team venture, as a reality that works best when all of the caregivers—doctors, nurses, therapists, technicians, counselors—construe themselves as a team working together for the patient.[43] The older sense of the doctor as almighty and of the other team members as underlings is much less accepted today. Attitudes—such as sexism—that work against this sense of a team of participants need to be broken down. There is also the need for the patient and the patient's family to be part of this team process. Can managed care, with its freedom from more traditional patterns of medical practice, help bring about this crucial sense of participation? Such participation may actually help health care to cost less, because patients will fare better if they see themselves as more involved in their own care. The reality of death—which we must all confront—can be faced with more acceptance and more faith-filled hope if it is faced with a sense of solidarity.

The ties of early managed care to the cooperative movement are quite fascinating. Members of cooperatives, whether trustees, physicians, administrators, nurses, patients, or family members, surely knew that they were in the health-care venture together. On the cover of Walt Crowley's history of Group Health, there is a wonderful picture of one of the early organizational meetings that helped establish Group Health.[44] Even without knowing the context, it is impossible to look at the picture without experiencing an overwhelming awareness that these were people who had come together for a critically important common purpose. Today, the breakdown of trust between physicians and patients is very noticeable. But some of the early forms of managed care evidenced a strong solidarity among doctors and between the doctors and patients. The question is whether this communal spirit can be recovered and linked with modern managed-care systems.

These comments evoke for us some of the basic Catholic themes about society that we considered earlier: the themes of participation, solidarity, and commitment to the common good. If an approach to medicine can help foster true participation and solidarity, such an approach has strong links to the fundamental Catholic vision about the corporate nature of society. Managed care does not accomplish all of this perfectly. But if managed care can stimulate a more corporate vision of community, this is surely for the good. When we talk about medical care, we are not talking about just any human commodity. We are talking about the very meaning of human life and death. The usual models of organized business and technological solutions to problems may not work in this vital area of human existence. The potential—and sometimes the actuality—of managed care offering us a model of medicine more focused on human solidarity ought not to be dismissed lightly, no matter what managed care's problems may be.

*Managed Care and the Quality of Care*

Almost from the beginning, managed-care models of health-care delivery began their focus on "best practices," that is, on approaches to medical care that really seemed to work for the patient's good. This concern for quality care for patients looked to much more than the latest scientific developments in medicine. The concern for quality stressed what types of care really worked, what care truly helped the patients fare better, either by curing the patients or helping them die well. The concern for quality also focused on preparing and recruiting doctors who were truly able to give patients good care.

It would be wrong to say that managed care has furnished the whole of the impetus that has led to the contemporary emphasis on quality in health care. Many factors have contributed to the quality movement, factors from within medicine, and factors external to medicine, such as W. Edwards Deming's work on industrial quality. But managed care has a natural affinity for the quality question. The very fact of groups of physicians working together in shared practices opens up a natural possibility for doctors sharing case histories and learning from one another. Group practice, even if managed from outside, also creates a natural interest in finding the best doctors possible. The whole practice—or the whole managed-care company—will suffer without such doctors.

There is still much more work to be done so as to discern the nature of true quality in health care. The effort to accomplish this task is evident in a number of different ways. *The New England Journal of Medicine (NEJM)* has published enough articles on quality in recent years to warrant the publication of a special collection of *NEJM* articles on quality.[45] Several national organizations on health-care quality have been founded. These include the Foundation for Accountability, founded by Dr. Paul Ellwood, and the National Commission on Quality Assurance (NCQA), which publishes a report on quality data known as the Health Plan Employer Data and Information Set (HEDIS).[46] The purpose of HEDIS is to help employers find out which plans are the better ones, so that they can offer quality health-care plans to their employees. It is hoped that the use of computer technology will make these measures of quality even more reliable in the future.

Critics note that a large part of the budget of the National Commission on Quality Assurance comes from accreditation fees paid to the commission by the managed-care companies, meaning that there may be pressure for the commission not to set its quality standards too high, a step that could cause some HMOs to fail the accreditation and cease being payers of dues. Perhaps some measures could be taken to ensure the autonomy of those who evaluate the presence of quality care. But whatever the criticisms, it is undeniable that managed-care organizations have helped stimulate the current focus on quality. A simple fact can be cited in this context: Managed-care organizations have placed a strong focus on the need to have health care provided by board-certified physicians. The percentage of board-certified physicians is significantly higher in managed-care organizations than is the percentage elsewhere in the practice of medicine.

Earlier we touched on the notion of a profession and the autonomy that goes with a profession. Autonomy protects the independent judgment on specific cases that belongs to any professional person. But "professional autonomy" means more than individual judgment. It also refers to the freedom and responsibility of any profession to grow as a whole by developing its standards of practice. In medicine it can be argued that professional judgment has too often been simply equated with scientific judgment and technological progress. The quality issue is more focused on practical wisdom in the daily exercise of professional judgment. If it is true that managed care is helping keep the quality question on the table, it can be argued that managed care is enhancing the medical profession. This enhancement is surely a morally responsible activity, an activity that is in keeping with the classic Catholic desire to support the professions.[47] If the quality of medical care goes up, it is the patients who will come out the winners, no matter whether they are in the process of being cured or in the process of dying.

*Preventive Measures and a Wholistic Notion of Health*

From the beginning, managed-care organizations have emphasized the use of preventive measures to promote human health. The very term "health maintenance organization" suggests this theme of enhancing health through measures such as education and prevention. Some experts suggest that as much as 90 percent of human health is dependent on a combination of good health habits (proper nutrition, adequate rest, and sufficient exercise), basic preventive steps such as immunizations and timely physical examinations, and environmental factors such as clean air and clean water.[48] So preventive health matters are a value in and of themselves. It also seems clear that preventive health measures can serve to reduce the cost of health care, with this too being an important human concern.

Beyond these fundamental arguments in favor of preventive health care, there are two deeper reasons why preventive health-care measures should be seen as a human and moral value. The *first* reason is this: If we do not include prevention in our understanding of the meaning of health care, health care is too easily construed as no more than a set of technological interventions aimed at repairing the human body (or the human mind) when something goes wrong. This point is not a criticism of modern medical technologies in and of themselves. But there is more to health care than technology. Health and health care raise profound human questions about who we are, how we live, and what human life ultimately means. Connected with these questions is the reality that health is a gift that we are called to care for. We are never certain as humans how long we will have the gift, and we often fail even to think about the gift of health until a crisis appears and we then realize that we may no longer have the gift of our health. There are many instances of people achieving whole new levels of appreciation of the gift of human health once a crisis causes them to stop taking the gift for granted. The issue of our mortality, of the meaning of human living and human dying, comes to the fore when we begin to ask these sorts of questions.

Preventive health-care strategies will not automatically connect us with these questions of moral and religious meaning.

But a larger notion of health care that includes prevention and education may raise these questions more easily than a totally technological construal of the meaning of medicine and health. In contemporary U.S. society it has become commonplace to hear strident attacks on the health-care delivery system. Some of these attacks may be justified. But it is hard not to wonder whether some of the attacks come from a refusal to accept the deeper meaning of health as a fragile gift that is connected with the mystery of human life. If managed care, with its focus on themes such as prevention and education, can make some people move away from trivialized notions of health, managed care will have done an important human service. The ability to ponder the fragile mystery of our health is enhanced by a context of communal human solidarity. Managed care has the possibility of promoting this context of solidarity.

The *second* reason to praise managed care's interest in preventive health care is that the turn to prevention opens up some very significant links with the contemporary scientific and theological concern about the environment.[49] It may not be going too far to argue that the contemporary shift toward an ecological consciousness is one of the most important developments in human thought to occur in the past 500 years. Since the time of the Renaissance, human beings have tended to look on the material universe as infinitely manipulable raw material, as material that exists so that we can do whatever we please with it in the name of progress. But in the past several decades, the construal of the universe as raw material has begun to break down. Environmental thinkers such as Rachel Carson and Bill McKibben have raised our consciousness.[50] The outstanding Protestant ethician James Gustafson has called on us to form a theocentric understanding of the universe, instead of staying with the older anthropocentric understanding in which we saw ourselves as the center of everything.[51] Pope John Paul II, in *Sollicitudo Rei Socialis* and elsewhere, has become the first pope to raise the issue of responsible care for the environment.[52] In sum, ecological consciousness, sometimes linked to feminist consciousness, has emerged as a major social concern as the new millennium begins. There can be no doubt any longer about the importance of ecological concern.

I have mentioned the need for deeper and fresher understandings of medicine, health, life, death, and human solidarity. Managed care, because of its different approach to health-care delivery, has the potential to help us think differently about health, solidarity, the meaning of life. It would be too simple to suggest that modern ecological thinking can offer us every single perspective we need to reformulate our approach to medicine and health-care delivery. There are some areas of medicine that will continue to depend heavily on medical research and on technological perspectives. Nonetheless there is a high level of interrelationship between ecology and the need for a new vision of health and health delivery. As philosophers would say, the question of ecology and the question about the meaning of health have about them a co-naturality. Recall that as soon as I introduced managed care's interest in prevention, I needed to explain *prevention* by discussing issues such as clean air, clean water, proper nutrition, and adequate rest. These issues—about our food, our air, our water, our noise, our pace of life, and our use of energy—are clearly tied both to our health and to ecology. Managed care's interests help put ecology on the table; this must be seen as a step forward.

### Managed Care and the Reduction of the Cost of Health Care

Managed care strives to keep health-care costs down. This is an important value, not only from the economic perspective, but from the broader human perspective as well. The Catholic moral tradition, long before today's debates, listed high cost as a factor that can make health care extraordinary rather than ordinary.[53] The insights behind this Catholic position are threefold. *First,* there is recognition that, despite the great good of medical care, death is a part of human life, so that there is a reasonable limit on what we should do and how much we should spend to prevent dying. *Second,* there is a Catholic awareness that, precious as it is, health is only one human good among many, so that society needs to avoid being so focused on health that it neglects other human goods. *Third,* there is a deep Catholic concern to exercise wise stewardship over health-care resources so that there will be sufficient resources available to care for all persons, especially the poor. These Catholic insights can be filled out in many ways, and important insights can be mentioned from other sources. But as long as a reasonable standard of health care can be maintained, the reduction of health-care cost is a good thing in and of itself.

The reduction of health-care costs was a significant development in the mid- and late 1990s in the United States. Sometimes this reduction of health-care cost occurred through a reduction in the rate of increase of health-care expenses, so that these expenses were not outpacing the cost of living and the rate of increase of people's incomes. But in other cases, such as Medicare spending in fiscal 1999, the actual outlay of money went down.[54] While factors other than managed care contributed to these cost reductions, managed care should be given credit for its role in helping keep health-care costs down.

There are several points of controversy connected with managed care and the lowering of health-care costs. Some critics point to the practice known as "cherry picking" (the best and the healthiest cherries) and argue that managed-care plans reduce cost by finding ways to recruit only the healthiest groups of patients, whose health care costs less on average. Other critics point to the very high rate of patient turnover in some managed-care plans. These critics argue that the high turnover rate shows that the plans with high turnover are saving money by failing to offer quality care. Still other critics point to the significant increase in the number of uninsured (from 37 million to 44 million since 1994) that has taken place during the same years in which managed care has become such a large factor in the delivery of health care in the United States.[55] These critics do not claim that managed care is the entire reason for the increase in the number of uninsured Americans, but they see managed care as a factor that contributes significantly to it.

There is another question about managed care and the cost of health care. Some scholarship argues that health-care structures that use the fee-for-service model cost only very slightly more than managed-care plans.[56] But even if it is true that today's fee-for-service plans and managed-care plans have almost the same cost, this has happened because fee-for-service medicine has learned to use the same strategies that were pioneered by the managed-care organizations. I refer to strategies such as the reduction of the length of hospital stays, preventive health care, and careful utilization of specialists. Whatever else is to be said for or against it, I think it is an unassailable fact that managed care has created a climate that has contributed significantly to the effort to keep health-care costs down. For all of us, and for our common humanity, this concern about costs must be seen as good in itself. It is an exercise of good stewardship.

In summary, I believe that the five factors I have cited (care of common people, solidarity, quality, wholistic health, and cost management) result in a substantial case in favor of managed care, a case with clear affinities to the Roman Catholic tradition. But there are two questions or two areas of doubt. *First,* is the case for managed care too much based on what managed care once was? Does the case ignore what managed care actually is today? And *second,* is the case too much based on a not-for-profit understanding of managed care rather than on the for-profit approach to managed care, which increasingly dominates the contemporary world of health-care delivery? These questions will be considered in the next chapter, which will discuss both the problems associated with managed care and potential remedies to these problems.

# Chapter 3
# MANAGED CARE: PROBLEMS
# AND POTENTIAL SOLUTIONS

## INTRODUCTION

The previous chapter made it clear that managed care has an impressive history. In light of this history, the frequent and sharp criticism that managed care receives today is very striking.[1] In the popular media, hardly a day goes by without one or more media sources launching a new critical attack on managed care. Scholarly sources are less sensational, and there are some scholarly defenders of managed care. But even the scholarly literature reflects the growing tone of criticism of managed-care systems.[2] Some media sources assert that managed care has failed completely and that its days as a health system are numbered. Others, such as the respected Princeton health economist Uwe Reinhardt, argue that the predictions about an early death for a managed-care approach to health delivery are very much overstated.[3]

The popular media strive to sell their product, and some of the attacks on managed care may be categorized as hype aimed at higher sales figures. But at a deeper level, the increasing criticisms of managed care reflect genuine concern about the current practices of managed care. Hence we must take a serious look at the problems of contemporary managed-care organizations and at possible remedies for these problems.

The first half of this chapter considers the contemporary criticisms of managed care. These criticisms are presented in five sections. The first section discusses difficulties with managed care from the viewpoint of the patient. The second reflects on the pressures and even self-identity issues that managed care can create for physicians. The third section comments on the problems with managed care that are experienced by hospitals. The fourth assesses concerns about the economic foundations of managed care, with special emphasis on the question of whether a theological anthropology of health care can ever be reconciled with large-scale for-profit approaches to medicine. The fifth and last section turns to the theme of social justice and assesses the compatibility between managed care and society's responsibility to provide universal access to a reasonable standard of health care.

The second half of this chapter considers possible remedies for the problems raised in the first half. Is it possible for these criticisms to be remedied so that managed care can prove to be a sufficiently just means of health-care delivery? Four possible routes to the reform of managed care will be discussed. *First,* what about vigorous activity on the part of patients and families? Can such patient and family action reform managed care? *Second,* what about the role of the doctors? Can a recovery of the ideal of the good doctor help reform managed care? *Third,* what about the managed-care providers themselves? Can they find ways to become the agents of their own reform? And *fourth,* what about the role of public policy vis-à-vis managed care? Can state or national government action be a means to reform managed care? The real question will be whether all four of these routes can coalesce so as bring about a more just managed-care system.

## MAJOR CURRENT CRITICISMS OF MANAGED CARE

### Patient-Centered Criticisms

At the level of the popular media, it is the problems of individual patients with managed care that attract the most attention. The issue of *Newsweek* mentioned in chapter 2 strongly emphasizes the patient, with its cover picture and strident headline proclaiming, "HMO Hell."[4] To describe the patient-related complaints about managed care, we will divide patient concerns into two categories: (1) surface presenting problems (what patients explicitly talk about), and (2) underlying substantive issues (the deeper matters at the heart of what troubles patients). In the category of presenting problems, five themes will be considered: (1) choice of physician, (2) access to specialists, (3) length of hospital stays, (4) access to emergency care, and (5) external decision makers.

To begin, the popular rhetoric about managed care frequently speaks about the desire of each patient to choose his or her own physician. This issue works differently in diverse managed-care settings. Some plans limit choice to only those physicians who are part of the specific plan, meaning that the patient has no option to choose anyone outside the plan, even for an additional copayment. Sometimes, even within a plan, the physician may be assigned to the patient without any decision by the patient, but there are also many cases in which the patient's choice of doctors from within a plan is not limited. So there are variations, but patient choice is an issue for many managed-care subscribers.

The concern about free choice of physician is understandable because the strength of the physician-patient relationship is a key element in successful health care, an element that relates closely to the underlying human dignity of the patient.[5] But it may be an overstatement to tie the issue of patient choice too closely to managed care. In any delivery system, patient choice will be limited. The physician the patient desires may not have time to take any more patients. She may be too far away from where the patient lives or works. He may charge more than the patient can pay. In addition, in some managed-care settings, patients and physicians develop very productive relationships. I am not denying the importance of the physician-patient relationship, nor am I denying that sometimes managed-care systems can create special problems of patient choice—for example, the case of the patient who changes jobs and cannot continue a long-term relationship with a much trusted physician because that physician is not covered in the patient's new health plan. Yes, patient choice of physician can be an issue in managed-care settings, but it may be an overstated issue, especially in sensationalized media interventions such as the famous "Harry and Louise" ads of the mid-1990s, sponsored by the HIAA, which featured the couple as opponents of the Clinton plan.

A second issue raised by patients is their desire to make their own decisions about seeing specialists. There is a place for clear recommendations about specialists from primary care physicians. Also, today's highly technologized vision of medicine may create in some patients a level of false expectation as to what specialists might be able to do for them. But we must remember that ultimately medicine is more an art than a science, so that the instincts of patients may sometimes be correct when they find that they are not at peace with what their primary physician recommends. The Germans have it right when they call the doctor *Das Artzt,* a term related to the English word *artist.* There are many situations in which the true standard of quality medical care is not clear, even if there has been significant progress in defining medical quality. In these cases, it is hard to contest the position that a specialist may be a better judge of the best medical course of action to follow. If managed-care plans exclude access to specialists in these specific circumstances, the criticism that the plans receive may be justified, at least in part.[6]

A third point of criticism raised by patients and their families has to do with the length of hospital stays. The general reduction of hospital stays in recent years is a good thing. I have rejoiced on a number of occasions to have been promptly released from a hospital. But are the early releases always good, always medically indicated? Or has the climate of early releases progressed to the point that some releases take place too soon? In spite of the many obvious values of early hospital releases, some releases do happen too soon for the patient's good. Most readers will be familiar with recent legislation that provides for longer hospital stays for mothers who have given birth. But is there a sufficient possibility for a longer stay in all cases in which a longer stay is medically indicated?

A fourth patient criticism of managed-care concerns access to emergency care. Do managed-care plans provide sufficient access to emergency care when the location of the patient makes it impossible for the managed-care plan's physicians and hospitals to be used to furnish the emergency care? In many cases, this criticism is now obsolete, because a majority of managed-care plans provide broad access to emergency care. A number of state laws have been enacted to require this sort of emergency care.

The fifth surface issue that patients raise in the context of managed care has to do with who makes the actual care decisions. Does the patient's doctor make the recommendations on her own, or are the care recommendations controlled by a source external to the patient-physician relationship? This is probably the most significant of the surface questions that individual patients will ask. It is also a question that is asked with equal or even greater frequency by doctors, since it so clearly relates to the professional identity of the physician. We will defer our consideration of this question until we have turned to the physicians' concerns about managed care. There have been some recent signs of change in managed care's approach to the question of who makes the final care decisions, and these signs of change will be considered when we take up the issue of who makes medical decisions in more detail.[7]

Each of these five surface concerns may sometimes be overstated, but each also bears significant weight as a criticism of specific aspects of managed-care plans. It also seems clear that even simple policy changes on the part of the managed-care providers could fairly readily address all of these surface issues. In some cases, this has already begun to happen.

Each of these five concerns hints at more substantive underlying patient concerns about managed care. Patients may frequently not be explicit in raising these deeper concerns, but the concerns are surely there. There are three major underlying patient concerns about managed care: (1) the autonomy of patients, (2) the need to trust physicians, and (3) a sense of ongoing confusion about how managed care works in the first place. I believe that managed care's ability to meet the concerns of patients will depend on how it addresses these deeper issues rather than on how it addresses the surface issues.

The first more substantive patient criticism of managed care focuses on patient autonomy. A great deal of recent biomedical ethics literature has stressed patient autonomy, as opposed to the pattern of earlier times when patients often reacted to their care with complete passivity.[8] In particular, the recent literature has stressed informed consent, that is, the right of the patient to direct the course of his or her care. Not every aspect of the modern stress on patient autonomy has been fully adequate. A reduction of medical ethics to a one-sided focus on autonomy is problematic. Medical ethics is not just about how patients decide (we hope with a genuine autonomy). It is about the underlying values that ought to guide patient choice. It is about broader social values, such as the appropriate use of limited health-care resources by the health-care providers, who are called to exercise wise stewardship of these resources. But the emphasis on autonomy is important. There should be no return to the days when all sense of self-direction stopped when someone crossed the threshold of the doctor's office or the hospital.

Traditional Catholic theological anthropology helps establish an important background for today's concern about autonomy and informed consent. Catholicism has long taught that human freedom is among the most central of all our human capacities. The Catholic interest in spiritual direction and confession came out of a recognition of human freedom and of the need to help shape human freedom. In the twentieth century one of the most significant of the Catholic documents was the *Declaration on Religious Liberty* from Vatican II.[9] While the specific concern of this document was religious liberty, the document's methodology applies to a whole range of human issues. Catholic thought is also helpful in focusing on human freedom as conditioned and limited by the very nature of our finite humanity. No area of human decision making is ever totally free, because we are historically limited persons.[10] Hence Catholicism would not see us as completely free in the area of health care. Catholicism would expect that we would both be free and subject to reasonable limits when it comes to health-care decision making.

To play out these thoughts about freedom and autonomy in the context of managed care, it can surely be argued that it is reasonable for systems to place some limits on patients' health-care decisions. Any exercise of human freedom has its limits, and some of the complaints about the freedom-limiting policies of the managed-care providers are not justified. But many people today believe that the total combination of freedom-limiting strategies used by managed-care companies has reached an unacceptable level, and the limits on patient choice are no longer just and reasonable. Recall that when I reviewed the surface complaints of patients about managed care, many of the complaints were rooted in a sense of the loss of patient autonomy. The statements, "I can't choose my own physician," "I can't decide when to see a specialist," and "I can't get emergency care," all relate to the autonomy issue. For many persons, even those who accept the principle of reasonable limits on patient choice, some forms of managed care seem to limit autonomy to the point that the fundamental dignity and freedom of the human person is undermined. If so, there is a clear moral problem.

There is an irony in all of this, namely that much sound scholarship about health believes that, when patients do have an adequate sense of freedom, they will commit themselves more fully to the treatment plan and fare better as a result.[11] Health care is very much a team process, with doctors, nurses, family members, and the patient all needing to work together to accomplish the best result. The patient herself or himself needs to have the experience of being an active agent in the pursuit of good health-care objectives. When the patient does have an adequate sense of self-direction and the treatment plan moves well, the end result may also be that the treatment will prove to be less expensive, meaning that the interests of the managed-care company and the general public are better served. Many managed-care companies have learned this lesson, and are making remedial efforts to keep their limits on patient autonomy at a reasonable level.

The second more substantive patient concern about managed care has to do with the theme of trust in one's physician. The physician-patient relationship is of its very nature a relationship that calls for trust. When a person goes to see a professional—any professional—for help, the person makes two very basic assumptions: (1) that the professional is competent in the matter at hand, and (2) that the professional will unquestioningly and unhesitatingly act in the best interest of the person who has come to the professional for advice. The person seeking help places a radical trust in the professional, and the person can be deeply hurt if the trust proves to be unwarranted.[12]

Because of my many years as a seminary professor, I have had some sad opportunities to see how terribly hurt people have been when their priests failed them. The same kind of hurt is possible in those cases in which a doctor fails in her bonded commitment to the patient. For Catholics, I would argue that both doctors and priests are placed on an especially high level of trust as professionals. It used to amaze me how frequently people in hospitals—staff members, patients, and family members—would call me "Doctor" and call some of the doctors "Father." I think this slip of speech occurs because of people's very high regard and trust level of both doctors and priests. It can hurt badly when this trust is broken.

Underlying many of today's patient complaints about managed care is a fear that patients can no longer trust their doctors, because the doctors have to respond to the goals of the managed-care organization rather than always acting for the good of the patient. It is not true that all external challenges to doctors' judgments are inappropriate. Even in the early history of managed care we saw some legitimate challenges to the ways in which doctors practiced medicine. But patient trust is pivotally important. It is fair to say that managed-care organizations need to be structured in such a way as to maintain that trust. Here too managed care will probably save money if it fosters a climate of patient trust.

The third substantive patient concern is that many patients are confused about how managed care really works. This confusion makes them worry about whether they are getting proper care. As an example of how confused people are, one recent study reported that 54 percent of persons currently enrolled in an HMO stated that they have never been members of an HMO, and 68 percent of persons currently enrolled in a PPO stated that they had never been members of a PPO.[13] Another factor adding to patient confusion about managed care is the climate of rapid changes and turnovers in managed-care plans. It is by no means unprecedented for a managed-care plan to come into a geographical area, set up shop, enroll perhaps several hundred thousand patients, and then leave the area, all with in a few years' time. This has happened frequently in the case of Medicare HMOs, which ought to have a special loyalty to their senior citizen patients. For the general population, unexpected changes can come from even very highly respected managed-care companies, as was the case with the November 1999 decision of the Tufts Plan to stop covering patients in Maine, New Hampshire, and Rhode Island, so that about 150,000 people had to find new providers. Still other examples of patient uncertainty about managed care—what it is, what it covers, and how it works—could easily be cited. The lack of understanding—and the related lack of confidence—can easily leave people frustrated.

If we recall the classic Catholic understanding of the person, the theme of human knowing quickly emerges as deeply central in the Catholic approach to the meaning of our humanity. Debates have flourished in Catholic thought across the centuries about whether human freedom or human knowing is more definitive of who the human person is. Even in our own times a scholar like Karl Rahner can be seen as representing the intellectualist position, whereas Cardinal Joseph Ratzinger can be seen as representing the voluntarist side of the debate.[14] But what is not debated is the importance of both intelligence and free will. Earlier I spoke about the lack of human autonomy in health-care decision making and how problematic this lack is because of the importance of human freedom in a key area such as health care. The same point should be made about the lack of human understanding of today's health-care systems. Because health care is so central, there seems to be a clear responsibility of health-care providers to make their systems as clear and comprehensible as possible. Human dignity surely requires this.

We began this with some simple patient concerns about managed care. These surface issues are all capable of being addressed by suitable changes in the design of managed-care plans. The surface concerns have led us to deeper issues, such as genuine freedom, trust in physicians, and human understanding of health care. These deeper concerns can also be addressed, if managed care chooses to do so.

*Physician Concerns about Managed Care*

Because of a fairly thorough ongoing dialogue in the medical journals and elsewhere, physician concerns about managed care are more focused than are the concerns of patients. Hence we can move directly to three fundamental physician concerns about managed care, all of which are related to the professional judgment of the physician as he seeks to act for the patient's good. Physician professionalism includes a variety of issues that go beyond the specific question of physician judgment about patients. But judgment about individual cases is a crucial concern for physicians as professionals. Many of them fear that their judgment can be compromised in managed-care systems by one or some combination of the following three factors.

*First,* physicians worry that someone other than themselves will make the final decisions about which treatments their patients will receive. I am not implying that all outside review of physician decisions should be rejected. In some cases there may be overridingly clear medical standards that the individual physician is not following. In other situations, where a given medical treatment is clearly optional, a plan might legitimately decide in advance not to cover such a treatment, a fact that should be known in advance by both physicians and patients. In still other cases, a treatment may be experimental, so that no one can say for sure whether the treatment will help the patient. A plan may legitimately decide not to cover such a treatment. In other cases it may be valuable for a physician to have her decision reviewed retrospectively. This would not change what the physician has recommended, but the review may help the physician give additional consideration to the course of treatment that should be followed in similar future cases.

But even with these qualifications, there is still the situation of a treatment that is covered in a given plan and that the physician clearly believes will be beneficial to the patient. Is it ever ethical for someone other than the patient's physician to decide whether such a patient will or will not receive such a treatment? As a matter of both justice and professional respect for the physician, no managed-care company should remove the decision about such a treatment from the physician-patient dialogue. If the physician recommends in this kind of case, and the patient agrees, the treatment should be given.

One of the major managed-care companies has recently announced that it will no longer remove these kinds of decisions from the physician-patient dialogue.[15] It will be important to see the exact details of the new policy, and also important to see whether other managed-care companies follow suit. It is quite intriguing that the company's study of the matter showed that it cost more to review the physician decisions than was saved by the vetoing of physicians' decisions. As happens fairly often, responsible ethical behavior turns out to be more responsible financially.

The *second* source of physician worry is that, without actually removing decision-making authority from them, managed-care companies will place significant financial pressure on physicians to decide in certain ways, especially ways that save money. It frequently happens that, when a managed-care company enters into a contract with a physician group, the contract will provide the group with a sizable additional income if the group meets certain financial targets. This managed-care strategy is sometimes called "risk sharing," because it places physicians at financial risk depending on how they perform. Especially if a group is fairly small, and if there is not a strong program of stop-loss insurance, one or two cases may be all that's necessary for the group to miss its target and lose significant income. Some of the scholarly literature reports that the premiums paid to a medical group for financial restraint can run as much as 25 percent, a figure that may cause the doctors' actual income to go up by as much as 50 percent or even more, when we consider their fixed costs for employees, buildings, and medical equipment.[16]

When we hear numbers like this, it is hard not to remember that doctors are human beings too, often with spouses, children, and aging parents who may need financial support. How can a doctor's medical judgment not be at risk of being compromised, if the financial incentives for non-treatment decisions are very great? I am not rejecting all financial incentives for doctors, because fiscal prudence is part of the stewardship

that is an important underlying health-care value. From its earliest days, the Kaiser Plan (in which the doctors were not
employees of the plan) always placed the member doctors at
some financial risk for their overall practice decisions, and
this step was considered an important factor in Kaiser's success. So what I am rejecting are financial incentives of a size
great enough to compromise the doctor's basic commitment
to his patient, thereby creating an actual conflict of interest.
To offer a specific number, I am inclined to agree with the
position of Dr. Ezekiel Emanuel and his co-authors that incentives that increase a doctor's income by 20 percent or less after
stop-loss insurance is figured in probably are not great enough
to compromise a doctor's medical judgment. But incentives of
more than 20 percent would seem to be unethical, because the
risk of compromised medical judgment becomes too great. A
top incentive of 10 percent may be an even more ideal figure
to work toward. To further reduce the risk of financial conflict, Dr. Emanuel and his co-authors add that for additional
reduction of conflict in capitated payment schemes, the smallest group of capitated patients should be 250 patients and the
smallest group of physicians receiving capitated payment
should be fifteen physicians.[17] It should be noted that in June
2000, the U.S. Supreme Court refused to rule out the payment
of financial incentives for physicians by managed-care companies, although the court left open the possibility of state
and/or federal regulation of such incentives.[18]

The *third* concern doctors sometimes express about managed care is less specific than the first two. This concern is that
some doctors, even if there are no specific review mechanisms
or financial incentives, find today's health-care climate to be
coercive, so that they feel subtle pressure not to follow their
best medical judgment if that judgment involves a costly
course of treatment. There even seem to be cases in which a
managed-care company is ready to approve a given procedure,
but the doctor hesitates to recommend it. To say this in
another way, doctors fear that today's health-care context will
not respect their professional medical judgment. Recent
research suggests that even the tone of today's medical schools
is very different. Already in medical school the students are

learning to be careful about not recommending too many medical tests and to be careful about not utilizing too many medical services.[19] This raises troubling questions about whether future generations will see sufficient numbers of well-motivated and well-qualified young people choosing careers as physicians. I have one doctor friend who says that he worries that the climate is such that young people who are bright enough to get into medical school will also be bright enough to decide to do something else with their lives.

I am not implying that all of the pressures on physicians are strong enough to create conflicts of interest for physicians. Some of the changed climate that helps make doctors and medical school students more cautious about ordering too many tests is actually for the good, because it saves the patient from unnecessary procedures and practices stewardship over valuable medical resources. Nonetheless, it is fair to say that at times the pressures are great enough to raise the specter of compromising the physician's professional judgment.

As with patients' concerns about managed care, all of the physicians' concerns appear to be remediable if managed-care organizations choose to remedy these concerns. It is possible to come up with designs that avoid unreasonable limits on doctors' professional judgments. It is possible to avoid unreasonable financial incentives. There is nothing inherent in the nature of managed care that necessitates the policies that many doctors find so troubling. The hope is that suitable reforms will keep on happening so as to address the doctors' legitimate concerns.

## Managed Care and Problems for Hospitals

I have focused attention on patients and doctors because the issues that affect them are fairly easy to understand. But hospitals can also have difficulties with managed-care organizations. Some of these difficulties are exactly the same as those experienced by patients and doctors. Hospitals can find it very difficult when a managed-care organization denies a patient something that is perceived as truly necessary treatment. Sometimes such cases force a hospital to stretch its charity budget to levels that may threaten the stability of the hospital. But hospitals also have their own unique difficulties with managed care. A managed-care company may set its reimbursement rates for some procedures at levels substantially below what it actually costs the hospital to provide the treatment. Managed-care organizations may run far behind schedule in paying a hospital for its services, so that the hospital's income, which it needs to pay its employees and suppliers, may be running millions of dollars behind schedule. The seriousness of these problems is such that there are frequent news reports of hospitals discontinuing their contracts with certain managed-care companies, because it seems impossible to do business under the terms that the managed-care company is following. Such a step may mean that large numbers of patients—again hundreds of thousands of people—will need to find new insurance carriers if they want to keep using their traditional hospitals. All in all, hospitals can have serious difficulties in the managed-care environment.[20] Perhaps the underlying issue is that while the delivery of health care needs to be based on sound business practices, health care is more than a business. It is a commitment to serve the common good, something which managed-care companies cannot ignore in their relationships with hospitals.

*The Economic Structure of Managed Care*

In chapter 2, I outlined the origins of the managed competition model, with its emphasis on cost control and related techniques. This model has drawn criticism from a number of sources. The more one envisions health care as a reality grounded in a strong sense of communal solidarity, the more one is inclined to question whether a market-based model of health care can succeed as a just and moral undertaking. This question needs to be asked of any market-based approach to health-care delivery, but it is a question that applies most especially to for-profit systems of health care. In the context of managed care, while not-for-profit entities dominated the earlier days of managed care, the for-profit companies now account for more than half of all managed care, and the for-profit percentage of the managed-care marketplace is growing quickly. Hence the question about market economics and managed health care becomes steadily more significant.

I want to be clear that not-for-profit systems of managed health care have different underlying motives and values and thus are not the same as for-profit managed-care companies. But it is nonetheless true that many of the not-for-profit health-care providers have begun to make use of some of the for-profits' financial and management techniques, so the ethical use of market-based methods is a question for the not-for-profit health-care providers as well, although certainly to a lesser degree. It may well be that the primary reason that European health-care systems have developed so differently than those in the United States is that, throughout the entire postwar period, the Europeans have construed the fundamental meaning of health care out of a much stronger sense of social solidarity, a sense that permits far less market thinking to enter into the delivery of health care. Some critics state that in the United States the delivery system for health care has been designed to meet our underlying market assumptions about economics, whereas Europe structures the economic systems that support health care so as to meet the underlying assumptions about the need for social solidarity as the basis for the delivery of health care.[21]

The question about the justice of the for-profit approach to health-care delivery is not simple. In many ways the current economic approach to health care has worked. The rate of increase of health-care costs has declined significantly. The U.S. economy improved dramatically in the latter half of the 1990s, in part due to the fact that health-care costs increased much less rapidly, or even showed actual decreases. There are significant and thoughtful defenders of a market-driven, for-profit approach to health care, defenders who argue that only the discipline of the market can pull the U.S. health-care system out of its recent chaos. Prominent defenders include Regina Herzlinger, Uwe Reinhardt, and Alain Enthoven.[22] Part of the argument advanced by defenders of for-profit health care is that it is too simplistic to assert that profit making is the only function of modern for-profit health systems. Instead, there are many stakeholders to whom modern health-care corporations are responsible: patients, doctors, hospitals, the general public, and of course the shareholders of these corporations. The argument holds that all of these stakeholders can be simultaneously served in a climate of true justice.[23]

On the other side are those who argue that the nature of health care is uniquely focused on human life, human dying, and the very meaning of human community. As such, health care can only succeed when it occurs in an atmosphere whose primary context is shared social concern. This means that the quest for true justice in health care can never be fully compatible with a market approach to health-care delivery. Persons who argue along these lines claim that for-profit managed care will never be able to work as a health-care model, and we must begin to look for something else. The anti-market thinkers on health care often point out that the construal of health care as pure science and technology can easily link up with the market model of health care, so that health care's chief goal becomes the effective marketing of new technologies. Even if this is an overstatement, the union of market forces and technological forces can make a whole vision of health care all the more difficult to achieve.[24]

My own approach falls somewhere between the strong defenders and the all-out critics of a for-profit model of health-care delivery. Nothing in Catholic thought absolutely rules out a for-profit approach to health-care delivery. It is clear that some good has come to health care through the vigorous management techniques associated with profit-making. Some segments of health care clearly seem to work effectively in a for-profit context, even if other segments do not. A small group of physicians may be defined as a for-profit enterprise; the profit is not for stockholders, but rather to supply the income on which the doctors and their families live. Surely, no one could object. If we grant the value of medical research, investment (and a resulting profit) to help fund such research may be reasonable. These examples do not address the question of very large for-profit managed-care companies, which, in addition to covering hundreds of thousands or even millions of people, are also responsible to their stockholders. But even at the level of these very large companies, I do not think it is possible to offer a simple univocal judgment.

So I am anxious to avoid a simplistic answer. This should not obscure the fact that some of the recent practices of managed-care companies are outrageous from the moral point of view. In the past several sections, we have talked about unreasonable denials of patient freedom, excessive constraints on the professional judgment of physicians, and payment strategies that prevent hospitals from living out their mission of providing quality care to people. While these practices can be found in many types of managed-care companies, there is no doubt that they are driven by the business strategies of the for-profit managed-care companies. Even the custom of describing necessary medical care as a loss makes it very clear that the bottom line rather than a sense of mission is too often what drives today's managed-care companies.[25] All things considered, the public's growing outrage about managed care is clearly understandable and justified to a considerable degree. It is hard not to feel that we have come a long way down the wrong road from the moral heroism of the early managed-care doctors such as Sidney Garfield, Sandy MacColl, and Michael Shadid, who were so deeply committed to the bringing of good care to their patients.

But the possibility of morally responsible for-profit managed care cannot simply be ruled out. If government were to play its historic role in prudently regulating the excesses of for-profit managed care, for-profit managed care could be an ethical approach. The concept of combining free enterprise and government regulation into an ethically responsible approach to economic justice is very well grounded in Catholic thought, for example, in the theme of socialization and the tradition of social liberalism. At the same time, in light of the discouraging signs noted, the possibility of for-profit managed care becoming a moral success is a possibility that is subject to very grave doubt. There is a growing credibility to the position of those who argue for a fundamental irreconcilability between the nature of large-scale profit-making businesses and human health care as an activity rooted in human community and human solidarity. This judgment could still be proven wrong, if for-profit managed care can address the current complaints without creating new issues that are equally or even more problematic.

Earlier I stated that all of the patients', doctors', and hospitals' criticisms of managed care appear capable of being remedied if managed care changes its ways. I also believe that it is possible for managed care to set aside the excesses associated with its sometimes one-sided emphasis on profit-making and managing competition. But the challenge of setting aside these excesses is substantially greater than the challenges related to the patient, doctor, and hospital issues. And the challenge is less likely to be met successfully, especially without adequate government regulation.

The challenge is greater for two reasons. *First,* to make these deeper changes, managed care, especially for-profit managed care, will need to add significant elements of balance to the profit-making ideology that drives so much of it. *Second,* managed care in all its forms will need to become more mission-driven. It will need to develop a new and richer vision of the meaning of medical care, a vision less focused on constant technological progress and more attuned to dying as part of the human story, a part of the story we must accept, even though we can and should continue to make all reasonable efforts to prevent our dying. Daniel Callahan has developed this theme of a new vision with his call for a sustainable medicine.[26] The efforts to achieve a sustainable medicine are going to be particularly complex, because it is not only the managed-care industry, but also the whole of contemporary U.S. society that is in need of a conversion on this theme of the true meaning of health care. As I mentioned earlier, the profit theme and the technology theme seem to stimulate each other in an unhelpful symbiosis.

I hesitate to make these remarks sound too pessimistic, because of my great regard for managed care, especially in its earlier not-for-profit history. But the reasons for doubt are grave. Is the combination of profit-making and technologically dominated medicine a fatally flawed combination? Will managed care have the moral strength to avoid being dominated by the imperatives of profit and technology? Or will it be more likely that a different management system for health care will emerge to lead us toward a more socially responsible approach to health-care delivery? Only time will tell.

One more point: Since the beginning of 1999, several Catholic bishops have issued policy statements about hospital mergers involving the Catholic hospitals in their dioceses.[27] There is one common theme from these bishops' statements that is quite striking. All of them stipulate that they will not accept formal mergers between Catholic health-care facilities and investor-owned, for-profit health-care providers. While Catholic principles do not answer every conceivable issue about profit making and health care, at least several thoughtful Catholic bishops have concluded that the current tone of the for-profit managed-care industry cannot be reconciled with Catholic health-care sponsorship.

## Managed Care and Universal Access

Universal access to a reasonable standard of care is an issue of signal importance in terms of the Roman Catholic approach to health-care justice. We have already noted the sad and crucial fact that in the past five years—years of very rapid growth for managed care—the number of uninsured Americans has increased from 37 million to 44 million. The reasons for this increase are complex and cannot all be laid at the doorstep of managed care. But the dominance of managed care and the high number of uninsured persons come together to raise a key question: What is the possibility that managed care can organize itself in such a way as to help increase access to health care, help move the United States nearer to the goal of universal access? The more likely it is that managed care might help the move toward universal access, the more positive should be the moral evaluation of managed care. And vice versa.

At first glance there seem to be many reasons to doubt whether managed care can serve to enhance universal access. Particularly if we consider the profit-making motive of many managed-care organizations, care for poor people who cannot pay would seem to be a very remote priority for managed care. So it is hard not to have grave doubt about the potential of managed care to help foster universal access. In a more general sense, any health goal of a broader social nature, any goal without a specific economic lobby to help support it may have a hard time under managed care. For instance, hospitals that sponsor medical education—and in the process are likely to care for poor people—have a hard time enrolling managed-care patients because the managed-care companies do not want to pay the higher costs that teaching hospitals may need to charge.[28] Such an approach is short-sighted, because everyone will lose if there is not good medical education, just as everyone will lose if society is destabilized because of the outrage of the millions who lack access to health care. Some of the difficulties here are due to governmental cutbacks in support for medical education, which was traditionally seen as a common-good issue and was supported by the United States, especially through Medicare. But it is very hard to get managed care to focus on a broader social goal such as medical education, which lacks any immediate prospect of economic payoff.

But there are features of managed care that may help the move toward universal access. Managed care's ability to save health dollars is a plus. At least in theory, some of the savings could be used to care for the poor. Managed care's concern for preventive care may also help achieve justice. Its strategies of reducing the wasteful utilization of health services and finding out more clearly which services offer the best quality of care may help reduce costs and thus make more resources available for the poor. So there are reasons to think that managed care has elements that may help address the lack of access to health care by the poor. The key question is how socially responsible managed care, especially for-profit managed care, is willing to be. Will the drive for profit be so strong as to cut off all possibility of broader social responsibility? Or will market-driven managed care be able to take the longer view and see the need for strategies without which there may be no market left?

It seems unlikely that managed care will take on the stance of broader social responsibility all by itself. Part of the question may be how far we as a society will be willing to go in managing managed care. Some critics assert that the problem today is that managed care is becoming more and more a form of purely free competition instead of managed competition.[29] Might it be possible to use the strengths of managed care in combination with social pressure and direct regulation to bring about a more just system of access to health care? While doubt must remain, it is possible that this question will one day be answered in the affirmative.

## POSSIBLE STRATEGIES FOR THE REFORM OF MANAGED CARE

The rest of this chapter considers four possible sources for the reform of managed care. These sources are (1) patients and families; (2) doctors, hospitals and other provider groups; (3) managed care itself (as aided by the quality movement); and (4) governmental regulation.

### Patients and Families

Often the literature that talks about patients and families as sources of health-care reform speaks of them, and of the companies that employ them, as "consumers." This term suggests a certain narrowness of vision, with its construal of patients as purchasers of goods. The human dignity issues that are so much a part of health and sickness are overlooked by the use of the consumer analogy, an analogy that shows how strong the market orientation is in today's health-care world. When most people seek health care their focus is on very deep issues about what life really means, and they are not thinking of themselves primarily as consumers. The term "consumer" applies more reasonably to the employers who purchase coverage for their employees, but one would hope that employers would be working from a different attitude when they seek to provide health-care coverage. For the company's work, an employer may need to purchase steel, lumber, or parts. These decisions are more purely market decisions, whereas justice would see a decision about employee health care as relating to a different level of human good.

At first glance it would seem that patients and families will be able to have relatively little effect on the structure of today's managed-care systems. Since most decisions about specific health-care plans will be made by employers, the influence of patients and families will be mostly indirect. For the most part, people need their jobs and have little choice other than to accept the plan (or range of plans) that the employer offers. In addition, the complexity of today's health-care environment makes it very difficult for most patients and families to understand their health-care plan with any real depth. Patients are very often not in any position to offer intelligent and reflective critiques of their plans. My favorite comparison has to do with the difference between buying an automobile and buying health care. Most people who buy automobiles will be able to learn enough about the different carmakers' products to buy the vehicle they want at a reasonable price. But can they have the same level of knowledge about health care, which is much more complex, and likely to be needed at times of great stress that make it all the harder to understand all the issues clearly? Employers may be able to know a little more, but even for them, particularly for small businesses, there may be limits in their ability to mount effective criticism of the practices of today's managed-care companies.

These cautions should not lead us to dismiss the ability of patients and families to help bring about change. There is a tradition of patients and families acting as stewards of their own health care. It may not be easy to know which health-care plan will work best, but it is surely possible to know when something is wrong. Even though many patients still describe themselves as satisfied with their health-care plans, a growing number seem to be learning, through unhappy experiences, that something is wrong. This awareness is awakening many employers who care about their employees, so that the employers are trying to make better decisions and trying to push the managed-care companies toward more just practices. The managed-care companies themselves seem to show some sensitivity to patient complaints. From a market perspective, patient dissatisfaction is seen as bad business for the managed-care companies. Some of the companies have begun to use surveys on patient satisfaction and to make the results of these surveys a factor in the decisions about whether to award additional financial compensation to physician groups.[30]

Besides the general impact that patient concern can have on the structure of managed-care plans, two other patient-related themes deserve mention. The first is patient education. The more that patients and their families learn about the problematic side of managed care, the more articulate patients and families will become, and the more likely it is that managed-care organizations will respond to patient concerns. Even though the popular media's reports can sometimes generate more heat than light, they are helping to raise patient awareness. In addition, more serious publications are giving increasing treatment to managed-care issues.[31] Public interest groups and others such as churches are also doing more to educate patients and families about managed care. For all these reasons, patient awareness is growing, even though it will always have its limits.

The second theme is that, even apart from the knowledge of individual patients and families, a number of organized groups focus on health care from the patients' perspective. Among such groups are the American Association of Retired Persons and Families USA. The Catholic Health Association has a primary focus on Catholic health-care providers, but many of its interests support the health needs of families. The same is true of some of the stances taken by the American Medical Association. When all these groups are considered, there is a significant potential for patient- and family-driven approaches to the reform of managed care. Especially if patient and family interests are linked with other sources of reform, there is reason for cautious hope that managed care can change. But there is real doubt as well.

*Doctors, Hospitals, and Other Providers*

What about doctors and the problems of today's managed-care systems? Can doctors bring about change? It might seem that there is relatively little that doctors can do to influence managed care. Doctors are small-business persons, and the managed-care companies are large industries that therefore seem more powerful. The managed-care companies control which doctors patients are allowed to see, meaning that in order to maintain a supply of patients, doctors need to go along with the policies set by the managed-care companies. Otherwise, the doctors might not be able to get very many patients. The former days, when doctors exerted a great deal of control over the structure of medical practice, seem largely to be gone.

In spite of these obstacles, there are significant ways in which doctors may be able to influence the managed-care environment for the better. Even if the social standing of doctors is not as high as it once was, doctors, as professionals, are still very much respected in contemporary society. As a group doctors are more trusted than are managed-care companies. They may help determine which forms of managed care (HMOs, PPOs, PHOs) win greater acceptance by the public. If doctors—as individuals, in groups, and even in national organizations such as the AMA—can make their concerns about managed care known to the public, the doctors' concerns may influence public opinion and therefore increase the pressure for changes in managed care. In addition to this kind of information sharing, some doctors are moving toward more aggressive efforts to confront managed care. Fairly frequently one reads accounts in the media of doctors' groups that are refusing to accept patients from certain managed-care companies, because the doctors find the practices of these companies to be unacceptable.[32] In addition, there are recent reports that the California Medical Association, with the support of the AMA, has sued three of California's large investor-owned insurance companies, claiming that the interference in doctor-patient relationships by these insurers is a violation of federal anti-racketeering laws.[33] This follows earlier, narrower suits by state medical societies in Georgia and New York. It is hard to predict the long-term outcomes of such strategies. Will these strategies cause some doctors to be frozen out of the marketplace, or will the actions of the doctors and the medical societies be a catalyst for systematic changes in managed care? It is hoped we will see the latter result.

In general, the law construes physicians as independent businesspersons who cannot form unions, except for unions that represent doctors who are employees of hospitals or of the large medical groups used by some managed-care companies. The legislation restricts union membership for doctors because of fears that union doctors would engage in price fixing and restrain free trade. Such a restriction made eminent sense in the days when fee-for-service models dominated medical practice. But today, when the managed-care companies are so powerful, independent doctors and small group practices can feel overwhelmed, and look to find ways to join forces. There are some serious legislative proposals afoot that would permit doctors to unionize or at least bargain collectively. It will be interesting to see what happens to these proposals and to see how they affect doctors' ability to influence today's managed-care climate. The House of Representatives has passed legislation that permits doctors to bargain collectively, but it is uncertain whether this legislation will actually become law.[34] There are some serious issues to be debated here—for example, whether the unionization of doctors would serve to further commercialize medicine, thereby adding to some of the problems mentioned earlier.[35]

Hospitals are in a significant position on the matter of being agents for real change in today's managed-care environment. While managed-care companies own some hospitals, in most places managed-care companies need to negotiate contracts with existing local hospitals so that these hospitals will care for the managed-care companies' patients. This means that hospitals need to court managed-care companies, since a given managed-care contract may mean millions of dollars of income for a given hospital. But there is a two-way street here. To stay in business in a given locale, the managed-care companies need the local hospitals to agree to accept their patients. By staying independent of control by managed-care organizations, strong local hospitals, and even more so independent networks of local hospitals, are in a position to exert substantial leverage to help move the managed-care companies toward more ethically responsible standards of practice. Such leverage may even have some effect on issues as basic as care for the poor. Since the hospitals know that care for the poor and uninsured is a fundamental human necessity, might they be able to negotiate contracts that obligate managed-care companies to provide care for the poor? Some places have begun such arrangements, with managed-care companies obligated to pay into a state fund from which hospitals can obtain monies to help offset the expenses they incur in providing charity care. Unfortunately, such funding is usually used for health crises instead of the basic care that would serve to avoid more costly crises. But this example—along with other examples about fair reimbursement for complicated cases and about more freedom in making care decisions—shows that hospitals may be able to have significant impact on the character of managed care. Hospital employees can sometimes feel very limited in the face of large and powerful managed-care organizations, but there is reason to hope that hospitals, especially corporately owned groups of hospitals, may be agents for change.[36]

Besides doctors and hospitals, there are other groups that are part of the larger provider community. These include the sponsors and owners of health-care services, which may be religious organizations, universities, foundations, or community-based groups. The ability of these groups to influence today's managed-care scene has been less well analyzed, but it is clear that many of the non-public owners of health-care services come from sectors of society that are often held in quite high esteem. If the religious groups and universities are able to make their voices heard on managed care, they may be able to influence the public debate. Even the broader issues on which doctors and patients may have little impact (medical education, care for the poor) might be brought to the fore by these important provider groups. In the context of the churches, it is hard not to wonder about the potential impact of joint efforts by the hospital sponsors (often religious communities) and church leaders (bishops, judicatory heads) to speak for health-care justice. Such joint efforts might prove to be an important catalyst for change. The role of informed laypersons and parish-based groups may also have an important impact.

We should take note of the alternative providers that are growing and flourishing at the start of the new millennium. I speak of entities like home health services, hospice care, parish-based nursing programs, emergency clinics, and wellness centers. In some ways these groups have been aided by the advent of managed care, but managed care can make it difficult for patients to access these alternative services, even though such services may serve to lower the cost of patient care. This difficulty of accessing alternative services is especially present in managed-care models that do not fund services from outside the managed-care network. Many segments of the public are sensing more and more the value of these alternative services. This public esteem opens up the opportunity for these alternatives to influence the debate about managed care.

### Managed Care Reforming Itself

What about managed care, especially in its for-profit guise, serving as the agent of its own reform? Frequently, managed care is heard to say that it will do just this. While some of the managed-care industry's statements about self-reform may be classified as self-serving, there are two major ways in which managed care may be capable of some self-reform. *First,* managed care may be able to accomplish some self-reform by getting in touch with its historic roots. Three of these roots may have significant reform-oriented potential. The first root is managed care's long-standing interest in seeking to discern which medical care is truly quality medical care. The more that can be learned about this, and the more often lower quality medical interventions are avoided, the more likely it is that more people's health-care needs will be met. The second root is managed care's equally long-standing concern with promoting human wellness. If managed care joins with hospitals and others in accepting a larger degree of social responsibility to care for the poor, it may seek to apply some preventive measures to the poor out of a sense that this may be less expensive. Finally, there is managed care's rich history providing care to persons who really needed it and were not likely to get it through normal channels. If managed care can recover this heritage, it might become a source of significant social reform in health care. But the basic question remains: Will the strong market orientation of today's managed-care systems permit such a heightened social consciousness to come to the fore?

The *second* way in which managed care might move to self-reform is by engaging in a genuinely listening dialogue with its critics. Previously, we described the bonafide problems that many groups—patients, families, doctors, hospitals—have with the current tone of managed care. What about managed care's genuinely listening to all these groups and responding to their concerns? Good businesses in many fields know that they ought to do this. It may be fair to say that managed care has reached a "shape up or ship out" situation. Either it will address the legitimate concerns of others, or it will fail. There are some encouraging signs, such as the decision of one very large managed-care company to leave medical judgments to doctors and stop using an external approval process. It will be important to see the details of this changed policy, and I personally find it difficult that the new policy does not apply to mental health professionals.[37] But still, decisions such as this show a receptiveness to public opinion on the part of managed care. There is also an irony in the fact that the decision to follow the public's wishes and eliminate the approval process may end up being less expensive. So when all is said and done, there are some reasons to hope that managed care can reform itself.

### Public Policy as a Means to the Reform of Managed Care

The role of public policy in the reform of health care in general is a crucially important role that touches all aspects of health care, not simply managed care. Later we will review the overarching issue of public policy as a means to health-care justice. Here, the purpose is simply to offer some brief reflections on the potential of public policy as a means of reforming today's managed-care environment. Nowadays, many of the thousands of pieces of state or federal health legislation introduced in the

United States every year are aimed at managed care.[38] So our review of the possibilities of reforming managed care would be incomplete if we did not give some consideration to what state or federal legislation might be able to do.

Legislation alone could never be the sole source for the reform of managed care, or for the reform of any other broad social problem. The fundamental claim of Christian ethics is that every human person has a human right to a reasonable standard of health care. This claim is rooted in the concept of society as participative, as based on human solidarity. Unless the human community can come to this underlying notion of social life through a genuine conversion of hearts and minds, mere legislation will never be an adequate route to reform. As much as legislation has helped advance the civil rights of racial minorities and (to a lesser degree) of women, legislation alone can never fully resolve the underlying attitudinal issues related to racial and gender justice. Similarly, while legislation can help address certain environmental issues, the fundamental environmental issue (a realization that the world is God's world, not ours) will never be fully addressed by legislation. In the end, law as a means to the reform of managed care will need to work in tandem with many deeper personal, religious, and social values.

These cautions about legislative reform of managed care should not obscure the fact that law can and should be part of the process of reforming managed care. Some of this has already happened. Consider, for example, the great concern that surfaced in the mid-1990s about managed care's policy of limiting most mothers of newborn children to only one day in the hospital. Nearly every state now has outlawed this practice. Consider also the concern about physician gag orders, a policy of not permitting physicians to discuss with patients any treatment options that the managed-care plan is not willing to cover. Here again, many places have passed legislation that outlaws such gag orders. Other recent and successful pieces of legislation could also be cited.

Besides these examples of already enacted legislative reforms of managed care, some of the currently pending proposals for legislative reform are quite promising. One example that deserves special mention is legislation that would give patients and families the right to sue managed-care companies as means of contesting denials of care by the managed-care companies. By way of background, past federal legislation has been very concerned to assure the stability of company pension plans. Under the well-known Employee Retirement Income Security Act (ERISA), the self-funded plans of many companies are protected from lawsuits by the employees or retirees. Since many companies' health-care plans are also self-insured, ERISA immunizes the carriers of these plans against lawsuits.[39] This seems to be an example of legislation passed at an earlier time for a very good purpose that turns out later to have an undesirable side effect, that is, the inability of patients to sue their managed-care plans. Legal reform clearly seems desirable here, even if the reform might need to set reasonable limits and procedures in the matter of suits against managed-care companies.

So there have been legislative successes, and other potential successes loom on the horizon. But there is also great doubt as to how much legislative reform of managed care we will actually see, especially at the national level. There are so many special interests hovering around Washington, D.C., that one cannot help wonder whether truly substantial legislation will be able to pass. The first session of the 106th Congress (1999) may be an example here. In the House of Representatives, a coalition consisting of about one-third of the Republican majority and a large percentage of the Democrats succeeded in passing a very significant piece of legislation, including a right of patient lawsuits against managed care.[40] But the strategy of the Republican House leadership, in consultation with the U.S. Senate, helped make the final passage of any bill very unlikely, and during the second session of the 106th Congress, the Senate, voting along party lines, rejected managed-care legislation.[41] It is regrettable that the tradition of the common good and of government's responsibility to act for the common good did not come into stronger play in the final decision about this legislation. Early in his presidency, George W. Bush expressed support for a patients' bill of rights, including the right of patients to sue managed-care companies under rather limited conditions. In the 107th Congress, both houses have passed patients' rights legislation with the House's more cautious bill favored by President George W. Bush. It remains to be seen how the differences between the two bills will be resolved and whether the president will sign the bill which comes out of the House/Senate conference.

A fascinating side point is that among the Republican members of the U.S. House of Representatives, there are several health-care professionals. It was this group that was able to marshal a significant number of Republicans to join with the House Democrats in passing the 1999 bill. The efforts of Congressman Charles Norwood, a dentist from Georgia, and then Congressman Tom Coburn, an obstetrician from Oklahoma, were especially important in getting the bill passed. It is hard not to think that these legislators understood the issues better than did a number of their colleagues.

My expression of pessimism about national legislation makes it important to pay careful attention to managed-care legislation at the state level. The individual states are not subjected to as many special interest pressures as is the national government. This fact may give the states greater freedom to pursue creative legislative strategies vis-à-vis managed care. Several different legislative patterns seem to be emerging at the state level, and some of these patterns may prove to be successful in the managed-care environment. One new pattern, occurring in states such as Massachusetts and Washington, is that doctors and other groups are backing ballot initiatives seeking to reform health care and guarantee universal access to health care.[42] Successful legislation at the state level may prove to be an important step in paving the way toward more comprehensive national legislation. There are doubts about the legislative approach to the reform of managed care. But there are also reasons to hope that legislation may be of help.

## CONCLUSION

These comments bring this book's main treatment of managed care to an end. In summary, over its longer history, managed care has had enormously significant social and moral successes. In the current era, managed care has become infested with some grave social and moral problems, especially due to the for-profit ideology that drives so much of managed care today. There are some promising routes to the reform of managed care, but there is also well-founded doubt about how far these routes to reform will take us. The biggest issue is whether the for-profit motive of many managed-care providers can ever be reconciled with the fundamental human responsibility to offer reasonable access to health care to all people. The future stability of the United States, and of the world as a whole, may depend in part on the successful development of policies that provide reasonable access to health care. The jury is still out on managed care. It may reform and become part of the road to truly just health care. Or it may fail, so that we will have to look elsewhere to find the path to true health-care justice.

# Chapter 4
# THE ETHICS OF MERGERS, JOINT VENTURES, AND OTHER RECONFIGURATIONS

## INTRODUCTION

At the beginning of this book, I mentioned three major trends that have marked health-care delivery in the United States since the collapse of the Clinton proposal in 1994: the rapid growth of managed-care systems, the equally rapid increase in mergers and joint ventures, and the tendency toward piecemeal government interventions coupled with overall reductions in government financial support for health care. Chapter 4 offers an ethical assessment of the almost breathtakingly fast realignment of health-care services through mechanisms such as mergers and joint ventures. At times it seems that realignment decisions are happening so fast that someone interested in health care has to check every morning who owns whom today. Even with a slight decline over the past year or so, merger activity remains the outstanding business activity of hospitals today.[1] The chapter contains four major sections. *First,* we shall describe several different types of reconfigurations and make some general comments about the reconfigurations, especially as they affect Catholic health-care providers. *Second,* we shall discuss the reasons for the mergers and the values that they have achieved or at least hope to achieve. *Third,* we will talk about the problems associated with the realignment decisions, especially from the viewpoint of ethics and religious values. *Fourth,* we will consider some of the difficulties that realignment decisions can create for health-care organizations that are sponsored by the Roman Catholic Church, with its very strong and deeply historic moral commitments on the nature of health care. The difficulties for the church are by no means insoluble, and with more than 15 percent of all U.S. hospital beds owned by Catholic sponsors, it is impossible to think about health-care realignment without Catholic health care being part of the picture.

## DIFFERING TYPES OF REALIGNMENTS

Realignment arrangements can occur in various ways, both in terms of structures and in terms of the parties in the realignment. Six common realignment structures deserve mention. In describing them, we shall move from the loosest type of partnership toward the most tightly linked structures. The first and simplest type of realignment is a loosely affiliated *provider network*. In such a network, several health-care providers agree to work together and help support one another's interests. They may refer patients to one another and share certain services such as billing and payroll, but they have no formal ties to each other. Such networks operate mostly on the basis of good will, and the network will collapse if good will collapses.

A second quite simple structure is a *joint operating agreement.* In such an agreement, a group of providers, while remaining distinct entities, put in place a legally structured agreement that establishes a common management and a common operation of some or even all of their activities. Perhaps two or three local hospitals agree to a common billing operation, common payroll system, and common purchasing agency. Such a joint agreement might go so far that all the daily activities of the several hospitals take place in common. But the agreement might also be more limited, so that only certain activities become shared functions. The joint operating agreement is a stronger structure than a nonbinding provider network, but on the whole it remains a fairly loose structure. The worry that many persons experience about joint operating agreements is that they may too easily collapse because the ties among the original providers may not be that strong. In many joint operating agreements, there will be quasi-independent teams of management personnel. This helps assure autonomy to the partnering entities, but it may not assure truly integrated working relationships.

A third structure, related to a joint operating agreement, is a *joint venture.* Joint ventures usually refer to situations in which some health-care service or services are lacking in a given area. Rather than any one provider taking on the needed service(s), several providers together establish and own laboratories, outpatient clinics, hospice programs. Even a new hospital in a growing area may be a joint venture among the earlier providers. Ethical conflicts can arise in the area of joint ventures if the public is unclear on who owns such a service and why there is a tendency for patients to be referred to that service instead of to a competitor. But joint ventures can be a helpful way of making necessary health-care services present in a given area. Especially if some new lines of service are needed, joint ventures may be the way to bring these services into being.

A fourth and significantly stronger relationship occurs when two or more providers undertake a *revenue merger.* In this case the assets of the providers remain legally distinct, but for practical purposes the merged entities are acting as one company with one management team. Even if a new board of directors is put into place, the owners of the assets will retain certain powers related to the appointment of the officers and board members. There may also be agreements that specify certain revenue streams not to be shared, even though most revenues are shared. This is the famous "carve out" arrangement that we will need to consider when we talk about Catholic health-care providers entering into shared revenue mergers with providers whose practices are not fully in accord with the *Ethical and Religious Directives.*[2] A revenue merger creates a very coherent structure, and it assures a truly common operation, which hopefully works for the good of all people, especially the patients who need the care.

A fifth and even stronger form of merger occurs when the assets of the health-care providers become part of a new company that is no longer owned by the original owners. A new board of directors and a new set of officers are put into place.

The previous owners may hold some board seats into the future. But the newly created company will run itself. This is the boldest type of new venture, but it may also be the most likely to succeed. Even though simpler arrangements may be better in some circumstances, if a fresh new approach to health care is needed, an *asset merger* may be the best way to achieve this approach, because it will create a more unified and coherent system of health delivery. Asset mergers call for a letting go by the earlier owners of a health-care service. This occurs because the former owners will no longer have the control they once had.

The sixth type of realignment happens when facilities/services owned by one provider are sold outright. In these times of enormous financial pressures on health care, it frequently happens that a given owner cannot continue to operate a facility or set of facilities. Sometimes this situation leads to a closure of a health-care facility. But frequently the sale of the facility that cannot continue as is will be the better choice. The facility may still close in the end, but at least many of its services and programs will be saved even if transferred elsewhere. Sometimes a sale may lead to a revitalization of a moribund facility so that it again becomes a strong and vital health-care provider. Decisions concerning such sales frequently take much moral courage for both the seller and the buyer. The seller may need to face up to the fact that the best way to save the historic and ongoing contributions of a facility will be to sell it to someone else rather than letting it run itself into the ground. The buyer may need to take some significant risks, both financially and humanly, so as to save and revive the facility.[3]

In the Catholic context, the sale or purchase of health-care facilities may work in several different ways. Sometimes one Catholic party will purchase a facility from another Catholic party. Sometimes a formerly secular facility will be purchased by a Catholic party and become subject to the *Ethical and Religious Directives.* In other cases, a Catholic group may sell a facility or facilities to a secular group. Any one of these courses of action may be appropriate depending on the circumstances. It should be mentioned that, when a Catholic group receives income from the sale of health-care assets, there is a general moral responsibility that the income be used in a manner that fosters the mission and ministry of the church.[4] In addition, it is frequent for there to be legal requirements about how such income, often based in part on tax benefits, is put to use.

Our comments so far have concerned the different possible types of realignment structures. There are also different types of parties who may be involved in the structures. There are frequent hospital-to-hospital transactions or system-to-system transactions. Many of our subsequent comments will be focused on these transactions. But there can also be transactions between hospitals and doctors' groups, between hospitals and managed-care organizations, and between managed-care organizations and doctors.[5]

In the mid-1990s, hospitals had a very strong interest in purchasing physicians' practices. The thinking was that the purchasing of these practices was an essential step in the hospitals remaining competitive. Relationships between hospitals and physicians remain very important, and hospitals frequently employ physicians to help the hospitals meet specific needs. But there is less enthusiasm today for outright hospital purchases of physician practices. While the hospitals want to work closely with these practices, the goals of the hospitals and the doctors may not be close enough for actual ownership of the practices to be the best solution, even though it still happens. Even from the financial viewpoint, solutions other than hospital ownership of physician practices may be better. Earlier we spoke about physician-hospital organizations in which hospitals and doctors work together on the basis of a joint agreement, but without ownership of the practices by the hospital. This may often be a better approach.

Managed-care companies usually work with hospitals on the basis of annual contracts. But there are cases in which managed-care companies own their own hospitals (a long time practice in some of the Kaiser organizations). There are also cases in which managed-care companies seek to purchase already existing hospitals as the managed-care companies grow and expand in a given area. And there are partnerships between hospitals and managed-care companies that are stronger than simple annual agreements. Yes, hospital and hospital system mergers very quickly catch the public eye. But there are many other significant partnerships as well.

It should also be noted that proposed hospital transactions are often hotly debated in the public arena. Normally, civil regulatory approval is needed before a transaction can be consummated. Many transactions, such as the relocation of hospital beds to another site, call for the granting of a "certificate of need." The approval of a certificate of need has to go through a public process with hearings, state review, and other steps. When one hospital or group of hospitals is seeking a certificate of need, other providers in the area will often fear that they will be placed at a significant competitive disadvantage if the other hospital or hospital group gets its certificate. So certificates of need are likely to be highly contested, sometimes in a courteous manner, but sometimes with much acrimony. This aspect of hospital realignment is highly distasteful.[6] Health care exists for the common good of society, not for the aggrandizement of profit-seeking entrepreneurs. The public controversies about realignment are not all bad, as there is a place for reasonable public debate. But the tone of many of the public exchanges may be a sign that a concern about profit is all too present. This concern can put significant pressure on the not-for-profit providers, even if the basic mission of the not-for-profits is clearly different.

I have described the variety of types of arrangements so as to give the reader an overview of the sorts of things that can happen. It is not my purpose to give a deeper analysis of the differing types of arrangements, nor is it my purpose to make the case that some types of arrangements are always preferred. Every one of the specific arrangements may be the best choice in a situation. In what follows I will focus on mergers and other ventures as a global phenomenon. But sometimes I will need to reflect on one type of partnership as opposed to others.

As an integral part of this explanation of health-care realignment, it should be noted that Catholic health-care providers have become very much involved in the world of mergers and joint ventures. In the mid-twentieth century, most

Catholic hospitals were operated as independent entities, even if they were owned by the same religious community. Beginning around the 1970s this began to change. During that period most religious communities that owned hospitals joined these hospitals together into unified health-care systems. In the case of religious communities with a small number of hospitals, the merged systems were usually national systems including all of the community's hospitals in the United States. But some Catholic religious communities with large numbers of hospitals created different regional systems for different parts of the country. Not all of these Catholic systems were the same. Some of them were fairly loose organizations with a great deal of local autonomy. Some of them became quite tightly organized, with strong national or regional leadership, strong financial management systems, and unified personnel policies both for local leadership and for employees everywhere. Not all Catholic hospitals joined these religious community-based health-care systems. Some remained independent, and very successfully so.[7] But the majority joined these earlier Catholic systems. For Catholic-sponsored health care, the trend toward larger health systems did not just begin with the merger frenzy of the 1990s. The roots of integrated Catholic health-care systems go back twenty-five years and more.

This earlier history formed the basis for what may have been an even more important period of change and integration for Catholic health care during the 1990s. In the mid-1990s, several situations emerged in which the leaders of three or four different religious communities decided to put all of their assets together to form even larger Catholic health-care systems, sometimes with fifty or more hospitals and several billion dollars worth of health-care assets. This trend continued in 1999, when there were two cases in which two religious communities with large unaffiliated health-care systems decided to join their assets into larger unified systems.[8] The current health-care climate convinced these Catholic leaders that even their already quite well-organized health-care systems were not up to the pressures of today. In sum, we are now seeing a second generation of Catholic health-care systems that I call the mega-systems. The mega–Catholic systems have had some notable success, but they have also had some struggles, especially in the case of Catholic Healthcare West in California, which has had to cope with significant labor/management tensions and with the dissatisfaction of some member hospitals.[9]

Some observers of the trends toward unification in Catholic health care have wondered whether all the moves of recent times might ultimately lead to some sort of single nationally unified Catholic health-care system. This will be unlikely, because of local and regional differences in health-care needs, and because the fascination with ever-larger health-care organizations may be coming to an end.

These comments have touched on cases of new relationships between Catholic hospitals and groups of Catholic hospitals. In addition, in many geographical areas in the United States, Catholic health-care services have formed new relationships with other local providers. The ethical questions raised by these mergers with other than Catholic parties are discussed at the end of this chapter.

It may be helpful to comment here on the concepts of Catholic sponsorship of health care and Catholic ownership of health-care assets. When a religious community formally commits itself to a certain ministry in the church, it is said to be "sponsoring" that ministry. A ministry may be sponsored by one religious community or it may be sponsored jointly by two or more religious communities. The community that sponsors the ministry may also own the assets used in carrying out the ministry. But a community may decide to place the ownership of the assets in the hands of its health-care system or in the hands of the individual hospitals. It is to be noted that ownership of assets in the technical or civil sense is not exactly what Canon Law considers when it seeks to determine who controls a given set of assets. Canon Law uses the concept of a public juridic person who is responsible for the oversight of the assets.[10] In this context it may be the case that, even if a subsidiary corporation owns a set of hospitals, Canon Law will still regard the council of the sponsoring religious community as the public juridic person who is responsible for the assets.

These concepts of sponsorship, ownership, and public juridic personality are important in the context of mergers and related transactions because of the fact that when the assets of a religious community are sold or transferred to someone else, such a transaction may require the approval of either the diocesan bishop or the Holy See, depending on the canonical status of the religious congregation that owns the assets. The specific language of Canon Law is that when the "stable patrimony" of a religious community is alienated, church approval is required if the value of the property to be alienated exceeds a set amount (currently $3,000,000 in U.S. dollars).[11] Some of the arrangements described above (joint operating agreements and so on) do not require such church approval. Even certain actual transfers of assets may not require such approval, particularly those cases in which the religious community (the public juridic person) remains the sponsor and also clearly retains the ultimate direction of the assets. But other transactions, such as a sale to someone else or a withdrawal from sponsorship, are an alienation of property in the canonical sense. The cases that do require formal church approval should not be construed as unreasonable interference by the church. Rather, the church wants to be sure that church assets are not transferred to parties whose purposes are deeply at odds with the church's values. The church also wants to be sure that religious congregations do not lose the resources ("stable patrimony") that are necessary to support the members of the congregations, especially after they retire. I have found Catholic bishops to be unfailingly helpful to religious congregations in these situations. Here we will not enter into a complete analysis of all of the canonical issues that may come into play when a religious community is working through a hospital reconfiguration decision. But the canonical question of alienation of property is important enough that it deserves mention.

## WHY ALL OF THIS REALIGNMENT?

*Patient-Centered Reasons*

So far our focus has been on describing the different types of realignments that are taking place today. But why is all this realignment happening? It can be hard not to have a wistful longing for the good old days of simple local hospitals unaffiliated with anyone else. In the past, many people identified a specific hospital as *their* hospital. They may have been born there and gone there a generation later to bear their own children. Their parents may well have died there. In the same era, people had long-term relationships with their physicians, relationships that may have lasted for thirty to forty years, or for the entire professional career of the doctor. Many examples of this memorable past could be cited. One example that I hear over and over has to do with women who clearly remember details about the hospitals where their children were born.

The times I am describing are past, and they will not return. But the memory of the past raises important questions: Why all the change? Why all the realignment? For what purposes is this being done? Here I will outline three major reasons for the rapid realignment of health-care services. The first reason has to do with the need to make available to people truly integrated systems of health delivery. The second reason has to do with making health-care delivery more effective and efficient, both in terms of human and medical resources and in terms of managing financial costs more prudently. The third reason focuses on the importance of creating larger hospital organizations so that these organizations can be in a stronger position to deal with the pressures imposed on hospitals by managed-care organizations.

We begin with the first reason: to make quality health care available to people in an integrated fashion. To understand this issue, it will help to review the modern history of medicine. Modern health care began in the latter part of the nineteenth century because of two key developments: (1) the creation of effective antiseptic procedures under the leadership of physicians such as Joseph Lister, and (2) the discovery of effective anesthesia under the leadership of physicians such as Crawford Long. These two advances made surgery possible and laid the groundwork for many of the spectacular advances in medicine that occurred during the twentieth century. As we begin the new millennium it is easy to forget how simple and primitive medicine was just a century ago.[12] Doctors tended to be somewhat of an underclass, often earning less than the farmers who constituted most of their patients. For many doctors the biggest annual operating expense was the annual upkeep of their horses and buggies. Many of these doctors were great moral heroes, making long journeys to visit patients, staying up with sick patients all night in the patients' homes. But there was little that these doctors could do for their patients in terms of what we today think of as standard medical care. In 1900, life expectancy around the globe was only about forty-five. Recall that in the world as a whole, between 1800 and 1950, about 1 billion people died from just one disease: tuberculosis.[13]

Even though the roots of modern medicine date to the late nineteenth century, medicine remained fairly simple for the first half of the twentieth century. One statistic that helps show the character of mid-twentieth century medicine is that until after World War II a strong majority of all doctors were trained as what people then called "general practitioners."[14] Yes, there were some residency programs for medical specialists, but specialists were a definite minority. Medicine was quite familial and communal. In that context small unaffiliated hospitals really worked. They worked wonderfully well.

My next words sound like those of the great theologian Karl Rahner: "Today all this is quite different."[15] Medicine has become enormously technical and specialized. Even though recent years have seen a revival of family practice, medical specialization has become predominant. Relatively few patients develop a long-term relationship with a family doctor. Patients are likely to deal with a whole series of physicians, often in discrete short-term encounters with little opportunity for building trust. A patient who is in the hospital with multiple symptoms may have several different doctors involved in her care, with no one of these doctors having a complete picture of what is happening. Related to this development of special-ties, medicine has grown like Topsy since the middle of the twentieth century. In many cities a wide variety of hospitals, clinics, rehabilitation centers, and auxiliary support services have grown up, often with very little integration and fre-quently with overlapping or redundant services that raise health-care costs. There was a climate of relatively unregulated competition between hospitals and other medical services, so that if one local hospital opened a line of service, other hospi-tals felt that they had to follow suit, lest they be placed at a competitive disadvantage.

These happenings made the medical system very compli-cated and very difficult for the individual patient. Even when a patient successfully accessed one medical service, he might still be uncertain as to where to go to obtain other needed services that were not offered at the original care location. The traditional method of physician referral helped alleviate some of this difficulty, but the problem remained. Physicians themselves were subject to the same difficulty of not always being familiar enough with complex local service patterns to make the best possible referrals.

With this background, we can begin to see the most basic reason for today's very strong impetus toward the creation of integrated delivery networks (IDNs) in local areas. The basic reason is so that the patient, as soon as she seeks health care, has access to an integrated network of services that, except in very unusual circumstances, will be able to furnish the patient all the health care she needs in an integrated, uncomplicated, high-quality manner. The integrated network is trying to offer the patient the sense of trust and security that used to be avail-able through a family physician. Relationships between patients and physicians are still a key element in a successful approach to health care. But in today's world, it is impossible for the doctor-patient relationship to provide the same wholis-tic sense of health care it once did. So the goal is to help the patient make contact with an integrated high-quality pattern of services. This need to provide quality integrated care for patients is the first major reason underlying today's very rapid realignment of health-care services.

There are other reasons for health-care realignment. But these reasons should not obscure the fact that the move to health-care realignment has begun out of a desire to better serve patients. Health-care realignment has not been a complete success. But if the health-care system can become more accessible—for ordinary people and without constant confusion—this will be a great step forward. A return to the 1950s is a naïve pipe dream. Fully integrated, easily accessible health-care networks may be one of our last best hopes for achieving a coherent approach to health-care delivery. The ideal is for there to be two or three such networks in each of our major metropolitan areas, so that the different networks stimulate each other to provide high quality health care. A multiplicity of networks may not be possible in smaller cities or rural areas, but even in these locales access to networks may be the key to comprehensive health care.

*Systemic, Social, and Financial Reasons*

The second set of reasons for realignment is focused on the broader social nature of health care and on the need of today's health-care systems to exercise wise stewardship of health-care resources. The haphazard development of health care from the mid-twentieth century onward tended to create chaos for individual patients. But the chaos was also very bad for health care itself. Some services, even very costly services, were excessively present in given geographical areas. One example is that in the early 1990s there were more magnetic resonance imaging machines (MRIs) in Los Angeles County than in the entire country of Canada. Hospital beds were frequently in oversupply, especially as medical progress created the possibility of shorter hospital stays (or no hospital stays) for many health-care situations. Creative realignment planning has often been a better way to lower the number of hospital beds, and such realignment may help the space used for such beds to be employed for services such as skilled nursing or assisted living. Without such planning the excess beds were more likely to simply disappear through wars of attrition that hurt everybody.

More will be said later about the cost of pharmaceuticals, but there is one point about drugs that should not be put off. A significant amount of the money spent in the development of drugs is spent for the development of drugs known as "Me too" drugs. A drug is called a "Me too" drug when one drug company, probably at a cost of millions of dollars, has developed an important new medication. Other drug companies fear that they will be placed at a disadvantage by their competitor's new drug. So they in turn spend their own millions of dollars to develop a similar drug so they can compete with the original drug for sales. The second (and perhaps the third and the fourth) new drug is a "Me too" drug, whose research cost everyone in the United States ends up paying for. It is true that some "Me too" drugs turn out to be significantly better than the original product, but this does not deny the reality of the inefficiency of the way in which drugs are developed in the United States.[16] On the whole it seems clear that a more integrated approach to the development and production of drugs could serve both to reduce patient cost and improve patient care.

In addition to beds and pharmaceuticals, many other aspects of the health-care system became highly inefficient and excessively costly. Some of these problems and duplications of services were addressed through processes of natural attrition. But for the most part it was and is far better to accomplish the necessary efficiency through coherently planned strategies. Coherent health-care networks are important not only from the viewpoint of eliminating the duplication of health-care facilities, goods, and services. Well-designed networks also offer the possibility of providing health-care services in a better-organized and more cost-efficient fashion. There are several steps networks can take to help foster efficient care and cost reduction. Necessary hospital supplies may be purchased at better prices. Administrative overhead can be reduced. Measures to assure the provision of best practices and truly quality care can be introduced. Liability insurance costs can be pooled over a number of institutions and probably reduced. Just benefits may be able to be provided to employees at a lower total cost.

Programs to lower the rate of medical errors may be more easily put into place.[17] Personnel may be able to be more readily moved from one location to another so that they end up where they are truly needed. These comments make it clear that, in addition to providing better clarity and accessibility for patients, well-designed health-care networks can be more coherent and cost effective. This sort of stewardship can help everyone.

In summarizing the possibility of greater efficiency, I have used the term "networks." In health-care parlance, the term "integrated delivery network" (and its acronym IDN) has become the catch phrase for describing all the advantages possible through more coherent approaches to health-care delivery. But recall that there are a variety of realignment mechanisms: joint ventures, joint operating agreements, revenue and asset mergers, and so on. Every one of these mechanisms has the possibility of achieving better service for patients and wiser use of resources. Differing mechanisms may be better in different circumstances. I am not using the popular term "network" to create the impression that I am only in favor of loosely affiliated health-care networks.

*Mergers and the Confrontation of Managed Care*

A third reason for health-care mergers is that mergers may help to put the larger merged groups of hospitals in a stronger position to negotiate contracts with managed-care companies. Such contracts can enhance quality health care and foster the quest for justice. The needs for patient service and efficiency have not disappeared, but the need to concentrate power so as to be able to confront the managed-care companies looms larger and larger as the years go by. Many recent commentators on mergers stress the role of mergers as a strategy for confronting the issues raised by managed care.[18] We need only reflect back on the problems associated with managed care to appreciate the role that hospital mergers might be able to play if the merged hospitals can act as challengers of managed care.

## SOME PROBLEMS WITH HEALTH-CARE REALIGNMENT

The case for health-care realignment is a credible case that deserves support. But has realignment of health-care services in the United States unfolded in a fully acceptable fashion? Has the process of realignment been free of problems and difficulties? There have been significant successes—for example, new health-care entities that have reduced patient cost and improved the quality of patient care. But there have also been difficulties in two major areas: (1) realignment decisions that have taken place without sufficient forethought, and (2) realignment decisions that have not taken account of the problems associated with very large increases in the size of health-care service systems.

Once realignment strategies began to get up a full head of steam in the middle part of the 1990s, it was hard not to get the impression that, at least in some situations, there was almost a frenzy to put together realignment packages. It seemed that there was often too little reflection on whether a given realignment structure would really work. In any realignment decision, a number of crucially important questions need to be studied in detail. If the services owned in a local area by two or more providers are put together into a network, is the network designed so that the result really will be the integrated continuum of services that the community needs? Or will the network fail to create this integrated continuum and possibly even create greater holes in the local health-care delivery situation? What about the prospective financial savings? Are these real or only a matter of speculation? What about the quality of care? Will the network improve it? What about the cultures of the two organizations? Can the cultures be integrated? Often, hospitals have had significant historical rivalries. It can be quite difficult for them to come together. It will sometimes help if a third party is introduced into the mix of a merger. This third party may be able to help modulate the historic rivalries.

Similar questions need to be asked about realignments that create broader regional or even national health systems. When health-care realignments are under consideration, the legal term "due diligence" often comes into play. Due diligence refers to a period during which someone, especially someone who is buying someone else's hospital, has the opportunity, before consummating the transaction, to examine all of the financial and legal structure issues of the hospital to be purchased. What I am suggesting here is that, in health-care merger transactions, a broader sort of due diligence is necessary to be sure that all of the human and service-oriented aspects of a transaction have been given an in-depth assessment, especially from the viewpoint of mission and ethics.

In many transactions the climate of haste to accomplish some sort of merger has led to merger decisions that have not worked out successfully. The sad result is that some of these mergers have come undone in fairly short order. Recent examples of merger situations that did not endure include the Optima Health Network in New Hampshire, the agreement between Penn State University and Geisinger, and the withdrawal of the Daughters of Charity from the Unity Health System in Rochester, New York.[19] These mergers failed for a variety of reasons. Sometimes the cultures of the two organizations were just too different. Sometimes the pressures of the given marketplace were too much for the merged entity. Sometimes the partners were not able to reorganize their services into a coherent and productive pattern.

Strong efforts will be made to assure good futures for these providers after the failure of their mergers. But the point remains: Sometimes there is too much haste to accomplish mergers and too much fear that if a given hospital does not merge, it will inevitably be at a competitive disadvantage when compared to other nearby hospitals. There has been more caution in the past year or so, as the health-care community has learned lessons from those mergers that did not succeed. But it is fair to list uncritical haste as one of the negative elements that can come to the fore in mergers.

The second major weakness in some of today's realignment decisions has to do with an excessive fascination with ever-larger health-care systems. While it is true that larger size may help a health-care provider accomplish some or all of the values I described earlier, size in itself is not a virtue. Without careful planning, the larger size of a health-care provider can create a sense of alienation on the part of its patients. It can create a new level of complexity, making the health-care system harder to fathom. These sorts of things do not always happen when realignment takes place. They can be avoided with careful planning so that health care remains sufficiently personal and sufficiently understandable. But the risks are there. Just as there can be undue haste in assembling new health-care networks, so also there can be an excess fascination with sheer size. It is too early for in-depth studies of why some merged health-care organizations have failed. But along with uncritical haste, a major factor contributing to merger failures is the lack of mitigating steps to offset the problems that can arise due to the larger and potentially more dehumanizing size of a health-care organization.

Larger size is not bad in itself. Certainly some quite large health-care organizations have been able to maintain high levels of patient satisfaction. But larger size can have its pitfalls, especially when the hurry to assemble a merged health-care organization leads to insufficient planning. In this context it is hard not to think about the wisdom of the traditional Catholic principle of subsidiarity that we discussed in chapter 1.

## SPECIAL ETHICAL PROBLEMS FOR CATHOLIC PARTIES IN HEALTH-CARE MERGERS

*Introduction*

Earlier I noted that there are some specific canonical and legal issues that Catholic health-care providers must face when they enter into health-care mergers. These issues concerned sponsorship, ownership, and the alienation of church property. But there is another, perhaps even deeper set of issues that Catholic health-care providers must confront when they consider mergers with health-care providers that have not previously been Roman Catholic. This deeper set of issues concerns the place of the *Ethical and Religious Directives* in the resulting merged entity. Because of the importance of this matter, we will discuss it in some detail. After some preliminary notes, we will consider the fundamental ethics of cooperation, the common Catholic approach to cooperation on fertility and human life issues, and strategies for working together on broader social moral issues.

*Preliminary Notes*

Two preliminary points should be mentioned. *First,* there is a popular concern about how issues like abortion, euthanasia, and sterilization will be handled in a merger between Catholic hospitals and other providers. But it must be remembered that the Catholic issues of importance in a merger negotiation go far beyond the issues of fertility and human life that immediately strike the popular mind. Catholicism has a very deep commitment to care for the poor, to justice for employees, to the spiritual care of patients, to quality care for dying persons, and to a reasonable balance of scientific medicine and basic human care for the sick.[20] If any of these issues is being treated in a deeply inappropriate manner by a potential partner, one would hope that the Catholic provider (and the local diocesan bishop) would have grave reservations about a merger, with these reservations sometimes being as serious as the reservations about issues such as family planning that surface more quickly in the media and elsewhere. Later we will offer some suggestions about how these broader social moral issues might be addressed in a merger negotiation between a Catholic health-care provider and someone else.

The *second* preliminary point is this. A number of scholars would wish to add some significant nuances and qualifications to some of the themes of Catholic moral teaching raised in the *Ethical and Religious Directives* and other documents that summarize Catholic moral teaching. Some scholars would push even further and, without questioning any foundational Catholic moral values, propose reformulations of some specific elements in Catholic moral teaching.[21] In the proper context, these sorts of discussions may be of genuine service to the Roman Catholic moral tradition. There is important reflection taking place today about how best to situate these discussions so as to prejudice neither the need for clear Catholic teaching nor the place of sound theological reflection.[22] As a moral theologian, I am very naturally interested in all serious efforts to understand and express Catholic moral teaching more adequately.

But this task of ongoing study and possible reinterpretation is not our purpose. Instead the purpose here is to accept the stated Catholic moral teachings on biomedical ethics, and then to ask the following question: Are there ever circumstances in which a Catholic health-care provider may enter into a business arrangement with another provider whose practices are not fully in accord with official Catholic moral teachings? Without doubt, the answer can be Yes, but it is much too simple to state the Yes without explanation. The Yes must be grounded in an explanation of the Catholic moral tradition's approach to cooperation. Hence we turn to a summary of the Catholic concept of cooperation, both as a theoretical issue and in terms of specific cooperation decisions in the field of health-care ethics.

## The Catholic Theory of Cooperation

For centuries, Catholic thought has recognized that at times a person or institution may legitimately cooperate in the evil action of someone else for the sake of a greater good.[23] Perhaps the most common popular example has to do with the person who happens to be driving past a bank just as the armed robbers emerge with the money they have stolen. The robbers accost the driver and threaten to shoot him unless he drives the robbers to their hideout. Obviously the value of the driver's life and health is of paramount importance, and it is surely acceptable for the driver to cooperate in the robbery by driving the car so as to stay alive. While this example may sound too simple, it underlines the fact that we can all face complex situations in life in which it is reasonable to go along with something we do not accept for the sake of the greater good. This is the basic notion of cooperation.

Several important distinctions should be added here to help fill out the concept of cooperation. Suppose, for example, that the bank robbers were a large and well-organized gang. In this case, they probably had their own getaway driver waiting for them outside the bank. The driver in this scenario did not actually rob the bank, but certainly this driver is in a different situation than the driver who came on the scene as an innocent passer by. Traditional language has described the driver who was part of the gang all along as a *formal cooperator* while the innocent passer by driver was a *material cooperator*. The tradition has also stated that no one may ever formally cooperate in a behavior that is known to be wrong, but that, for a sufficient reason, one may materially cooperate in a behavior that is known to be wrong. For example, a doctor could never actively support a managed-care program that unjustly limits patient and physician autonomy. This would be formal cooperation. But a doctor might reluctantly accept such a program as better than no health care at all, if the program in question is the only one available to the patient. This would be material cooperation.

Since formal cooperation can never be justified, the real question that emerges concerning cooperation is the question of when material cooperation can be justified. There are four key issues to be considered when making decisions about material cooperation, with the ultimate decision about material cooperation coming from the interaction of these key issues.

The first key issue has to do with the *level of duress* being faced by the person or institution that is considering a material cooperation decision. The greater the duress, the better the case for material cooperation. In the case of the innocent bystander who drives the bank robbers, the level of duress is very high. If a Catholic health-care provider, perhaps the last Catholic provider in a local area or even an entire state, faces almost certain closure without some sort of merger arrangement, the duress may also be quite high, since the Catholic provider may feel forced to act so as to stay open even if the provider would prefer not to become involved in merger negotiations. Perhaps this case is not the same as the case of someone who is having a gun pointed at her, but there is still a great deal of pressure in the situation. On the other hand, if a

Catholic provider, while finding a certain merger possibility attractive, could surely flourish without the merger, the duress is not so great. The degree of duress will vary from one scenario to the next, with no two cases ever being exactly identical. In every cooperation case, the level of duress must be considered carefully.

The second key issue has to do with the *weight of the evil or wrong* in which the person or institution is considering material cooperation. In the Catholic moral tradition, there has always been the understanding that some behaviors are more seriously wrong, sometimes much more seriously wrong, than others. This is also true about our good behaviors. Some are significantly better than others. The concern about the degree of wrong in a behavior is the solid point behind the well-known distinction between mortal and venial sin, even if we have not always explained this difference as well as might be desired. In the context of material cooperation, the crucial point is this: If a behavior is clearly less seriously wrong, lesser duress can be said to be sufficient to justify the cooperation. An obvious instance can be cited to help clarify the distinction between degrees of wrong. Roman Catholicism sees a substantially higher degree of wrong in direct abortion than it does in contraceptive activity, even though Catholicism opposes contraception and would prefer not to cooperate in it. Abortion is a direct attack on human life, while contraception directly acts against human fertility, which, for all its importance, is not quite the same as human life.

The third key issue has to do with the *degree of involvement of a material cooperator* in a behavior that the cooperator sees as wrong but considers supporting because of some significant reason or reasons. If the cooperator's involvement is remote, a lesser reason is required to justify the cooperator's involvement. But if the involvement is closer, a stronger reason is necessary. An example of remote involvement has to do with the purchase of clothing that has been made in a foreign country. While there is a significant likelihood that textile workers in the foreign country are being exploited, the purchaser's involvement in the evil is quite remote and may not need a high level of justification. But a company that buys the clothing for import to a country such as the United States is more closely connected to the exploitation of the textile workers and may not have a justifiable reason for cooperating. In health care, a nurse who actually assists a physician in a medical procedure to which he objects is a closer cooperator than an office assistant who merely schedules the procedure. A hospital that furnishes space on its own premises so that a doctor can perform an objectionable procedure is cooperating more closely than a hospital that has a partnership with some other entity that lets the procedure be performed on its premises.

The fourth key issue has to do with the *objective* that the material cooperator is seeking to achieve. Just how important is this objective, particularly in terms of underlying Catholic values? Does the good to be gained have a greater weight than the negatives that result from the material cooperation? Can the good be gained in some other way, without the cooperation? How strongly does the good to be achieved contribute to the mission of Catholic health care? No decision in favor of material cooperation can be made without this sort of assessment. In the context of health care, the decision for material cooperation must be based on the general goal of enhancing Catholic health care. But in the case at hand, just what is the specific enhancement of Catholic health care, and what is the cost, in terms of witness to the Catholic tradition?

Any concrete decision about the legitimacy of material cooperation will need to be based on the interaction of all four of the issues we have just outlined: the level of duress that raises the possibility of cooperating, the moral character of the activity in which cooperation is being considered, the degree of involvement that the cooperator will have in the activity, and value of the objective to be gained as a result of the cooperation. The complexity of the interaction of these four issues requires that cooperation decisions be grounded in two underlying themes from Catholic moral theology. *First,* in complex moral matters, Catholicism has always relied strongly on the principle of proportionate reason. The judgment on whether moral justification is present in a case of material cooperation is ultimately a judgment of proportionate reason. Traditional theology makes this point clear.[24] In the end the most formal moral question to be asked is whether there is a proportionate reason of sufficient weight to justify the material cooperation.

*Second,* in regard to concrete cases, moral decision making is ultimately more of an art than it is a science.[25] Even though different cooperation decisions may have similarities, there are probably no two cooperation cases in which the duress, the type of evil, the type of involvement, and the specific objective come together in exactly the same way. For this reason, while official Catholic moral teaching emphasizes proportionate reason and other clear moral principles about cooperation, it does not attempt to resolve all the specific application questions related to cooperation. The church knows that these specific application questions need to be resolved at least partly on the basis of the concrete facts of each case. Even when the church appropriately requires a wider ecclesial review of a cooperation decision, it sees this review as belonging especially to the office of the diocesan bishop who is present on the local scene and therefore in a better position to learn about and address the local facts. The diocesan bishop may need to consult his national episcopal conference or even the Vatican about the underlying principles that pertain to cooperation, but he and his advisors remain in a unique position when it comes to learning the local facts.

It should be noted that, both historically and in the contemporary world, the tradition of cooperation is important for a great many issues beyond the realm of hospital mergers. In politics, the decision to support almost any political party may well involve a person in cooperation with some of the party's questionable agenda items. In fund-raising, the value of joining an integrated funding campaign such as the United Way may be a form of cooperation with the raising of funds for activities with which a person or group (such as the church) does not agree. A decision to work for a given company may raise questions about whether someone can cooperate in all of the business activities of that company, especially if it is a multinational company with business activities in the third and fourth worlds. The decision to go online makes one a cooperator in some of the very objectionable forms of information that are available through the online services. Here I am not trying to resolve the matter of the rightness and wrong-ness of these cooperation decisions. The point is to make it clear that cooperation touches a great many other issues besides hospital merger issues.

### Catholic Teaching on Issues of Fertility and Human Life and Cooperation in Hospital Mergers

In view of these background thoughts on material coopera-tion, what about the situation of material cooperation by Catholic hospitals in the activities of their proposed partners? Can such cooperation ever be acceptable? Two immediate and potentially conflicting value orientations present themselves. *First,* the Catholic Church has some very significant moral teachings on a host of issues related to human fertility and/or human life: abortion, euthanasia, in vitro fertilization, sterili-zation, contraception, and so on. Since Catholic hospitals are public entities in the church, the leadership of the church has an understandable concern that Catholic hospitals bear very clear witness to all these teachings, even if the Catholic Church does not see the same weight of evil in actions against some teachings as it sees in actions against others. *Second,* Catholic hospitals are precious and important value centers. It is very desirable to preserve and strengthen Catholic hospitals in these times when, in some cases, mergers may be the only way in which Catholic hospitals can have a secure future as wit-nesses to Catholic values. Because of this precious character of Catholic hospitals, no one, neither the bishops nor the reli-gious communities nor the hospital leaders, wants to preside over the demise of Catholic hospitals, even though there have been and will continue to be some cases in which the closings of Catholic hospitals are unavoidable.

Once we reflect on these two value orientations, we see the classic kind of conflict that opens up the issue of material cooperation. From the viewpoint of basic Catholic teachings, it might be argued to be better that Catholic hospitals never cooperate in any mergers with parties whose practices depart from Catholic teaching. But from the viewpoint of preserving the wonderful mission of Catholic health care in our times, the case for material cooperation begins to emerge. To use the language cited earlier, the need to preserve and strengthen Catholic hospitals is the element of duress that makes it necessary to give material cooperation serious consideration.

I am not referring here to those cases in which a Catholic hospital actually purchases a hospital that was not formerly Catholic. In such cases the purchased hospital (which may have sold assets such as a family planning clinic to others before it was purchased) becomes fully Roman Catholic and therefore fully responsible for following the *Ethical and Religious Directives.* I have had several personal experiences of helping a formerly secular hospital become Roman Catholic and begin following the *ERD.* These experiences have gone smoothly, with a great deal of support from the doctors and others.

But what about the place of the Catholic commitment to the issues of fertility and human life in actual mergers between Catholic providers and other health-care providers? While some situations may be unique due to local circumstances, there is one common agreement pattern that is employed in the consummation of such mergers throughout the United States. The common pattern is this: Both parties agree that the non-Catholic partner remains free to offer contraceptive services and surgical sterilization in those facilities that have been put into the merger by the non-Catholic partner. Both parties also agree that no part of the merged entity will perform direct abortions or physician assisted suicide (should assisted suicide become legalized). Each of the two parts of this agreement pattern is significant and deserves some comments here.

On the question of contraception and sterilization, it seems that the Catholic parties considering mergers understand that in the realism associated with material cooperation, they must concede some points to the other party in order for there to be any possibility of consummating a merger agreement. Similarly, the local bishops who review and approve merger agreements understand that some material cooperation is reasonable. Earlier we noted that not all behaviors that the Catholic Church opposes seem to have the same degree of moral gravity. Fertility-related practices such as contraception and sterilization, even though the church opposes them, have a lesser gravity than human life issues such as abortion or euthanasia. Some years ago, Cardinal John O'Connor, while arguing for the legitimacy of Catholic efforts to change liberal abortion laws, stated that no Catholic bishop in the United States had any interest in the placing of legal restrictions on contraception.[26] Cardinal O'Connor's statement clearly shows that the Catholic Church has a lesser investment in the public policy aspects of contraception. This lesser investment helps show why it seems reasonable to many people that Catholic bishops choose to permit Catholic hospitals to materially cooperate in the contraceptive and sterilization services of partner hospitals. If we consider that in some cases Catholic hospitals may have no future unless they merge with others, the duress that permits material cooperation is present to a sufficient degree. The decision of the bishops to permit this sort of material cooperation does not mean that the bishops are unconcerned about contraception and sterilization; the decision simply means that, all things considered, they find this type of material cooperation to be a proportionate course of action.

Because of the nature of most hospital merger agreements, the general public will easily recognize that it is the partner hospital rather than the Catholic party that is providing the contraception and sterilization. Often the specific agreement will include measures that heighten this perception. For example, the practice of "carving out" the revenue allocation of the merged company in such a way that the Catholic party receives no income from the provision of contraception and sterilization has a very important purpose in and of itself. The "carve out" helps to create a real separation of the Catholic party from the contraception and sterilization. But carving out also makes the real separation clearer to the general public. The earlier tradition on cooperation frequently raised the question of scandal and stipulated that for material cooperation to be acceptable, the cooperation must not be a source of scandal to ordinary Catholics.[27] The fact that contraception and sterilization are readily seen as the action of someone else serves very well to eliminate the possibility of scandal. But if the design of a given merger so closely ties the formerly separate hospitals into one entity that a separation cannot be perceived, questions may arise as to whether material cooperation can be permitted.

To be more precise, the tradition of avoiding scandal means that what the public perceives about the merged entity is of special importance. Mergers may involve a variety of complex legal structures. When the public cannot perceive that someone other than the Catholic party is the performer of the sterilizations or other procedures, the legitimacy of material cooperation becomes questionable. But if the public does clearly perceive that someone else is providing these procedures, perhaps the precise legal details of the merger agreement may not be so significant, as long as the separation of the Catholic party from certain practices is clear.[28] Even an asset merger may not alter the public perception or the true reality of who is actually doing what. Recall that from the canonical viewpoint, a civil merger of assets may not involve a loss of canonical sponsorship or a loss of the sponsoring religious community's role as the true maintainer of Catholic values in the Catholic segments of the merged entity.

I think that both the Catholic health-care providers and the bishops deserve a great deal of credit for the prudence and discretion they have shown in accepting some instances of material cooperation in the contraception and sterilization procedures provided by partner hospitals. It is not as if the Catholic parties are inflexible in the merger negotiations. The clear fact is that, for the mergers to work, both sides have to make some concessions, and this is exactly what happens. In addition, since in most geographical areas there are several local health-care providers even after mergers, the charge that Catholics are forcing the removal of contraceptive services from many cities is highly overstated. Note that, except in cases related to caesarian deliveries, many managed-care companies prefer to furnish tubal ligations in non-hospital clinics at a time some weeks after a woman has given birth or at a time not related to birth at all. There may of course be the rare possibility of a remote rural hospital being purchased by a Roman Catholic sponsor and ceasing to offer contraception and sterilization in that rural area.

In the end, all of the specific decisions about material cooperation in contraception and sterilization are made locally and in dialogue with diocesan bishops. Catholic bishops and Catholic health care remain deeply concerned about the moral values that are called into question by contraception and sterilization. Even in the face of these concerns, both Catholic health-care leaders and Catholic bishops are open to material cooperation in contraception and sterilization when (and only when) such cooperation is appropriate.[29]

But what about the other aspect that is part of the common pattern of merger agreements between Catholic parties and other health-care providers, the aspect of every element in a merged entity agreeing not to perform direct abortion or physician-assisted suicide? For Catholicism, there is clearly a higher level of investment in human life issues such as abortion and euthanasia. From the Catholic viewpoint, the logic is that if the Catholic side concedes on the continuance of contraception and sterilization in some of the entities that make up a health-care partnership, it becomes very reasonable for the Catholic party to ask the other parties not to perform direct abortion or physician-assisted suicide. This Catholic request is usually put forward with both candor and care, and with appropriate nuance on questions such as the distinction between direct and indirect abortion and the distinction between abortion and the post-viability induction of labor for a sufficient reason, both of which topics are covered in the *ERD*.[30] The non-Catholic party in the merger discussion is usually very understanding of the Catholic request on abortion. Indeed, the other party often seems to welcome the opportunity to stop doing abortions. When proposed mergers break down over the abortion issue, the breakdown is often instigated by third parties whose interest is not in either of the providers seeking to merge, but rather in their own agenda. One of my great concerns is that, if substantial numbers of proposed mergers fail over this or related matters, the result may be that in some cases both of the potentially merging parties may ultimately close, leading to a situation in which the United States ends up with more and more cities with only one or two health-care providers. If this happens the quality of everyone's health care may suffer greatly, and Catholic values may be less well represented in the future of health care. The last situation may be worse than the first.

Moving these reflections to a deeper level, it must be said that, even if some persons disagree, the Catholic opposition to abortion is a very credible opposition. Neither the bishops nor any one else needs to apologize for such opposition or to feel obligated to mount a whole new defense of the position every time a merger or some other situation comes up. The United States has a strong tradition of voluntarism in health-care delivery, with a great many independent groups—foundations, universities, churches—involved in providing health care. All of these groups (and the public providers as well) are regularly and for a wide variety of reasons making decisions about which health-care services they will and will not provide. This is as it should be. Whatever future social policies may be adopted on the provision of health care, the actual delivery of health care should be left in the hands of these varied and often private groups. Once we accept the principle of voluntary health-care providers, it seems inevitable and fully appropriate that health-care organizations that are even partly sponsored by the Catholic Church will not furnish direct abortion or euthanasia, not even on the basis of the principle of material cooperation. Even though Catholicism may be open to cooperation on a variety of health-care issues, the *ERD* explicitly excludes cooperation in direct abortion, and the same position can be said to apply by analogy to physician-assisted suicide.[31]

Here I want to add two more points. First, while I was clear on the typical Catholic negotiation approach to issues such as contraception, sterilization, abortion, and euthanasia, I did not address the question of how in vitro fertilization by a partner hospital might enter into merger negotiations. I shied away from commenting on this issue precisely because there does not yet seem to be a fully clear pattern on it. Many persons, including bishops, seem more concerned about possible Catholic cooperation in in vitro fertilization than they are about cooperation in contraception and sterilization. This greater concern may be partly due to the increased technoligization and increased financial costs that are associated with in vitro fertilization, especially in an era when the cost and distribution of health-care services are such enormously important issues. But the more basic question is whether in vitro fertilization rises to the same level of concern for Catholicism as do human life issues such as direct abortion and euthanasia. In the end the bishops may well move toward a common judgment that in vitro fertilization is more of a human life issue than a fertility issue, so that it should be treated in merger agreements in a manner similar to abortion and euthanasia. But as of now, the pattern of Catholic practice on the relationship of in vitro fertilization to merger agreements is not fully clear. The Vatican recognizes that many persons who seek in vitro fertilization are doing so out of a worthy desire to have children,[32] but this pastoral sensitivity does not take away the fact that in vitro fertilization has a very strong relationship to the fundamental Catholic concern about human life.

The second point is this: The commonly accepted cases of Catholic material cooperation in health-care mergers are cases in which the Catholic party is cooperating in a rather distant fashion, that is, cooperating in something that is being done by a partner hospital. But what about the possibility of a closer form of material cooperation? What about a Catholic hospital, in an effort to consummate a merger, agreeing to cooperate by letting the doctors use its own facilities to perform a medical procedure that is prohibited by the *Ethical and Religious Directives?* Can this type of material cooperation, sometimes known as immediate material cooperation, ever be acceptable?

Several comments can be made. The older Catholic tradition does not completely rule out immediate material cooperation, especially if the duress is extreme. The passerby driver provides immediate material cooperation to the bank robbers because a shotgun is pointed at his head. The tradition would see the driver's immediate cooperation as acceptable because of the duress he is under. But can the duress faced by Catholic health-care providers be said to be similar to the duress of the innocent driver?

At the level of theory, there may not be a completely clear answer to the question of immediate material cooperation by

Catholic hospitals in procedures such as tubal ligation. But it must be acknowledged that the much more common practice of Catholic hospitals and by far the more common interpretation by bishops is that this immediate cooperation is not acceptable. Recent published reports about a Vatican review of a cooperation agreement made by a Catholic hospital in the state of Arkansas only serve to underline the more common position on this issue.[33] The question of immediate material cooperation will continue to be studied by Catholic theologians, as will the questions mentioned earlier about the adequacy of some of the specific teaching themes articulated by the *ERD*. It would go beyond our purposes to answer all of these questions here.[34]

### Toward Broader Values in Health-Care Mergers

The question of how the Catholic teaching on life and fertility issues impacts health-care mergers is of great importance. But it should also be noted that Catholic teaching and tradition care deeply about a number of other crucially important issues in health-care ethics: care for the poor, spiritual and pastoral care, justice for employees, and respect for the sacredness of the dying process. What about the place of these issues in a merger negotiation? If a potential partner hospital is not open to a practice on these issues that is similar to Catholic principles, a merger is probably unjustifiable, even if there are grounds for material cooperation on an issue such as sterilization. I am not claiming that both organizations have to be exactly identical on every one of these broader themes, but there needs to be enough similarity that it does not appear that a large portion of Catholic moral values are being called into question by the merger.

These broader issues raise the troubling question of whether a Catholic health-care provider may ever merge with a large investor-owned, for-profit health-care provider. Even if not every aspect of this complex question is fully resolved, mergers with this type of for-profit entity raise very grave doubts. We have already noted the decisions of several

Catholic bishops to reject such mergers in their dioceses.[35] These decisions could well be pointing the way to the future.

How can we determine whether a Catholic health-care provider and another party have a sufficient base of agreement on issues such as care for the poor and spiritual care? The two organizations may have very different cultures, and they may not understand each other that well as merger negotiations begin. My experience suggests that in the negotiations the two sides will need to agree on some sort of memorandum of understanding or set of joint operating principles to address these broader issues. The process of drawing up such a set of understandings may help the two organizations understand each other better and become clearer as to whether their cultures really are common enough to justify a merger. If such a written agreement about the social issues in health care is to be drawn up, the Catholic party may well need to take the lead in preparing the agreement, since the Catholic party may have more experience with issues such as care for the poor and pastoral care. But this is not to deny that other providers have a long tradition of concern about these issues. It is the providers who do have this long tradition that may turn out to be among the best partners for Catholic health care.

To close, I want to be clear that health-care mergers are not the answer to all the momentous problems that beset the health-care scene today. This is not the case by a long shot. But for many providers, mergers are an inescapable aspect of the effort to deliver high-quality, value-driven health care. I hope I have helped describe the main moral issues that arise in the context of mergers, especially for Catholic health care, with its precious traditions on both human life and social justice.

# Chapter 5
# PUBLIC POLICY AND
# CONTEMPORARY HEALTH CARE

This book's introduction named three trends that have dominated the delivery of health care in the United States since the mid-1990s: (1) the burgeoning growth of managed care, (2) the rapid rate of hospital mergers, and (3) a government policy of piecemeal changes in health care coupled with substantial reductions in the rate of government spending on health care. This chapter will assess the third of these trends: the role of public policy in today's health-care context in the United States. In recent years, the American public's concern about health care has become so strong that health care has become the biggest single item on the legislative agenda in the United States. In 1999, about 1,400 laws on health care were enacted nationwide, and 27,000 of the 140,000 bills introduced in the state legislatures were about health care. Similar figures occurred in 2000, with 16,000 of the first 104,000 bills that were introduced being about health care.[1] The need for ethical reflection on health-care legislation is crystal clear.

The chapter is divided into four sections: (1) an historical survey of the principal theological viewpoints on the role of government as an agent for social justice, (2) an outline of what is actually happening today in the United States on the question of health-care policy, (3) a theological assessment of current and potential developments in health-care policy, and (4) a reflection on the role that Catholic health-care providers and other value-driven groups might play as advocates seeking

146

to bring about meaningful changes in health-care policy, both at the state and at the federal level.

## THREE MAJOR CHRISTIAN OPTIONS ON PUBLIC POLICY

Fifty years have passed since H. Richard Niebuhr published his wonderful book *Christ and Culture*.[2] Even with the passing of years, Niebuhr's work remains the classic modern text on the differing ways in which Christianity and society interrelate with one another. This section will describe Niebuhr's three centrist approaches to the church-society relationship: the Augustinian/Calvinist approach, the Lutheran approach, and the Thomistic/Catholic approach. One of Niebuhr's other two approaches—the approach he describes as Christ Against Culture—continues to exert an important moral influence on believing Christians everywhere.[3] In our times, the Mennonite tradition most fully represents this theme of uncompromising withdrawal from society out of a sense that no secular society can ever fully embrace gospel values. Even if the Mennonite tradition does not present us with the same kind of policy options that we find in Augustine, Calvin, Luther, and Aquinas, every Christian must ponder the question raised by the Mennonites: Is the world around us so corrupt that dropping out of it is the only truly Christian thing to do? While I cannot answer this question affirmatively, I also cannot help but be challenged by the question on a daily basis.[4]

*A Calvinist Approach to Public Policy*

The first of Niebuhr's more mainstream approaches is the Augustinian approach, which was given special emphasis by John Calvin and his followers in the Presbyterian and related traditions. The basic mindset of the Augustinian/Calvinist approach is that God has decisively broken into human history in such a way that public policy ought to be construed as essentially a means of making God's will work in the world, of making the world a better place. In this vision the best people to be the political leaders are the holy and faith-filled people, since they will know what is right and be able to use their political role so as to make the world embrace this right. This theme of the holy persons as political leaders and creating a good society was the guiding spirit behind Calvin's Geneva. The same theme was carried into the American colonies, with the establishment of the Congregational Church in colonies such as Massachusetts and Virginia a sign that God had blessed America and that the kingdom of God had been founded in a special way in the New World. The U.S. Constitution's Bill of Rights did not forbid the states from having established churches, and the Congregational Church remained established in Connecticut and Massachusetts until well into the nineteenth century.[5]

There has always been something refreshing and attractive about the views of Augustine and Calvin on history, religion, and society. This segment of the Christian tradition has a very strong sense of social responsibility and social justice. It sees it to be the task of religious persons to lead society to true justice, and it is convinced that the experience of faith tells the true believers what should be done so as to construct a good society. In *Christ and Culture,* H. Richard Niebuhr describes the Augustinian/Calvinist approach as "Christ the Transformer of Culture."[6] While Niebuhr is very careful to avoid naming as his favorite any of the church/society models that he explains, I have long tended to think that he favored the transformationist model both because of its sense of the dynamism of human history, and because of its construal of the church as committed to ongoing action on behalf of justice. In the context of health care it is hard not to think that religious transformationists will have a strong sense of needing to find a way to transform the current U.S. health-care system, with its 44 million uninsured persons.

I have always had a very high regard for the transformationist model, with its sense of social responsibility and its sense that through the power of the gospel real social change is indeed possible. But another part of me has always been uneasy about the transformationist approach. Granted the faith-filled character of transformationism, does faith alone give us the answer to complicated questions of social policy? Isn't there a danger that faith without solidly adequate answers to complex problems will slide into an enthusiasm that may end up forcing unsuitable solutions on society, so that the last situation becomes worse than the first?

When we think about the transformationist heritage of U.S. colonial times, along with the good things, it is hard not to think about the witchcraft trials in Salem, Massachusetts, in the 1690s. It is also hard not to think about Nathaniel Hawthorne's classic book, *The Scarlet Letter,* with its story of Hester Prynne and her large red *A.* If we turn from colonial times to the twentieth century, it is similarly hard not to think about Prohibition. Alcohol abuse was and still is a significant social and medical problem. But was the banning of the sale of alcohol the proper solution to the problem? Can it not be argued that organized crime in the United States exists in significant part because of the foothold it was able to get during the Prohibition era? It is hard not to conclude that Prohibition's net effect was to bring about more harm than good to U.S. society.

These examples serve to point out that a spirit of faith may not be able to be effective if it does not rely on a sophisticated analysis of the issues, an analysis that often makes use of secular rather than religious sources. Especially in health care, it can be argued that zeal for justice will not be adequate for the reform of health care at the policy level. Health care involves many complexities, many issues that are extraordinarily difficult to resolve. Even the basic question of which aspects of health delivery are best managed through legislation and which aspects are left in private hands cannot be answered by relying on faith and morality alone. I do not offer this caution out of a sense that public policy has no role in the current health-care debate; on the contrary, public policy can and should have a role in the reform of health care. The point is that while a crusading enthusiasm may help drive the debate about health reform, it will not be adequate to bring about just health care.

The ancient Greek philosopher Plato argued that governments would work best if the philosophers were kings.[7] Setting aside Plato's monarchical assumptions, the question is whether any kind of government will succeed best when it is run solely on the basis of philosophy and religion. St. Augustine was versed in the tradition of Platonism, and Calvin's Geneva also seems to have a Platonist spirit about it. My admiration for the sense of social responsibility and for the civic spirit of the Calvinist tradition is very great. The value-driven quest for justice should mark our view of government and stand as a goal for any public policy issue, including health care. But the laudable motivation of a Calvinist approach to public policy will only succeed if this motivation can be coupled with a hard-headed assessment of what exactly is workable and unworkable in a field as complex as health-care delivery.

### Classical Lutheranism and Public Policy

Luther's writings about government, especially his famous *Treatise on Secular Authority*,[8] have a very different tone concerning government than do Calvin's writings. Even if Calvin was overzealous and at times naïve about the role of government, Calvin had a strongly positive sense about government. He believed profoundly that government could develop policies that would make the world a better place for everyone. Calvin, with his links to the humanists of his era, had a positive optimism, not only about government but also about human learning and human affairs in general.

For Luther, a much darker picture quickly emerges. The beginning point from which to understand the role of government is not a theology of creation and redemption; instead Luther bases his approach to government and policy-making on a deeply ingrained theology of human sinfulness. The starting point in a Lutheran theological anthropology is a vision of the human person as sinner, of the human community as a sinful community. Based on this, Luther sees that the main purpose of the state is to serve as a dike against sin,[9] as a check upon human wickedness. No one should expect that public policy can improve the human situation. Efforts to better human life through public policy are flawed from the outset. Luther asserts that it is only to be expected that politicians will be corrupt. He argues that it is part of God's providence that there be corrupt political leaders. Since the world around us is so corrupt, God ordains that there be wicked political leaders. Since these leaders personally know evil, they will be able to address it successfully. In explaining why God sends corrupt political leaders, Luther utters the famous sentence, "Frogs need Storks."[10] Once one understands that storks eat frogs, the force of Luther's words is clear.

Luther's pessimistic, sin-based view of government does not lead him to dismiss the role of government. The Mennonites shared Luther's sense of the sinfulness of the world, and they may have been more consistent in their decision to remove themselves from the world as much as possible. But Luther felt that since sin is so real, government has an important role as the challenger and preventer of sin. Once the Lutheran view of government is accepted, government emerges with a clear task in activities such as crime prevention and the punishment of criminals. Dealing with crime is government's way of addressing the problem of sin within a country's own borders. Government also emerges with a strong role in national defense, since this is the way for a state to protect itself from sinners outside its borders. Luther and his tradition put these themes of crime prevention and national defense together into a theory in which holding public office is seen as a genuine vocation for the Christian, since society as a whole needs the efforts of the state to prevent evil.[11] Even if some popular Lutheran thought sees the state as the left hand of God, the state is still a hand of God.

Based on all of this pessimism, classical Lutheran thought rejects the idea that the state should construe itself as an agency whose purpose is to enact positive policies aimed at improving the human lot. This makes the Lutheran tradition very different from the Calvinist tradition. In the area of health-care justice, the Lutheran position would not see it as appropriate for the state to try to envision and erect any kind of positive unified theory of how health care should work. If it is true that there is much evil in the current delivery of health care in the United States, Lutheranism would surely agree that public policy can play an important role by passing laws whose purpose is to help stamp out the evils in the current health-care system. Surely everyone would agree that this is a desirable objective. But is it the only reasonable objective for government in terms of health-care policy? This is what classical Lutheranism would claim, but others would expect a more activist role on the part of government.

In these remarks, I have deliberately used the term "classical Lutheranism," so as to indicate that there are many strains of thought in the Lutheran tradition, including important modern efforts to add clarifying nuances to the Lutheran position. Often these modern efforts will stress the theocentrism of Luther's position, that is, his view that politics, whatever else is to be said about it, is to be construed as being under God, especially under God's judgment. The writings of the twentieth-century martyr Dietrich Bonhoeffer stress this theme.[12] Modern scholarship will also point out that Luther did see the value of the state as a maintainer of order as well as a dike against sin. It does seem that every time a major political scandal comes on the scene, some scholars who are familiar with the Lutheran tradition will find a way to assert that Luther was right all along with his cynicism about politics and politicians. But not all of Lutheran political thought should be seen as an exercise in unbridled pessimism.

To be fair, there is something very helpful about the Lutheran cynicism about political life. Politics will frequently fail in its efforts to seek the common good. It is important to avoid a naïve optimism about what can be accomplished for the human good through efforts at political reform. Of the Protestant scholars in the United States in the twentieth century, a substantial case can be made that Reinhold Niebuhr was the most important figure. As a member of the German Evangelical Synod, Niebuhr did not come directly from the Lutheran tradition. But Niebuhr was able to use pessimism and cynicism with great effectiveness in his critiques of politics in the United States, from the days of Woodrow Wilson to the time of Richard Nixon.[13] Any wholistic theory of the relationship between morality and politics can benefit from a touch of Lutheran pessimism, just as it can benefit from a touch of the crusading zeal of Calvinism.

## The Aristotelian/Thomist View of Public Policy

The third major Christian viewpoint on moral vision and public policy is found in the outlook of Thomas Aquinas and his great intellectual predecessor Aristotle. On the whole, Thomas is much more like Calvin than he is like Luther. Because of the heritage of the natural law that he draws from Aristotle, Thomas believes profoundly in human goodness. He believes in learning, in science, in human community, and in the role of government as an agency that can help bring about the moral and human good.[14] Unlike Luther, Aquinas does not see law's only purpose as protecting us from our fellow sinners and maintaining order. Instead, like Calvin, he believes that law can also serve as a teacher and guide, as a helper in the task of creating a just society.[15] A great deal of modern political theory is based on Aquinas's theory that government can help bring about the good. Aquinas influenced the British philosopher John Locke, who in turn influenced Thomas Jefferson as he wrote the Declaration of Independence. Aquinas was not the only influence on the political beginnings of the United States, because the U.S. Constitution is also based on a fair amount of Protestant pessimism, which can be seen in the Constitution's commitment to the separation of powers and in the impeachment clause. But the influence of Aquinas on modern theories of government is very great, not only in the United States, but also in the world as a whole.

Granting the similarities between Calvin and Aquinas, there is also a very significant difference between these two great figures. Aquinas, with his roots in Aristotle (instead of in Plato and Augustine), believes that politics has a clear level of independence from religion. Aquinas believes that politics should do all it can to build a moral society, but he does not believe that philosophers or religious leaders should be the heads of government. The classic Thomistic phrase that expresses all this is the statement that government is "autonomous in its own sphere." This concept of autonomy, which was developed in the twentieth century by scholars such as John Courtney Murray, holds that politics, besides its responsibility to strive for the embodiment of moral values, has about it a level that falls outside the province of religion and morality. As we noted earlier, this level is sometimes called the level of practical feasibility.[16]

The concept of practical feasibility is this: Even if a proposed law has a moral objective, there are still a number of crucial questions to ask before the law ought to be passed. Will the law work? When considered in a broad context, will it accomplish more harm than good? Will the law be enforceable, and, if not, won't its passage serve only to undermine respect for law? Will the proposed law be enforced justly, or will it be enforced mostly against certain groups of citizens, such as the poor? Does law sometimes need to focus on preventing greater evils even if it might rather be focusing on moral goods? Can law realistically address all possible moral concerns? In a democratic society, are there enough votes to pass the law? If not, might it be better to come up with a compromise piece of legislation that will have enough votes to pass and will at least do some good? As these questions indicate, the Thomistic tradition understands public policy making as an extremely complex undertaking. Thomism is optimistic about public policy and society; it does believe that law can serve as a creative energy to bring about the common good. Thomism avoids the Lutheran pessimism about public policy. But Thomism also knows that lawmaking is not easy. It recognizes that legislators have to consider many factors besides the moral content of the law. The oversimplified enthusiasm of the Calvinist perspective is avoided, due to the recognized complexity of policy issues. It is this complexity that is the root of the Thomist insight that lawmakers need to be autonomous in their own sphere.

Thomism has about it a careful balance in its view of the relationship between morality and public policy. This balance deserves praise and makes the Thomistic perspective the most useful and flexible of the Christian perspectives on the way in which public policy and morality can interact. Our assessment of how health-care policy may become more fully moral will be based on the Thomist outlook, with its mix of optimism and pragmatic realism on the question of how public policy might address health-care justice.

## HEALTH-CARE JUSTICE AND PUBLIC POLICY
## IN THE RECENT PAST

The later 1990s saw two major trends on the issue of health-care and public policy: (1) the tendency toward smaller pieces of legislation and (2) the large-scale reduction of funding for health care, especially at the federal level. Each of these trends will be outlined here. Our reflections on the smaller pieces of legislation will focus on five characteristics of these legislative initiatives: they (1) are focused on individual aspects of health care, (2) problem-oriented, (3) politically opportunistic, (4) ignorant of and sometimes even promoting larger health-care difficulties, and (5) lacking an overall vision of where health care might move in the future.

### The Tone of Recent Health-Care Policy Initiatives

*First,* recent public policy initiatives have exhibited a strong focus on individual issues. An individual concern rises to the surface, and legislation is proposed and sometimes enacted to address the individual concern. People worry that mothers who have given birth are not given enough hospital time, and a law is passed requiring a minimum of forty-eight hours. People worry that many children lack health care, and legislation is passed to enhance the health care of children. People worry that not enough children are immunized against the major childhood diseases, and laws are passed to facilitate immunization. People worry that managed-care companies are not responsible in the care decisions they make, and legislation is proposed to render managed-care companies liable to suit for the decisions they make. People worry that if they change jobs they may not be able to maintain their health-care coverage, and laws are passed assuring the continuance of coverage after a job change. People worry that they will be denied access to health insurance because of some preexisting health condition, and laws are passed to prevent this from happening. And so on. Individual issues come to the surface and are addressed at the level of public policy. No doubt some of the laws passed through this sort of process are quite effective and highly desirable, so credit should be given when credit is due.

One word is often used to describe the legislative process that I have just outlined: the adjective *incremental.*[17] I have some doubts about the suitability of the word. *Incremental* implies a step-by-step process, in which one action builds upon another in a process of organic unity and wholeness. I do not think it can fairly be said that the types of legislation I have just outlined come together in an organic wholeness. As good as some of the recent laws may be, they are simply individual steps, often quite unrelated to one another, and very much discrete entities. They do not suggest a broad sense of the mission and purpose of health care.

*Second,* the current legislative atmosphere about health care is very much problem-centered, that is, oriented toward fixing problems. The whole idea seems to be that, if health care does something bad, public policy should step in so as to repair past damage and prevent further damage. This approach has some important roots in the Catholic tradition of subsidiarity, but much recent health-care legislation seems more reactive rather than constructive. From the viewpoint of the Thomistic tradition, the current public policy context seems a bit too pessimistic, too ready to assume that there is no positive role for government in enhancing access to health care. The role of government in recent years seems to have been that of watchdog, the role of protector of the people from evil behaviors by the health-care providers. This feels like the classic Lutheran concept of the state as a dike against sin. For all its difficulties, the Clinton health-care plan envisioned government as a positive enabler of better health care. But little of public policy in the years since has gone beyond the level of construing government as the protector of the citizenry from the evils of modern health care. Former Senator Bradley's proposal in the 2000 presidential campaign may have moved to a different level, but this was an exception to the pattern of the years after the failure of the Clinton plan.[18]

I have refrained from any extended discussion of the recent publicity and interest in the issue of medical errors.[19] Of course medical errors happen. Even the very best doctors, nurses, and other providers are human beings who sometimes make mistakes. This is part of the human condition, and medical errors can never be fully prevented. Of course, it would be desirable if the rate of medical errors could be reduced. Everyone involved in health care—individual practitioners, administrators, boards of trustees, accrediting agencies—should work to eliminate as many medical errors as humanly possible. Public policy may well be able to play a helpful and imaginative role that will contribute to the reduction of medical errors.

But I worry about the recent high profile publicity about medical errors. I worry that the publicity may bring about a naïve expectation that all errors can be eliminated, with this expectation furthering the inadequate understanding of medicine as a pure technology that can find the way to resolve every human health problem. I worry that this publicity will reinforce a popular understanding of government's health-care role as wholly focused on protecting us from evil. If the construal of government as a police agency against medical errors becomes a dominant construal, the understanding of government's health-care role as anything more than protection from evil may wane all the further. The popular media's flamboyance on medical errors may do more harm than good by promoting a largely negative understanding of the role of public policy vis-à-vis health care.

A *third* main characteristic of current health-care legislation is that much of it is politically opportunistic. The vast number of bills being introduced helps to show this. Some of the bills are well intentioned and may be passed and do some good. Many have very little chance of passing, but they may help legislators posture themselves in such a way as to impress certain constituencies. Besides this posturing, much of the current opportunism in health-care legislation belongs in the family of old-fashioned log rolling with powerful legislators negotiating for favored treatment for the folks back home. For instance, at a time when some large urban teaching hospitals are desperately in need of funding, house speaker Dennis Hastert was able to get his rural home county (Lee County) defined as part of the Chicago metropolitan area, so that Lee County could get part of the funding targeted for the Chicago area.[20]

Unlike this tradition of opportunism, the tradition of Saint Thomas holds that a key role for law is the role of teacher, the role of helping people understand issues so that they can relate to them appropriately. In today's health-care context, there is a need for this role of law as an educator. There are many misunderstandings about health care, particularly the tendency of many persons to think of health care as a series of endless technological innovations. This emphasis on a purely technological approach to health can serve to hide the fact that death is a part of life, so that the need to accept death is an essential element in the human story. For the United States to achieve a more just system of health care, people are going to need to go through an in-depth conversion of hearts and minds, a conversion that breaks down the individualism in which every person seeks the most possible for her or himself, a conversion that accepts human limits in all areas of life, especially in medicine. Legislation cannot accomplish this conversion all by itself. But thoughtful legislation can help with the conversion, as it helped in the case of civil rights. Health-care laws cannot simply focus on helping certain isolated groups of people get more and more of what they want. Health-care laws must also help us understand that such isolated efforts must be considered in the context of the good of the larger human community. This deeper kind of vision will not be possible unless we bring an end to the opportunism and posturing that mark so much of the current legislative atmosphere.

*Fourth,* significant elements of recent legislation have contributed, at least indirectly, to a further deepening of the injustices present in the modern distribution of health-care services. The issues of just health delivery are so vast and so out of control in the United States. The small pieces of legislation often tend to obscure the fact that access to health care is rapidly getting worse as the years pass. It is hard not to wish that legislators had a better long-term sense of legislative planning.

A classic example of this is the so-called CHIP (Children's Health Insurance Program), which has sought to provide more access to health care for poor children. It is good that significant numbers of children have been insured through CHIP.[21] But the fact is that since the passage of CHIP about 400,000 more children have lost access to health care because of funding reductions in other programs that used to cover children. It is true that this number of 400,000 would be substantially higher were it not for CHIP, so who is to say that CHIP is not a success? The problem is that we can all feel good about what CHIP is doing, and in the process lose sight of the fact that the problem of uninsured children is only growing larger. From this viewpoint, the cosmetic aspect of CHIP serves only to deepen the problem of children's growing lack of access to health care. Many other examples could also be cited. The piecemeal aspect of current legislation too often serves as a cover for the fact that the crisis in health care is deepening steadily.

*Finally,* a great part of today's public policy debate about health-care justice must be said to be lacking in a sense of overall vision about the purposes, goals, and long-term directions of the health-care system. Much in the legislation suggests that we have no idea where we are going in terms of future health-care delivery. To a significant degree this lack of overall direction comes from a lack of reflection on the deeper issues related to health care, issues such as the meaning of sickness and health, the appropriate and inappropriate uses of technology in health care, and the very meaning of life and death, as well as the meaning of ourselves as a community instead of an assembly of individuals. These questions about vision are not easy, but we cannot afford to run away from them.

The deeper questions about health care and economic theory are not easy. Is a privately financed managed-care system the most just way to deliver health care? Or might a single payer system ultimately prove to be more just? There are no simple answers, and the future of health-care economics is uncertain. There is an indisputable need for a broader and more visionary public dialogue about the future of health care. Without such a public dialogue and without a clear focus on the goal of universal access as a demand of justice, the legislative process will continue on its haphazard course, with the lack of just access to health care only growing more pronounced in spite of some partial successes.

To close these comments about the current legislative approaches to health care, I want to add a clarification. The tone of my remarks should not obscure the fact that some legislatures and some states have been quite visionary in their approach to health care. One thinks of Hawaii and Vermont,[22] which have come quite close to universal access, and of Minnesota, which, at least for now,[23] has outlawed for-profit managed-care companies. There are some important successes and we should learn from these successes, as well as from other countries around the world. Real legislative achievements deserve our praise. But the achievements do not take away the problematic aspects of the current legislative approach to health care.

## Public Policy and the Funding of Health Care

Up to now all of our comments on public policy and health care have been about government *regulation* of health care, whether at the state or the federal level. But there is a second major aspect to governmental health-care policy that has to do with government *funding* of health-care services. The question about funding is largely a question of federal activity, since Medicare is an exclusively federal program, and Medicaid, while administered by the states, is very much dependent on federal funding. Whatever legitimate criticisms one might make, Medicare has been the single most effective aspect of the health-care delivery system in the United States.[24] The track record of Medicaid, which was passed as an afterthought to Medicare, has been much more mixed, even though some good has been achieved.

The question here concerns government funding policy for health care from 1997 onward. This most recent period has seen sharp reductions in government funding for Medicare and Medicaid as part of the Balanced Budget Act (BBA). The goal of BBA was to reduce government funding of Medicare by $200–$250 billion over the first five years of BBA's existence. In 1999, actual Medicare spending was reduced for the first time in history, not just in comparison to the rate of inflation but in real dollars. While I want to offer some criticism of the BBA's approach to health-care funding, it should be acknowledged that not all efforts to reduce public spending on health care are wrong. In the first fifteen or twenty years after Medicare and Medicaid began in 1965, the psychological mindset of many health-care providers was that the government had an inexhaustible supply of cash to pour into health care, and the providers could keep raising prices and developing new lines of service because the government would always come up with the funds to pay whatever the providers asked. Certainly there were problems with this attitude. Ronald Reagan deserves credit for his effort to reduce the rate of health-care spending increases. The same credit must be given to some of the spending reductions in the years following Reagan.

But what about the current round of BBA reductions in health-care spending? While some health-care leaders have found the means to cope with BBA, other health-care providers are in frighteningly difficult situations, with some hospitals and other services teetering on the brink of extinction. The situation is especially fragile in large urban hospitals, with their high percentage of Medicare and Medicaid patients and the costs these hospitals often bear because of their programs for the training of the next generation of physicians.[25] Yes, there are cases in which a hospital's troubles may be due to its own poor management. But this is not the case with all of the hospitals that have been placed at such severe threat by the BBA. Even if some of the past efforts to reduce public health-care spending have been socially responsible, the BBA's strategy is simply not socially responsible, especially in an era of record federal budget surpluses.

Toward the end of 1999, the federal budget negotiations restored about $16 billion of the anticipated $50 billion BBA cut in federal health-care spending for the fiscal year 2000, with the restored funding aimed at some of the especially bad situations, such as the plight of large urban hospitals with teaching programs. A similar restoration happened at the end of 2000. These were good steps and at least a partial admission that the original BBA had gone too far. But there may not have been a sufficient restoration of funding, and the same type of restoration negotiations will need to take place in subsequent years, meaning that the individual decisions made at the end of 1999 and 2000 are part of the incoherent piecemeal approach to health-care policy.[26] There is plenty of rhetoric on all sides about using the budget surplus to save Social Security. But shouldn't there also be companion rhetoric about saving Medicare and (perhaps in a revised form) Medicaid, especially the original focus of Medicaid on care for the poor? Some of this type of rhetoric began to emerge during the presidential campaign of 2000. But one fears that some legislators will not want to do very much about BBA, Medicare, or Medicaid lest the other party claim credit for legislation that is well received by the public.

Beyond the BBA reductions, there is a deeper philosophical question about public funding and health care, namely the question about what segments of health care should be publicly funded and what segments of health care should be left to private funding structures. Those who favor a single-payer system of health care answer this question by asserting that all people's fundamental health-care needs should be covered by a government-funded health-care system. As concerned as Catholic thought is about true health-care justice, nothing in Catholic thought gives a definitive answer as to which type of economic system (public funding, private funding, or a mix of the two) is most ethically appropriate for the delivery of health care. On a question such as this, Catholicism prefers to listen with care, and then support what seems most practical and realistic in a concrete historical context. Recall our earlier comments about Catholicism's interest in a creative and practical interaction of the principles of subsidiarity and socialization. Today's concrete context clearly says that the health-care funding approach of the BBA is wrong and needs ongoing rectification. But this judgment does not answer all of the long-term questions about appropriate economic mechanisms for the delivery of health care in the United States. The Catholic flexibility on this last point deserves much appreciation.

## FUTURE ETHICAL DIRECTIONS FOR THE DEBATE ABOUT PUBLIC POLICY AND HEALTH CARE

What should U.S. health-care policy look like from a moral viewpoint as we move further into the new millennium? No one can be enough of a prophet to give a complete answer as to what public policy on health care will be like in ten years or so. However, there are certain basic themes that should characterize the debate about health-care policy in the years to come. Here I will outline five of these themes. If public policy is shaped by these themes, there is a reasonable hope that the United States can move toward a more satisfactory health-care system. The five themes are as follows. The health care and public policy debate should be (1) goal-centered, (2) willing to ask the deepest questions about life and health, (3) open to dialogue with all concerned parties, (4) coherent and sequential in its pursuit of justice, and (5) flexibly pragmatic about the steps needed to achieve a more just health-care system.

*First,* the approach to public policy must be goal-centered. There is one pivotal goal that shapes the debate about health-care justice: the goal of universal access, of a health-care system that is committed to a reasonable level of health care for all people. Based on the Catholic theory of human rights, nothing less than universal access to health care is an acceptable goal. This goal is a foundational claim rooted in the core dignity of each human person. It will not be easy to achieve universal access. There may be many partial successes and even some failures. But unless the debate has an unrelenting focus on universal access, there is too much likelihood that legislative proposals will obscure the true goal of health-care justice and make things worse by deluding us into thinking that we are achieving justice when we are not. It is hard to conceive of any policy planning for health care being truly productive unless it maintains a clear focus on universal access.[27] This goal, however it is achieved, remains the basic demand of the Catholic commitment to distributive justice.

*Second,* any future approach to a public policy for the delivery of health care must be willing to ask the deeper human questions that ground the meaning of health and health care. For years, I have tried to raise these deeper questions. So have other key writers, notably including Daniel Callahan.[28] What does human health mean? What does it mean that every one of us will one day get sick and die? Are we honest enough about the fact that death is a part of the human story? Do we too often pretend that death really doesn't exist? What does it mean that we are a community of human persons who need to act for the larger good of the community, the country, and the planet, and not just for ourselves? What is the place of technological advance as part of our approach to health care? Should there be some limits as to how far we go in our pursuit of technological breakthroughs in health care, especially if we reflect on health-care needs from a global perspective? Based on these questions, is there a reasonable standard of health care that we should try to meet for all people? Even if we admit that scientific, economic, and cultural standards may alter our understanding of a reasonable standard, can we at least make some progress in keeping the question of a reasonable standard in focus?

There is an understandable human temptation to avoid these issues. They make us uncomfortable, and we would rather not ask about them. But if we don't ask, how will we ever know what we should offer people in order to be just in the delivery of health care? In the last section, it was hard not to conclude that many of today's health-care initiatives were careening out of control without any sense of what should be done to make the health-care system better. People know that something is wrong with our health-care system, which explains the thousands of legislative proposals that have been introduced in recent years. Many of this vast number of proposals are well intentioned. But there remains a grave doubt as to whether these proposals can ever coalesce into a coherent pattern unless we can probe the depths of our common human heart about the appropriate meaning and purpose of health care.

I am not opposed to medical progress and technological medical breakthroughs. Remarkable things have happened in medical science over the past 125 years, and medical science deserves our support and our praise. But the deeper questions have to be asked, and it is hard to conceive of a reasonable future for health-care policy unless these questions are asked honestly.

*Third,* for a future health policy to succeed, the planning process will need to include the broadest possible dialogue between parties who have a genuine interest in the future of health-care delivery. If one thinks back to the collapse of the Clinton plan in 1994, it is clear that one of the sources of the failure was the atmosphere of secrecy out of which the plan was put together. From the viewpoint of Catholicism, there are many potential dialogue partners, including other churches and interfaith groups, as well as medical associations (such as the American Medical Association [AMA] and the American Hospital Association [AHA]), trade unions, and advocacy groups such as the AARP and Families USA.

But the dialogue partners should not be limited to the obvious possibilities. Early in the year 2000, the Health Insurance Association of America (HIAA) became a proponent of significant health-care reform and joined in a national meeting with groups such as the Catholic Health Association (CHA), the AMA, and the AHA.[29] Many readers will recall the "Harry and Louise" advertisements that the HIAA sponsored in 1993–1994, in which Harry and Louise opposed the Clinton plan because under this plan individuals would lose control of their health-care decisions. Harry and Louise never mentioned that the insurance industry (under managed care) would limit people's choices much more than would the Clinton plan. Harry and Louise have returned to television, this time as advocates for health-care reform.[30] A similar story can be told about the pharmaceutical industry, which at the beginning of the year 2000 dropped its long-standing opposition to the Medicare funding of senior citizens' prescription medications.[31] The point is simple: As the number of uninsured continues its steady increase and the health-care crisis deepens, more segments of society may be ready to enter a public dialogue about the reform of health-care policy. The broader this dialogue becomes, the better the chance that integrated reform of health care might be able to succeed.

*Fourth,* future policy initiatives for health-care reform will need to be coherent and sequentially oriented toward the goal of universal access. One of the significant difficulties with recent approaches to health-care policy is that many of the initiatives have had about them a piecemeal character, which ignores the complexity of the health-care system as a whole. The individual steps sometimes even slowed the progress of true health-care reform by obscuring the deepening crisis in the delivery of health care in the United States. This cannot be the case in the future. The individual steps taken need to fit together into a coherent whole, a whole that helps us see the ultimate goal of universal access, so that we choose individual steps that will move us toward that goal.

Several different adjectives are used by persons who argue for a more unified approach to health-care reform. I favor *coherent,* precisely because so much that has recently happened in the field of health-care policy has been incoherent, that is, the individual steps don't seem to fit together into a unified whole. Some have used the adjective *incremental,* implying that each step should be added onto the previous step, so that there is a linked chain of steps toward universal access. I have no problem with the concept of incremental steps, but there is doubt as to whether all of the steps that have been labeled as "incremental" really are incremental. Father Michael Place, the chief officer of the Catholic Health Association, has begun to use the adjective *sequential* to describe the individual policy steps that are truly ordered toward a wholistic process of health-care reform.[32] I like Fr. Place's adjective and would be pleased to see it become the predominant adjective in the discussion of suitable steps toward health-care justice. In this context, the test would be whether an individual health-care initiative can truly be seen as a link that leads logically toward the next step on the road to universal access.

In arguing for coherency or sequentialism in the development of health-care policy, I am not arguing against individual policy initiatives. Some individual initiatives will be necessary, and some initiatives will be good in themselves and part of a sequence that will move us toward universal access. Sometimes, too, an effort to take more than a sequential step will be counterproductive. The support of the public may not be present for more than the individual step, and if the step is both sequential and successful, it may open the public mind toward the desirable next step. And so on, in sequence.

An example of a sequential step toward universal access can be found in the proposal put forward by the Catholic Health Association at the beginning of the year 2000.[33] This proposal seeks to provide health-care coverage for an additional 15 million people in the United States between 2000 and 2003. The

CHA proposal contains four major elements: (1) the expansion of both Medicaid and CHIP, (2) a program of subsidies to help lower-income persons purchase private health insurance, (3) the expansion of the Federal Employees Health Benefits Program (FEHBP) so that more people can enroll in FEHBP, and (4) programs of additional safety-net funding for hospitals and clinics that care for the poor. There needs to be further discussion of the specific elements in the CHA proposal, but it seems to be exactly the kind of coherent proposal that is needed. It is good in itself and it moves toward the goal of universal access. The vision of the CHA proposal becomes clearer if one notes that President Clinton sought only to cover 5 million additional Americans during a similar time period.

The *fifth* characteristic that should mark the future public policy debate about health care is that the participants in the debate should be flexible and pragmatically realistic in their approach to the matter. There are two principal reasons for this call for flexibility and pragmatism. First, the economics of health-care delivery is an extremely complex reality. This complexity makes it unclear exactly which economic methodology is best for health-care delivery in the United States. Catholicism has no specific teaching that makes one economic theory better than another. Any economic methodology that is truly capable of organizing a just health-care system can be seen as acceptable. I have been sharply critical of the current managed-care environment from the viewpoint of ethics. But even with my call for the reform of managed care, I have not claimed that it will be impossible for managed care to get its house in better order so as to become a suitably just economic mechanism for the furnishing of health care. Catholicism does not approach fundamental economic theory with any preconceived notion as to what form of economics, be it more capitalist or more socialist, is more just. If someone enters the health-care justice debate thinking that only one economic theory is possible, one is being unfaithful to the Catholic tradition, with its recognition of the legitimate autonomy of a science such as economics. This kind of rigidity also lessens the likelihood that the debate about health care can come to a successful conclusion.

The second reason I call for pragmatic flexibility in the debate about health-care policy is that no reformed health policy will be able to succeed unless this policy has broad popular support. To gain this broad popular support, individual parties in the debate may have to concede to other positions in order for new policies to be put into place. When parties make concessions, they may hope that their positions will win greater acceptance at a later point. They may believe that the partial success of a compromise policy will enhance rather than restrict the opportunity for an even better policy at a later time. All of this makes the pragmatism involved in political compromise a true step in the art of practicing the virtue of justice.

In the United States in the twentieth century, the most famous example of a religiously motivated pragmatism was found in the works of the great Protestant theologian Reinhold Niebuhr with his system of Christian realism.[34] Niebuhr worried that Christian believers, with their depth of religious vision, might be too ready to propose ideal solutions to social problems, solutions that the world was not yet ready to accept. Niebuhr worried that such Christians, while deeply motivated, might end up with even less justice because they asked for too much. In this world, according to Niebuhr, Christians sometimes need to work for penultimate solutions to human problems. If an ultimate solution is not possible, a reasonable penultimate solution is surely better than no solution at all.[35] A dose of this sort of Niebuhrian realism may be a very necessary ingredient in the struggle to achieve a more just system of health-care delivery.

## CATHOLICISM AND ADVOCACY FOR HEALTH-CARE REFORM

What about Catholicism's role as an advocate for creative change leading to a more ethical health-care policy? Here we will consider five questions about advocacy. *First,* what is advocacy and why is it an essential part of the mission of Catholic health care? *Second,* who should be engaged in health-care advocacy from a Catholic perspective? *Third,* can Catholicism find appropriate partners in its advocacy efforts? *Fourth,* for what health-care goals should Catholicism advocate? And, *fifth,* is there a difference between advocacy and the lobbying that frequently takes place in the political arena?

*First,* the main purpose of advocacy is to undertake organized efforts to bring about change and thus achieve more justice in the delivery of health care. Advocacy often focuses on legislative bodies, seeking to get these bodies to adopt new legislative policies vis-à-vis health care. But advocacy can also be directed at regulatory agencies, with the goal of causing these agencies to adopt new rules of operation that will improve the delivery of health care. Advocacy can also be directed at health-care providers themselves, with the hope that the pressures from the advocacy groups will motivate the providers to adopt better policies on their own. Advocacy should be described as an essential element in the mission of Catholic health care. The core of Catholic social thought holds a deep belief that both government and private organizations can act for the greater good of the whole community. Unlike some segments of Protestant thought, Catholicism does not see either government or private entities as being so corrupt and self-centered that they cannot act in the interest of all people. Once Catholicism accepts this stance toward public institutions, it is not enough for Catholicism to try to offer good health care with its own resources, impressive though these resources may be. Instead, it is part and parcel of the Catholic ethos to enter the public dialogue about health care, trying to bring about change not only for the sake of the Catholic hospitals, but for the sake of all people. The Catholic spirit believes that decent public policy is possible, and it is incumbent on Catholicism to try to bring about this decent policy.

*Second,* once advocacy is defined, who should be acting as advocates for the Catholic concerns about health care? Catholic health-care providers own more than 15 percent of all the hospital rooms available in the United States. These providers have an acute understanding of the critical issues in health care today, and they should be strongly active as advocates for a more just health-care system. Catholic hospitals can exercise advocacy by themselves, in state associations, and through national groups like the CHA.[36]

As important as the Catholic hospitals are as health-care advocates, advocacy by the Catholic hospitals is not a sufficient fulfillment of the Catholic obligation to act as an advocate for health-care justice. If only the Catholic hospitals advocate for changes in health-care, they are likely to be perceived as acting solely for their own self-interest. But if the Catholic hospitals can join with other parts of the Catholic community, Catholic advocacy for health-care justice can be all the more credible and powerful. The Catholic bishops have a special role as advocates for health-care justice. The bishops have already acted as advocates for health-care justice, but even more action would be desirable. Catholic higher education also has a potentially very strong role in the quest for health-care justice. In addition to the field of theological ethics, consider the resources of the Catholic universities in fields such as law, economics, sociology, public policy, and medicine. It is hard not to dream about all these resources entering the dialogue about better ways to deliver health care. Consider also the informed Catholic lay community as a whole. This larger Catholic community has, at least implicitly, a taste for the Catholic belief in the place of public policy as a means to justice in a field such as health care. If the larger Catholic community can become an advocacy community—especially at the polls—the impact on the quest for health-care justice could be very great. Even this book, which hopefully will be read by health-care leaders, has had the focus of trying to reach a broad spectrum of informed Catholics who might become motivated to apply a Catholic perspective to health-care justice.

If we accept this broader notion of who among Catholics should advocate for social justice, a new sort of advocacy role emerges for the Catholic hospitals. These hospitals, in addition to their direct efforts for policy change, will need to serve as educators for the entire Catholic community. Health-care delivery is a very complicated issue, and its problems often seem arcane to the general public. Catholic health-care providers can help the Catholic public understand the issues and begin to see which policy options might lead to genuine progress toward health-care justice.

*Third,* what about Catholicism finding partners in its advocacy efforts about health care? There are cautions here, insofar as some of the groups agitating for new health-care policies are campaigning for their own interests. Catholic health care needs to be careful not to become overly identified with such groups. In particular, Catholic health care—and other not-for-profit health care—needs to take clear steps so that it will not appear to be approaching issues out of the exact same rationale as the for-profit health-care providers. A real loss would ensue if the Catholic providers are understood as being just like everyone else in health care.

Once this caution has been noted, the greater principle about Catholicism and advocacy is that it makes sense for Catholic health-care advocates to forge links with other like-minded groups. Earlier I referred to the need for a wide-ranging dialogue about the future of health care. Many other groups, even if their motivations are not the same, will want to join with Catholics in supporting some issues, and in politics one can use all the help one can get. Sometimes these other groups will be very close in their mindset to the Catholic perspective, with this being particularly true of other Christians and other religious groups. On other occasions the advocacy partners may come from more divergent backgrounds. In these cases the differences ought to be made clear, but the differences should not prevent joint efforts to achieve commonly shared purposes.

*Fourth,* on which sorts of health-care issues ought Catholic advocacy efforts focus? Precisely because advocacy is based on religious foundations, advocacy needs to place its main emphasis on core ethical issues such as justice in the provision of health care and compassionate care for those who are dying, care that tends to the spiritual as well as the physical aspects of illness. This focus of advocacy on the core health-care issues does not rule out the possibility of advocacy sometimes pushing for more specific and narrow proposals. But when advocacy does focus on more specific issues, it must always do this in a manner that reminds everyone of the long-term goal of health-care reform, the goal of universal access to a reasonable standard of health care.

*Fifth,* is advocacy for health-care reform, by Catholics and suitable partners, the same as lobbying? The obvious answer is No, since the law prohibits not-for-profit groups from lobbying, in the legal sense of the word. There are times when advocacy will look very much like lobbying, especially when advocacy is seeking to secure the passage of short-term pieces of legislation that are seen as suitable steps on the long road to health-care justice. But even with this similarity, advocacy and lobbying are not the same. Because advocacy is rooted in a religious/moral sense of justice, advocacy needs to be understood as a charismatic exercise of prophetic discernment. Advocacy cannot offer all of the answers to a complex problem such as achieving greater health-care justice. Recall what was said earlier about the legitimate autonomy of complex political issues, about the aspects of these issues that faith alone is unable to resolve. But in the debate about health care, religious advocacy can be said to have a privileged position. Because the religious perspective cuts so deeply, this perspective is particularly competent when it comes to pointing out evil and calling for ultimate goals. Pointing out evil and pointing to new goals is exactly what discerning prophets are called to do, even if they do not have all the answers about the best means to get to the goals. It is very much to be hoped that, when inspired and thoughtful religious leaders speak out on an issue, their utterances have a different character than the views of bankers, brokers, health economists, or insurance companies. Recall the role of Martin Luther King, Jr., and the other religious advocates for racial justice in the 1950s and 1960s. Even though there were other voices in the civil rights debate, King and his fellow religious leaders who sought justice took on a specific identity in the debates of that era. Their advocacy for justice was clearly more than lobbying for legislation by special interest groups. It was an exercise of faith speaking to power. Religious advocacy for health-care justice needs to have this same faith-based character. If the Catholics and their partners in the debate about health care are understood as just another group of lobbyists, they have surely failed.

To sum up, there are four main conclusions to be drawn from the chapter. *First,* even though public policy alone cannot address all the questions about health-care justice, and even though it is not clear exactly which future policy options will work best, there is no doubt that carefully developed public policy has a vital role in today's efforts for a more just health-care system. *Second,* the Roman Catholic tradition, with its positive sense of government and public policy, can be a helpful resource in the debate about health-care policy. *Third,* future directions on health-care policy need to be visionary and far reaching, willing to wrestle with fundamental questions such as the meaning of human sickness and dying and the meaning of justice. And *fourth,* to help bring about the necessary changes in our health-care system, Catholicism—and the other churches and religious groups—must be willing to play their historic and prophetic role as advocates for true justice. If these four conclusions can coalesce into a unified vision, public policy will surely be able to play an appropriate role in health-care reform.

# Chapter 6
# SOME PARTICULAR PROBLEMS
# IN HEALTH-CARE JUSTICE

The focus of this book has been on three overriding issues: managed care, rapid realignment of health services, and the lack of a coherent public policy on health care. Besides these issues, there are a significant number of other issues in health-care ethics that may not have the same degree of systematic importance but are very pressing, especially for people who have to deal with them directly. This chapter will offer some reflections on three such issues: (1) the rising cost of prescription medications, (2) the state of mental health care in the era of managed care, and (3) the prospects for medical education in today's health-care context. It is my hope that the consideration of at least three lesser issues will help awaken readers to the large number of subsidiary moral issues related to today's health-care delivery system in the United States.

## THE COST OF PRESCRIPTION MEDICATIONS

In the first half of the 1990s, the cost of almost every segment of the U.S. health-care system rose very rapidly. Double-digit annual inflation of health-care costs was the rule rather than the exception. The impression was that health-care costs were spinning out of control, and there were predictions that by somewhere around the year 2000, the United States would be spending 20–22 percent of its gross domestic product on health care.[1] Businesses in the United States suffered greatly due to the pressures of rising health-care costs. The defeat of

174

George H. W. Bush in the 1992 presidential election was due in significant part to the poor performance of the U.S. economy, and that poor economy was to a substantial degree brought about by rapid inflation in health-care costs.

Since the mid-1990s, the rate of increase in health-care costs has decreased dramatically. For the most part, health-care costs are increasing at a rate that closely parallels the rate of the economy as a whole, and the costs of some segments of health care are rising at a rate even lower than the inflation rate of the U.S. economy. Managed care can be said to have been a success, at least from the viewpoint of helping keep health-care costs down.

But there is one notable exception to this pattern of reduction in the rate of increases in health-care expenses. Since 1994, the cost of prescription medications has risen as rapidly as all the other health-care costs were rising in the early 1990s. In 1998, the average cost of prescription medications rose by about 15 percent; 1999's rate of increase was lower (only about 6 percent), but it remains to be seen whether or not this is a sign of lasting change in the rate increases for medications.[2] The recent history of pharmaceutical pricing may be an argument for managed care, since a field like drug pricing, where there is virtually no managed competition, has failed to come under control in a pattern similar to other health-care costs. If we grant that an economy based on profit-making will continue to be the best economy for the manufacture of drugs, some sort of cost management scheme may well be in everyone's best long-term interest.

Two special factors should be noted relative to the cost of drugs. *First*, a significant part in the cost is related to drug manufacturers spending large amounts of time and money developing similar and even redundant drugs so that they can compete with one another in the marketplace. Millions of extra dollars can be spent to develop competitive drugs that do very little that is new, and these costs are passed on to the patients. While it would be wrong to cut off all competitive research, perhaps some limits might be set. State regulatory agencies might limit the providers in their states to the use of no more than two or three similar products for a given condition, thus limiting the incentive for the drug manufacturers to develop too many drugs for the same purpose. Dr. John Kitzhaber, the governor of Oregon, has recently proposed a regulatory scheme for Oregon somewhat along these lines. Recently adopted legislation in Maine established a mandatory price control system for prescription medications if prices were not voluntarily lowered by October 1, 2001.[3]

The *second* special factor has to do with the enormous development cost of drugs. Even with regulatory schemes that restrict the number of drugs developed, vast sums of money will be spent on research for and development of new drugs. Most drug companies in the United States employ a two-tiered approach to the pricing of their drugs. In the United States, the drugs are priced to recover the cost of the research that was done to develop them. Some of this cost is recovered through government grants, and some through direct charges to the consumer; in either case the consumer ultimately pays for the drugs. When the companies sell the same drugs to other countries, a different pricing structure is often used, which pays for the cost of producing the drugs but not the cost of the research to develop the drugs in the first place. The result is that U.S. manufacturers frequently sell their products in other countries for far lower prices than they charge in the United States. One regularly reads accounts of U.S. citizens who live near the U.S. borders journeying to Mexico or Canada to buy prescription drugs.

There are two sides to this dual pricing structure. Other countries have very limited economic development and sometimes terrible health problems. For these countries, lowering the price of drugs is a socially responsible action on the part of the drug companies. One thinks of some of the countries on the Indian subcontinent or in Central Africa, where the life expectancy is still only in the mid-forties—what it was in the United States a century ago. In a few of the African countries, the AIDS epidemic has lowered life expectancy to the mid- to upper thirties.[4] An example of a socially responsible approach to the pricing of medications in such countries is the May 2000 decision of several major drug manufacturers to reduce the cost of AIDS medications for poor countries, especially in Africa.[5] But one also hears sadder stories, for example, of drug manufacturers ceasing to produce certain medications that are only useful in poor countries where little profit can be made.[6] Some published reports indicate that drug costs are actually higher in some of the very poor and disease-ridden parts of the world such as Africa.[7]

Besides these very poor countries with special social needs, there are other countries with highly productive economies. Some of these countries are involved in research to develop new medications, and they bear some of the costs associated with this research. But the United States, and in particular drug consumers in the United States, are asked to bear a disproportionately high share of the research and development costs related to new medications. It would seem more just to develop a formula that would cause all of the world's productive economies to share equitably in the cost of developing new drugs. Perhaps the U.S. drug manufacturers might develop two pricing structures for products they sell outside the United States, one for poorer countries and one for richer countries. Such an integrated approach would also have the effect of lowering drug prices for consumers in the United States, at least to some degree.

There are occasional reports of managed-care companies in the United States negotiating special price arrangements with the drug companies so as to pay less for drugs, less even than what the government pays for drugs in programs for the poor such as Medicaid. I do not question managed-care companies using economic leverage to help lower drug prices, but it does seem unreasonable that these price breaks are not extended to programs for the poor. According to some observers, it may even be illegal.[8]

Because there have been so many breakthroughs in the development of new medications, more and more medical conditions can be managed successfully through the use of medications. This is very good, provided that the medications actually are effective in doing what they set out to do. Compared with hospitalization, surgery, or simply putting up with poor health, the management of health issues through medications is quite attractive. Many persons have a higher quality of life because of the medications they take.

In spite of all this benefit, there is a significant negative aspect connected with the trend toward more use of prescription medications. The increased use of these medications means that many persons, especially in mid- and later life, may be taking a number of medications, even for relatively routine health conditions. The result may be a substantial expense, perhaps several thousand dollars a year, even for a fairly simple pattern of care. Working persons may have coverage for these costs, and so do some senior citizens. But many senior citizens, especially those whose only coverage comes from the traditional Medicare program, have no coverage for their prescriptions. Since these seniors are often living on fixed incomes, the cost of prescriptions is a heavy burden. When Medicare was established, prescriptions were used less frequently, and they cost much less. In that context, it may have been acceptable for the standard Medicare program not to have included a prescription benefit. But given the current state of prescription use, the practice of the United States' major health-care program for seniors not including coverage for prescriptions is in need of serious reexamination. Because of the growingly important place of prescriptions in today's health-care context, exclusion of prescription coverage cannot be defended as a matter of justice, at least for those seniors who have no other means to cover the cost of their prescriptions.

At the beginning of the year 2000, the major drug companies in the United States announced that they would no longer oppose the funding of prescriptions as part of Medicare.[9] This is a step forward, and it seems likely that some substantial change will occur in the near future on the issue of funding prescription drugs for senior citizens. There are questions as to exactly how this change will take place. Will a new approach to the funding of prescriptions for seniors be part of a larger, more integrated approach to health-care justice, or will it be another piecemeal effort that may help with one issue while the whole picture of health-care delivery in the United States continues to worsen? Will the program be very confusing, like some of the other health-funding issues are for seniors? Will the drug companies maneuver for special advantages in a new Medicare prescription program, so that the underlying issue of the high cost of drugs is not really addressed? Will the need of hospitals and others to recover more of the Medicare funding that was cut by the Balanced Budget Act restrict other health funding so that there will not be enough money left to fund a quality prescription drug program for senior citizens?[10] Only time will tell, but there are some strong indications that political pressures may cause both parties to support a Medicare benefit for prescription medications, at least for those who have no other coverage.[11] President George W. Bush has supported both a short term-emergency prescription plan for poor senior citizens and a longer, more thorough reform of Medicare. Some members of both political parties have opposed Bush's ideas, and the legislative outcome remains uncertain.

I introduced the subject of prescriptions because their high cost, while affecting many people, is a particularly burdensome issue for senior citizens and their families. There is another issue of high health-care cost that also imposes a special burden on seniors and their families. This is the extremely high cost associated with skilled nursing, especially if it continues for a period of many months or even years. It is good that important and less costly alternatives to skilled nursing, such as home care and assisted living, have emerged in recent years. But there are patients for whom skilled nursing will be the only option. And it is very expensive, often $5,000 per month or more. Many middle-class and poor families are not in a position to afford insurance for skilled nursing, so it becomes a question of families playing a sort of nursing home roulette, hoping that their loved one will not be the one who needs skilled nursing, at least not for a lengthy period of time. It is true that Medicaid will cover the cost of skilled nursing, but only after a person's life savings have been expended. There are ways around this, such as a patient's giving his life savings to his family at least three years before skilled nursing is needed, but this remedy is highly demeaning, and it does not address the underlying justice issues related to skilled nursing. There is also the problem of Medicaid paying low reimbursement rates for skilled nursing, with the result that nursing homes sometimes refuse to accept Medicaid patients or at least try to limit their number. These tactics by the nursing homes only serve to illustrate the depth of the funding problems associated with skilled nursing.

The moral outrage associated with the lack of a broader social plan for skilled nursing is as great or greater than the moral outrage connected with our failure to cover the prescription medications for senior citizens. The time may be farther away, but it is very much to be hoped that the growing consensus on the moral obligation to cover seniors' prescription costs will evolve into a consensus to provide coverage for skilled nursing.[12] Especially if the economic crisis faced by skilled nursing is joined to a moral awareness of access to nursing care as a justice issue, some change may be possible.

## CARE FOR BEHAVIORAL OR MENTAL HEALTH

So far I have made only a few passing comments about the current state of behavioral or mental health care. A complete treatment of the ethical issues related to mental health care is beyond the scope of this book.[13] But there are important moral considerations about mental health care as part of the overall context of health-care delivery. Some of these moral considerations on mental health care exist more as questions than as answers.

Recent years have seen two major developments in the field of behavioral or mental health care. *First,* there have been some spectacular discoveries in terms of the pharmaceuticals produced to help address a wide variety of mental health conditions. Pharmaceuticals have long been a part of the approach to mental health care, but never have there been so many effective medications targeted at so many specific mental health issues. This must be seen as a great step forward. Especially when we stop to consider how many persons suffer from mental health difficulties, the pharmaceutical advances deserve praise. Often when we think about illness, we exclusively limit our perspective to purely physical ailments. It helps to remember that a group such as the World Health Organization holds that neuro-psychiatric conditions constitute the most common long-term health problem found on Earth.[14]

Until the recent past, hospitalization, perhaps for lengthy periods of time, was the only answer for many persons with significant mental health difficulties. Today many persons who would have been hospitalized in the past are able to keep living in the world, staying with their families, perhaps continuing to hold jobs. It is very good that these persons are able to have a significantly improved quality of life at a reasonable financial cost and without hospitalization because of the new mental health drugs. At the same time, we need to ask whether there are any negatives about the new mental health drugs.

This *second* trend is that in the United States managed care has taken over the mental health marketplace to almost exactly the same extent that it has taken over the health-care marketplace.[15] Almost everything said in the earlier chapters about managed care can be repeated in the context of mental health. Costs have been kept down, and organized systems of mental health care have been put into place. But patient and physician choice have been limited, and even recent moves by managed-care companies to give physicians greater autonomy may not be extended to the mental health field.[16] The millions who lack access to health care in general lack access to mental health care, even though a right to a reasonable level of mental health care should be part of the overall human right to health care. On the whole, managed care can be said both to enhance and to limit mental health care.

The key question is, What happens when the two major trends of pharmaceutical development and managed mental health care are combined? Some good points will be observed when the new mental health pharmaceuticals and managed care of mental health are viewed as one reality. Managed care enables many people to get mental health care at a reasonable price. Many people are able to stay out of hospitals and keep functioning reasonably well in their daily lives. But there are some serious questions that need to be asked about mental health care in today's world. Because the pharmaceuticals are so readily available and because they cost less than hospitalization or long-term counseling, is there a tendency of managed-care plans to rely too exclusively on the new drugs as the means of caring for persons with mental health issues?

Might there not be cases in which a patient might be genuinely well served by a period of mental health hospitalization, even if the hospitalization involves a higher cost? Some of the modern mental health drugs are very powerful, and, in appropriate cases, persons may need to take them for a lifetime. Still, it is hard not to worry about some of the cases in which persons continue taking such drugs for many years, especially if a sizable number of these medications are being taken at the same time.[17] Many of these medications have major side effects. They can alter not only the difficulties but also the normal functioning of persons' emotional and affective lives. Passivity and loss of interest in the surrounding world are but one example of the difficult side effects that these medications can create. Recall that managed care as a whole has sought to keep patients out of hospitals or to reduce the length of hospital stays, even in cases where there is a clear social consensus in favor of the hospitalization. More research is necessary, but it is at least fair to ask whether there are cases in which managed mental health care turns too quickly to the new pharmaceuticals instead of to hospitalization. Even the question of homelessness in our society deserves mention. Are some of the increasing number of homeless persons in today's world persons who formerly might have been hospitalized as mental health patients? Would it be better if some of these persons could again be hospitalized?

Another issue is the role of counseling as part of the mental health recovery process. Some mental health issues involve physiological factors, such as chemical imbalances, and some patients need medication on an ongoing basis. But mental health is also an affair of the human spirit. Sometimes mental health patients need to develop new styles of living, new ways of approaching their problems. Catholicism has a high focus on spiritual direction. Spiritual direction is not simply the same as helping someone with mental health issues, and the proper distinctions need to be maintained. But there is an overlap. At least some aspects of mental health growth involve the reality of personal conversion, of accepting responsibility for who one is, and trying to move in new and more productive directions. The best members of the behavioral mental health profession, such as Dr. Karl Menninger, have always recognized this.[18]

From this perspective, mental health counseling—sometimes long and arduous mental health counseling—may fairly often be indicated as part of an overall mental health program. Sometimes this counseling may be accompanied by medications, even for a lifetime. But with mental health counseling, perhaps the total number or dosage level of the medications can be reduced. In some cases, the medications may even be able to be stopped completely. These steps may very well improve the quality of life of the person who is being treated. The side effects are reduced and the person acquires a greater freedom. He or she freely chooses to be the person he or she wants to be. This is where mental counseling and the life of the spirit in union with God come together.

Counseling may be expensive, and success is not always possible. But when counseling can help a person, it is certainly medically indicated, and it is a matter of justice. In our drug-oriented, instant-fix culture, it can be too easy to rely excessively on psychotropic drugs, valuable though these drugs may be in themselves. The cost-conscious outlook of managed care may serve only to fuel the easy reliance on mental health drugs, and it is regrettable that the moves to give more autonomy to managed-care physicians may not extend to the mental health field. For too long mental health care has been a poor stepchild in the overall field of health care. Even with the advances in pharmaceuticals and managed-care mental health planning, our ultimate goal in mental health care should be true quality care, using all the options that are best for a given patient, even when these options are not the least inexpensive ones.

There are three special mental health issues that deserve note. *First,* what about the use of medications in mental health care for children? No one would question that there are some situations in which medications for mental health purposes can be of significant value for children. Such medications are sometimes used to help with conditions such as attention deficit disorder and hyperactivity. The care for childhood depression may also be enhanced through the use of medications. But the temptation to overuse these medications can arise with children as well as with adults. A recent major study asserts that behavioral modifying medications are overused in a substantial number of cases involving children.[19] The overuse of psychotropic drugs in children is especially troubling. Not only are children our future; they are an enormously vulnerable population who cannot speak for themselves, at least not completely. Special vigilance is therefore required regarding the mental health treatment of children.

The *second* special issue concerns another very vulnerable population, persons who are dealing with behavioral issues very late in life, in nursing care centers or in similar situations. Some persons undergo significant behavioral changes as their health declines. Persons who throughout life have been highly cooperative may become very difficult to deal with. Quiet persons may become obstreperous. Inappropriate sexual contacts may occur in persons whose past lives have been exemplary. These and related behavioral changes may make it very difficult for the caregivers to get the patients to cooperate with the recommended course of medical care.

There is a related issue that arises rather frequently when health-care ethics reflects on the very old. I refer to the use of physical restraints, which are sometimes used or proposed to prevent difficult older patients from interfering with the course of treatment that the doctors wish to follow.[20] There are cases in which patients are at a very clear risk of harming themselves, so an absolute prohibition of the use of restraints is not possible. But physical restraints raise grave questions about human dignity and freedom. It is hard not to wonder whether in some cases the use of restraints is being proposed for the convenience of the caregivers (who want an easier time in caring for the patient) rather than for the true good of the patient. While I cannot rule out restraints completely, they are surely acceptable only as a last resort.

I mention this theme of physical restraints because some health-care providers feel that the use of heavy dosages of behavior modifying medication in the very old is more or less the same as using physical restraints, especially from the moral point of view. Like children, the very old are a highly vulnerable population over whom advantage can easily be taken. Some aged persons may be suffering from conditions such as clinical depression and may be helped through the appropriate use of behavioral medications. But the worry is that too often behavior modifying medications may be given to the very old for the convenience of the caregivers or the family. This is wrong, and special vigilance is called for on the whole question of the use of behavior modifying drugs for those who are very old and very sick.

The *third* special consideration has to do with the relationship between mental health and addictive behaviors. Some published scholarship has pointed out the links between mental health and addiction, be it to drugs, alcohol, gambling, or other compulsions.[21] Treatment plans for mental health must always be alert for issues connected with addiction. Treatment for addiction may frequently be a necessary part of an overall approach to mental health treatment. Once this fact is noted the question about how best to use medication in the treatment of mental health only becomes more pressing and difficult.

## SOCIAL JUSTICE AND MEDICAL EDUCATION

Our third special issue arises because social action programs to provide health care for the poor frequently have the added benefit of providing opportunities for the medical education of new doctors and other health-care professionals.[22] It often happens that the medical schools of major universities are connected with hospitals in large cities, where there are significant concentrations of poor people. Usually the medical schools establish programs in these hospitals that focus both on caring for the poor and educating the medical students. Special clinics and other outreach programs are often founded near the universities to further these dual objectives. To keep all these programs functioning, the medical schools and university hospitals are aided by public funding from programs such as Medicare and Medicaid. The tax monies that help fund the medical care of the poor also have a second benefit that redounds to the good of every taxpayer: these programs help educate the future doctors (and other health-care workers) whom we will all need someday, regardless of our financial status.

Some persons, on hearing that much of the care for the poor in the United States is tied to the medical education system, object that the system takes advantage of the poor because it subjects them to treatment by less experienced physicians, often medical residents. But the medical care given in the settings I have mentioned tends to be very well supervised, and in addition the medical residents can be very highly motivated to provide the best care they can. It helps to reflect that many persons besides the poor seek medical care in these education-based centers precisely because they may be able to access a level of sophistication unavailable anywhere else. It is very common to find patients from all over the world at the United States' medical school-connected hospitals. These patients are seeking a level of care that they cannot find anywhere else.

The poor are to be given the same human rights as any other patients in our university-based medical centers. These centers frequently—and appropriately—are interested in performing medical experiments. It is acceptable to ask the poor patients to take part in such experiments. But they should receive the same explanations of the experiments and be given the same freedom to say Yes or No as anyone else.[23] Senior doctors in teaching hospitals will frequently—and appropriately—wish to have the medical students become familiar with the specific illness situations of the different patients. The students' learning about the individual patients will help them become better doctors. But there are circumstances in which a patient and family will have a special need for privacy. When this happens, the poor patient should be treated the same as the well-off patient.

The current deep reductions in public funding for health care are creating special problems for medical education. For the 2000 fiscal year, some funding was restored to the teaching hospitals. But one questions whether the restored funds were sufficient, and the restoration of funding was only temporary, meaning that the peril for medical education will continue into future years. It is very shortsighted not to provide sufficient funding for medical education. This approach can serve only to hurt the quality of medical care in future decades. What good will it do to have all sorts of sophisticated medical technologies if we lack sufficient doctors to use these technologies for all people?

A related issue concerns the many physicians who were born and educated elsewhere in the world practicing medicine in the United States. Many of them are very competent physicians, and the practice of medicine is enriched by having physicians from different countries and cultures work together. There are no objections to qualified individual physicians from around the world coming to the United States to practice medicine; it is part of a very honorable American tradition of welcoming immigrants to our shores.

What I question is the United States following a broad social policy on medical education that serves to make the United States a net importer of doctors and other health-care professionals. In the world as a whole medical needs are so incredibly great. For a very rich country like the United States not to educate enough physicians so that it can be a net exporter of physicians clearly seems to be wrong. Whatever questions there may be, the traditional link between care for the poor and strong medical education ought to be preserved, since both of these goals are so worthy. I happen to be writing this section of the book in one of the Central African countries where health care is in such a desperately difficult situation. Not only are there the mega-problems such as malaria and AIDS, but the infrastructure to help offer health care as a whole is very weak. It simply seems morally untenable for the United States to weaken its medical education system to the point that, like oil, it ends up sucking in personal health-care resources from the rest of the world instead of generating a broad supply of doctors, nurses, and other practitioners, some of whom may be able so serve elsewhere. I recognize that some individual U.S.-born and educated health providers do practice in other countries, but my concern is the net balance. Both from the U.S. perspective and the global perspective, quality medical education programs in the United States are a crucial priority.

Many other issues could be added to the three I have mentioned. One might consider the question about the impact on health care of the growingly multicultural character of the U.S. population. One might consider the need for spiritual and pastoral care as a more integral part of health care. It is hoped that the specific issues that we have discussed will bring our attention to the host of issues that are part of health-care ethics today.

# Chapter 7
# TOWARD SOME OVERALL CONCLUSIONS
# ABOUT HEALTH-CARE JUSTICE TODAY

It is time to move to the overall judgments and opinions to be drawn from this book. These will be presented in two sections. *First,* throughout the book I offered a number of particular conclusions that were grounded in the materials considered in the different chapters. It will be helpful to summarize these conclusions to see how they coalesce as a whole and whether they offer a coherent overall picture of health-care justice in today's world. I call this first set of conclusions "sequenced conclusions."

Once we have articulated these sequenced conclusions, I will move further and offer some deeper conclusions, which come to the fore once the sequential conclusions have been seen as a whole. This *second* set of conclusions will reach further into the future of just health care, both in the United States and globally. This second set of conclusions will not be as well grounded in the logical structure of the book, but then the more distant future never is as clear. Some of these second-level conclusions will clearly be matters of my own opinion, perhaps evoking the tone of Kierkegaard's famous "Concluding Unscientific Postscript."[1] If we agree that Christian ethics is as much an art as it is a science,[2] it is entirely proper to offer judgments that contain an element of speculation. In the eighteenth century, Roman Catholicism developed its famous tradition of probabilism,[3] which recognizes that in the search for truth, high probability may be a very important tool, even if hindsight later corrects earlier probable judgments offered by theologians who are trying to open up the mystery of God's action among us. I call the second set of conclusions "probable intuitions" about the future of just health care.

## SEQUENCED CONCLUSIONS

The first sequenced moral conclusion about health care is that, both in the United States and elsewhere, access to a reasonable level of health care remains a clear obligation of distributive justice, an inviolable human right, and a basic requirement of the common good. This conclusion does not answer the question of which health services constitute a reasonable level of care, nor does it tell us which means of distribution is best in a given society at a given time in history. The questions about level of service and means of distribution are essentially economic, scientific, and medical questions that reach beyond the competence of moral theology. Only in cases where the specific proposals of economics, science, and medicine prove to be completely inadequate for the goal of universal access would the concrete proposals become a moral issue in themselves, and in such cases the proposals are not good economics, science, or medicine in the first place.

The delivery of health care is a *moral* issue at the level of principle, that is, the level where questions about the dignity and respect due each human person are considered. Therefore foundational reflection on the delivery of health care cannot be left simply to discussion and analysis by economists and other scientists. A large part of the problem with health-care delivery in the United States is that it has been looked at too exclusively as a matter of economic theory, so that other voices, including the voices of the moral thinkers, religious leaders, and common people are not sufficiently heard.

The first sequenced moral conclusion argues clearly that access to a reasonable level of health care is a human right. Some approaches to human rights are highly tinged with an unacceptable rugged individualism. A number of scholars, including Daniel Callahan,[4] have been moving away from human rights in their analyses of health-care justice. But for the Roman Catholic tradition, the understanding of human rights is organic and wholistic. The individual and her/his rights are seen as part of an integrated continuum with the greater good of society, and individual rights are always to be understood as calling each person to a broad sense of social responsibility. From this perspective, it continues to make good sense to describe health care as a human right,[5] especially in the United States, where rights thinking has played such an important part in our historical past.

The second sequenced conclusion concerns managed care and justice. Managed care has an honorable history in the United States, especially in its early manifestations such as Kaiser Permanente and Group Health. Even today, managed care has accomplished significant moral goods in areas such as quality control and cost reduction. But managed care in its current form raises very serious moral questions. These questions concern the dignity and autonomy of the patient as a human person, the professional identity of the physician, and the provision of reasonable access to health care to all people. The lack of access to health care has increased dramatically during the ascendancy of managed care. It would be inaccurate to say that managed care is entirely responsible for this increase, but it would also be inaccurate not to acknowledge that managed care has been a significant factor in the increasing lack of access to health care.

There is grave doubt about what sort of future managed care ought to have from the moral viewpoint. It seems likely that some aspects of managed care will endure into the future. But it is deeply uncertain whether managed care has enough moral character to retain its dominant position in health-care delivery in the United States. This doubt applies to all of managed care, but especially to the for-profit segment that is so strongly associated with the problems experienced by millions of Americans as they try to cope with managed care. Catholic social teaching is not committed to any one economic system. Managed care, even in its for-profit form, could develop in such a way as to be morally acceptable from the Catholic viewpoint. The Catholic question is not about the theories that ground managed care; the Catholic question is the practical moral question, that is, the question about the troubling facets of the actual practice of managed care. Some of the economists who espouse managed care argue as if the for-profit aspect of managed care is more or less an article of faith.[6] The structure of Catholic thought calls on all of us to suspend any advance economic or moral judgment, so as to concentrate on how managed care actually works from the moral viewpoint.[7] It is possible that managed care may find ways to address its moral problems well enough to remain the dominant model of health-care delivery in the United States. But there is grave moral doubt as to whether this will actually happen.

Our third sequenced moral conclusion concerns the rapid realignment of health-care services that has been taking place in the United States. Some of this realignment has happened for worthwhile reasons. Among the important accomplishments of realignment are a focus on quality, the reduction of health-care costs, the provision of easier patient access to a continuum of health-care services, and the creation of health-care power bases that are strong enough to challenge the seamier side of managed care. As realignment moves into the future, Catholic health-care providers will often be able to negotiate arrangements that respect the Catholic commitment to the *Ethical and Religious Directives.* Realignment decisions are likely to bring about new models for the sponsorship of Catholic health care, models in which several religious communities sponsor a health-care ministry or models with completely new types of sponsorship.

The main caution around realignment is that realignment is not a value in itself but only a means to other worthy objectives, such as making health-care services more readily available to more people at a more reasonable cost. The temptation to see realignment as an end in itself must be avoided, as must the fascination with constant growth to a larger size.

The fourth sequenced conclusion concerns the place of public policy in the achievement of health-care justice. The classic Aristotelian/Thomist viewpoint (also shared by Calvinists) holds that public policy can play a significant role in enhancing the human good. The negativism and cynicism that mark many aspects of today's policy debates about health care are to be avoided. Policy reform will never be the whole answer to the achievement of just health care. Some aspects of health policy may embrace, at least in part, the corruption that the Lutheran tradition has seen to be so inherent in public policy. Public policy involves technical, scientific, and secular elements, so that public policy can never be based solely on religion or morality. But, even with these cautions, public policy in health care can function in an enlightened fashion that helps foster the human good.

For public policy on health care to be a success, it will be essential for public policy to avoid the piecemeal approach that has been so common in recent years, and which frequently has only served to make matters worse by obscuring the underlying problems that beset the U.S. health-care system. Also, for public policy on health care to be a success, the debate about health-care policy needs to involve the widest possible range of participants.

The fifth sequenced conclusion is that there are a host of other crucial issues that cry out for health-care justice. We only took time to sketch out three of these issues: the cost of medications, care for mental health issues, and the future education of doctors and other health-care professionals. But beneath these issues there are many more matters of grave concern, issues that can only be addressed if we work from a framework that runs along the lines proposed in this book. These additional issues only serve to raise the high stakes about health-care justice even higher.

These five conclusions represent a summary of this book. The question is whether the argument can be moved any further to bring the book to its conclusion. To answer we will move to our set of intuitions.

## INTUITIONS ABOUT THE FUTURE

The first intuition has to do with the future of managed care in the United States. Will managed care be the dominant mode for health-care delivery in the United States, or will the country ultimately move in some other direction? No one can give an absolute answer, and, as election pollsters say, it is a very close call. In the presidential election of 2000, George W. Bush said relatively little about health care, other than calling for a prescription drug plan and for Medicare reform. Bush's general philosophical support for private enterprise and for subsidiary solutions make it likely that, along with some legislative reform proposals on matters such as lawsuits, he will try to give managed care the opportunity to evolve itself into a more just system of health care. This likely stance by the new president is surely defensible. My own estimate is that the odds are slightly against managed care remaining the dominant mode of U.S. health delivery. There are some resources with which managed care could reform itself and become more morally acceptable. But I think the odds are against this by about 60 to 40.

I have two main reasons for casting the odds in this negative direction. *First,* the overall tone of the business mentality associated with profit-making is very powerful, very difficult to overcome, and very difficult to reconcile with the passion for justice that is essential for genuinely moral health care. Even in the not-for-profit segment of health care, it is hard not to let the ideology associated with profit-making become the dominant rationale. Catholic providers are usually successful in avoiding domination by the negative aspects of the profit motif. But it is very hard for the Catholic providers to avoid the temptations associated with profit-making. All the more so, it seems unlikely that other health-care providers without such an explicitly religious motivation will be successful in avoiding the temptations associated with profit-making.

My *second* reason for doubting the long-term moral potential of managed care has to do with the rugged individualism that is so prominent in U.S. culture today. We very much live in an "every man and woman for himself or herself" kind of world. In such a world it is hard to generate much passion for a broader social goal such as universal access to health care. Often political campaigns are successful when they appeal to self-interest rather than to broader social goals. There may not be enough moral fiber in contemporary culture to create the matrix out of which the problems associated with managed care can be successfully challenged. I can certainly see possible routes to the reform of managed care, but the current individualistic tone of the United States makes it less likely that these routes will be taken.

Many of the inspiring stories about the early moral successes of managed care come from the World War II period. In that time period, a very powerful sense of community was created by the need to respond to the overriding issues of totalitarianism and economic depression. Americans had a much stronger sense of social solidarity, out of which persons as diverse as Henry Kaiser, Sidney Garfield, and Amadeo Giannini could join in a common effort to provide cost-effective, broad-based access to health care. But do we have the social solidarity today to bring about a truly just reform of managed care? My view is to have slightly more doubt than hope.

My second intuition is that in the future it may happen that the United States will need to create some sort of national insurance system to cover the basic health-care needs of every citizen. Such a national health insurance system is not an ineluctable necessity based on Catholic social principles, but it may emerge as a practical necessity based on the current social situation of the United States. Catholicism's belief that law can serve as a teacher and guide for people is important here. Precisely because there is so much individualism in the United States, it may well take the rule of law to create the funding mechanisms necessary to assure every citizen of access to health care.

In asserting the probability that by 2010 or thereabouts the United States may need to consider a national health insurance system, I am not arguing for the actual delivery of health services by the government, but only for a unified funding system that covers all people. I remain deeply convinced that the actual provision of health care should remain in private hands, at least for the most part. Keeping the doctors, the hospitals, and other resources private (or only with local public ownership) will keep health care more personal, it will enhance competition between providers, and it will lead to higher quality. Even though government may well need to become involved in the access question, I do not believe that there will ever be a case for socialized medicine in the strong sense, that is, with medical services largely provided by the government itself.

Should my intuition of a unified national health insurance system prove correct, there could still be a wide variety of ways in which such a system might work. For instance, just what level of coverage should such a unified insurance system provide? Should persons who can afford it be permitted to seek services beyond what the insurance system covers, and, if so, how much additional service should they be permitted to seek? The answers to these questions will depend on issues related to the performance of the U.S. economy and to the state of medical science. The level of services covered will need to be high enough to give everyone a sense of being treated justly, but not so high as to create excessive cost burdens and undue pressure on the U.S. economy as a whole.

How might a unified national insurance system be administered? How much autonomy ought to be given to state and local governments, especially since there are some important regional differences in peoples' health needs? How much should a national financing system make use of private intermediaries (for example, insurance companies and managed-care plans) to handle the actual disbursement of monies to the health-care providers? What sort of taxation policy should be used to fund a unified national health insurance system? Should general tax revenues be used? Should there be an expansion of Medicare and Social Security? What about an employment-based tax for those who work? Or might a combination of several financing mechanisms work best? All these questions make it clear that any greater government involvement on the access side of health care might occur in many different ways. If there are to be changes, politicians, economists, and health-care professionals will be more competent than theologians in determining the more concrete aspects of any policies that are enacted into law.

My third intuition flows from the fact that most of this book has focused on the situation of health-care delivery in the United States alone. This isolated approach should not continue into the future. The focus in future discussions about health care will need to be far more global, more open to issues of health-care justice throughout the world. How can the United States and other highly developed countries continue to have a morally suitable health policy without addressing issues like the very low life expectancy and poor public health standards that continue to be present in many parts of the world? Will the United States and other well-off countries be able to continue to spend vast sums to benefit small numbers of people with relatively unusual health problems when so many basic public health needs are not being met on a global basis? Will U.S.-based corporations and other multinational companies be permitted to continue environmental policies that have devastating effects in certain parts of the world? Will the purchase of military weapons and high international debt so mark the situation of poor countries that these countries will have very little chance to address health-care issues in a meaningful manner?[8] Will we continue to prop up leaders in poor countries who are committed to doing very little to promote the health of the people? What percentage of our resources can we commit to global health problems such as AIDS or malaria, even if the use of these resources restricts some of our options for health care here at home? Can we enhance our medical education programs, so that we become a stronger exporter of gifted health-care providers to needy parts of the world? Can we find ways to make drugs and medical equipment more available at relatively cheap prices throughout the underdeveloped countries and continents?

This list of questions is not exhaustive, and readers may well be able to propose even more penetrating questions. Even though health care involves each one of us in very personal ways, our future consciousness about the matter of justice in the delivery of health care will need to be a global consciousness.

I am not implying that there has been a complete lack of global consciousness about health care. There have been some important past steps by groups such as religious communities and the Peace Corps. Contemporary groups such as Doctors Without Borders are making momentous contributions to a globalization of the concern for health-care justice. But in our times the global consciousness about health-care justice simply must move to a whole new level. No other approach will really work.

My fourth intuition concerns the relationship between health-care justice and the broader stability of society, both nationally and internationally. Many critics say that in the United States tensions between racial and ethnic groups are increasing as the new millennium begins.[9] These tensions are often connected with the fact that some racial and ethnic groups do not have the same economic resources as other groups. The more clearly access to a suitable standard of health care is understood as a human right, the more the lack of this right can serve as a destabilizing factor for a country such as the United States. Even some of our most precious institutions, such as the belief in democracy and the commitment to a vastly productive economic system, may be placed at risk if we continue a situation in which so many millions of people in the United States lack access to health care. The lack of health care alone may not be enough to destabilize our society. But in conjunction with other factors such as poverty and discrimination, the possibility of destabilization is surely present. The United States needs a sober realism about this fact. In the end a stronger social program for health-care delivery may benefit the rich as much or more than the poor by helping assure the stability of our social institutions.

If we reflect on the question of health care and social stability from a global perspective, the considerations are even more sobering, in large part because the health-care situation is so much worse. While the U.S. media offers occasional reports, many persons in the United States are quite unaware of the great amount of civil unrest and even open warfare that is occurring on our planet as a whole.[10] The factors behind this unrest and warfare are multiple, varied, and complex. But the lack of decent health care cannot be excluded as one of the underlying causes of the political instability that exists in many parts of the world. If health-care standards are very bad, and persons expect only to die at an early age and without much opportunity for human development, there may be little to prevent the impression that war may be the way to make things better. So at least subconsciously the lack of health care may tempt poor countries to go to war against richer nations, perhaps even with weapons of mass destruction. I am concerned not to make all this sound overly dramatic, but we cannot afford to ignore the links between global health-care justice and world peace. This theme of the link between health justice and global peace will come more and more to the fore in the years ahead.

My final intuition is that for true health-care justice we need to find something even deeper than the issues that have so far preoccupied us. Much in the book has been based on economic theory, Catholic social teaching, and Catholic theology. These themes are important, and they are steps on the journey toward a more just health-care system. But true health-care justice will not be possible unless people can move through an experience of moral and spiritual conversion. This conversion will need to have two main elements. *First,* all people, but especially persons in the developed countries, will need to work out a new inner attitude toward death and dying, an attitude that learns to accept our dying as an integral part of the human story. Unless this peaceful acceptance of death takes place, people will never give up the romantic dream that medicine can solve all human problems.[11] Without the acceptance of death, people will continue to make unrealistic demands of medicine, demands that cannot be sustained, demands that will ultimately place the whole fabric of society at risk.

I want to be clear that I am not opposed to responsible medical progress. Surely such progress will find ways over time to cure or at least ameliorate some of the diseases that beset the human community. But still there is a question of personal attitudinal conversion so that medicine is viewed as only a partial answer to the meaning of our humanity, not an ultimate and therefore unachievable answer.

The *second* element of the personal conversion is that people must wake up to a deeper and much more global sense of community, a sense out of which we become more free to act on the basis of what is good for the entire nation and planet, not just for the individual. This is what the Catholic tradition of the common good is all about. Without this deeper sense of community, people who are dealing with health issues will have nothing to say except to ask for more, more, more for themselves, without reflecting on what their personal agenda might do to the rest of the planet and to future generations.

I thought for a long time about how best to end this book, since there are many pivotally significant issues that must become part of the ongoing journey toward more just health care both locally and globally. But at a core level I do not see how any of the steps to the reform of health-care delivery will be possible without a moral and spiritual conversion of hearts and minds, a conversion that comes to terms with both our mortality and our communal identity. Hence it seems most fitting, in the midst of all the structured social issues, to end with a call to personal moral conversion. And in the end is not this conversion what faith in God is all about? Throughout my lifetime, I have had an enduring fascination with that wonderful section of Genesis 49 that describes our God as the desire of the everlasting hills.[12] The image of the everlasting hills calls us beyond ourselves, calls us to a new level of trust in God and openness to each other. If we can believe in a God who calls us beyond the everlasting hills, we may at last be in a space where we can be free to pursue a truly just system of health care.

# ABBREVIATIONS USED IN NOTES

| | |
|---|---|
| *C&C* | H. Richard Niebuhr. *Christ and Culture.* New York: Harper and Row, 1951. |
| CHA | Catholic Health Association |
| CHIP | Children's Health Insurance Program |
| *CHS* | *Comparative Health Systems: Descriptive Analyses of Fourteen National Health Systems.* Marshall Raffel, ed. University Park, Pennsylvania: Pennsylvania State University Press, 1984. |
| *CIB* | *Contemporary Issues in Bioethics.* 5th ed. Tom Beauchamp and LeRoy Walters, eds. Belmont, California: Wadsworth Publishing Company, 1996. |
| *CJC* | *Code of Canon Law.* Latin-English Edition. New English Translation. Washington, D.C.: The Canon Law Society of America, 1998. |
| *CST* | *Catholic Social Thought: The Documentary Heritage.* David J. O'Brien and Thomas A. Shannon, eds. Maryknoll, New York: Orbis Books, 1992. |
| DRG | Diagnosis Related Group |
| *DV2* | *The Documents of Vatican II.* Walter Abbott, ed. New York: America Press, 1966. |
| *EB* | *Encyclopedia of Bioethics.* Warren Reich, ed. New York: Simon and Schuster Macmillan, 1995. |

ECMC      *Ethical Challenges in Managed Care: A Casebook.* Karen Gervais, et al., eds. Washington, D.C.: Georgetown University Press, 1999.

EJP2      *The Encyclicals of John Paul II.* Edited with introductions by J. Michael Miller. Huntington, Indiana: Our Sunday Visitor Press, 1996.

EM        *Ethics in Medicine: Historical Perspectives and Contemporary Concerns.* Stanley Reiser, Arthur Dyck, and William Curran, eds. Cambridge, Massachusetts: MIT Press, 1977.

ERD       *Ethical and Religious Directives for Catholic Health Care Services.* 4th ed. Washington, D.C.: United States Conference of Catholic Bishops, 2001.

ERISA     Employment Retirement Income Security Act

EV        Pope John Paul II. *Evangelium Vitae.* March 25, 1995.

FH        Daniel Callahan. *False Hopes: Why America's Quest for Perfect Health Care Is a Recipe for Failure.* New York: Simon and Schuster, 1998.

FJW       United States Catholic Conference Domestic Policy Committee. "A Fair and Just Workplace: Principles and Practices for Catholic Health Care," *Origins* 29 (1999), 181, 183–88.

FLE       *Managed Care: Financial, Legal, and Ethical Issues.* David A. Bennahum, ed. Cleveland: The Pilgrim Press, 1999.

HCR       Philip S. Keane. *Health Care Reform: A Catholic View.* New York: Paulist Press, 1993.

HEDIS     Health Plan Employer Data and Information Set

HIAA      Health Insurance Association of America

JAMA      *Journal of the American Medical Association*

JCAHO     Joint Commission on the Accreditation of Healthcare Organizations

M&MP      Kenman L. Wong. *Medicine and the Marketplace: The Moral Dimensions of Managed Care.* Notre Dame, Indiana: University of Notre Dame Press, 1998.

M&C            John McHugh and Charles Callan. *Moral Theology: A Complete Course.* London: B. Herder, 1929.

MCR            *The Managed Care Resource: The Language of Managed Care and Organized Health Systems.* Minnetonka, Minnesota: United Health Care Corporation, 1994.

MDHC           Regina Herzlinger. *Market Driven Health Care.* Reading, Massachusetts: Perseus Books, 1997.

NCCB           National Conference of Catholic Bishops (see USCCB)

NEJM           *New England Journal of Medicine*

NYT            *New York Times*

OMM            *On Moral Medicine: Theological Perspectives in Medical Ethics.* 2nd ed. Stephen Lammers and Allen Verhey, eds. Grand Rapids, Michigan: Wm. B. Eerdmans, 1998.

PMG            John G. Smillie. *Can Physicians Manage the Quality and Costs of Health Care? The Story of the Permanente Medical Group.* New York: McGraw-Hill, 1991.

RMC            *Regulating Managed Care: Theory, Practice and Future Options.* Stuart Altman, Uwe Reinhardt, and David Schactman, eds. San Francisco: Jossey-Bass, 1999.

SMR            *The Social Medicine Reader.* Gail Henderson, et al., eds. Durham, North Carolina: Duke University Press, 1997.

STAM           Paul Starr. *The Social Transformation of American Medicine.* New York: Basic Books, 1982.

TI             Karl Rahner. *Theological Investigations.* 23 volumes. London: Darton, Longman and Todd, 1961–1992.

TTH            Kenneth M. Lundmerer, M.D. *Time to Heal: American Medical Education from the Turn of the Century to the Era of Managed Care.* New York: Oxford University Press, 1999.

USCCB          United States Conference of Catholic Bishops (formerly called The National Conference of Catholic Bishops [NCCB]).

# NOTES

AUTHOR'S NOTE: Throughout the notes, when citing newspaper articles, I have consistently not provided page numbers. Most readers may look for these articles online, where page numbers are most commonly not used. Some papers' online editions include only the exact articles on the exact days they appeared in print. Other papers put slightly different versions online. We hope that editorial and citation practice on these matters will become clear over the course of time.

## INTRODUCTION

1. My earlier book (cf. *HCR*) was an explanation of the moral issues that were at stake in the context of the integrated approach to health care that appeared to be possible in the mid-1990s. Words such as *integrated* or *unified* imply that a number of different approaches might be able to achieve the goal of universal access, and that a nationally managed health-care system is not the only possible way to achieve integrated or unified health care in the United States. For other overviews on the Catholic tradition and just health care, cf. Jose Lavastida, *Health Care and the Common Good: A Theory of Justice* (Lanham, Maryland: University Press of America, 1999) and B. Andrew Lustig, "Reform and Rationing: Reflections on Health Care in the Light of Catholic Social Teaching," *OMM*, 960–73.

2. This figure was reported by Reuters Health in September 1999. For the details, cf. ch. 2, n. 40.

3. The figure of 44.3 million was the estimate of the Census Bureau in the second half of 1999. The percentages in the text are my own calculations, based on the Census Bureau's data for 1993

and 1999. In the fall of 2000, after this book had been written using the 44.3 million figure, the Census Bureau, for the first time since the mid-1980s, reported a decrease in the number of uninsured to 42.9 million. It remains to be seen whether this decrease marks the beginning of an actual change or whether it is only a statistical blip.

4. Rosie Mestel, "Despite Big Spending, U.S. Ranks 37th in Study of Global Health Care," *Los Angeles Times,* June 21, 2000.

## 1. A SUMMARY OF CATHOLIC PRINCIPLES FOR HEALTH-CARE JUSTICE

1. Cf. abbreviation *ERD.*

2. Many of the nuances of this statement (e.g., What are the roles of government and of the market in securing the right to a reasonable standard? How does the concept of the common good fit in?) are treated as the book unfolds.

3. New York: The Macmillan Company, 1916.

4. For a recent republication of *Rerum Novarum,* cf. *CST,* 14–39.

5. Pope John XXIII, *Master et Magistra,* no. 127, *Pacem in Terris,* no. 64. (*CST,* 81–130, 131–62.)

6. For an interesting treatment of the relatively low social status of medicine in the mid- and late nineteenth century, cf. *STAM,* 82–91. Starr notes (p. 83) that in earlier times doctors (who did not have that much medicine to practice) often held public office, but this trend has ended. As we shall see, the twenty years since Starr's book was published have included the election of quite a few doctors to public office.

7. This article, originally published in the *Journal of Religious Ethics,* has been widely reprinted in the major medical ethics anthologies. A good current source is Gene Outka, "Social Justice and Equal Access to Health Care," *OMM,* 947–60.

8. *OMM,* 955–56.

9. *Rerum Novarum,* no. 34 (*CST,* 31).

10. Both of these seminal documents contain a good deal of sexist language that we would not find acceptable today.

11. One helpful reflection on the problem with some modern human rights thinking is Mary Ann Glendon, *Rights Talk: The Impoverishment of Political Discourse* (New York: Free Press, 1991).

12. John XXIII, *Pacem in Terris,* esp. nos. 11–27 (*CST,* 132–34). Second Vatican Council, *Declaration on Religious Freedom (Dignitatis Humanae),* esp. nos. 4–7 (*DV2,* 675–96).

13. Carl Wellman, "Rights: Systematic Analysis," *EB* 4, 2305–10.

14. Churchill's March 1943 intervention on health care is described in Martin Gilbert, *Churchill: A Life* (New York: Henry Holt and Company, 1992), 742. Roosevelt's January 1944 State of the Union Address spoke of "the right to adequate medical care and the opportunity to achieve and enjoy good health." Quoted in Carleton B. Chapman and John M. Talmadge, "The Evolution of the Right to Health Care Concept in the United States," *EM,* 566.

15. *Pacem in Terris,* no. 11 (*CST,* 132).

16. In his very helpful book, *False Hopes* (cf. abbreviation *FH*), Daniel Callahan argues that the rights model of health care has declined in the United States over the past twenty years or so (228–29). In the context of critiques by authors such as Glendon (cf. n. 11), Callahan's point makes sense. Callahan then goes on to discuss a solidarity model for health-care justice. I would argue that the Catholic view of human rights as opposed to the secular model is based precisely on a sense of social solidarity. Hence I believe that the Catholic understanding of a right to health care continues to make good sense.

17. *Mater et Magistra,* no. 65 (*CST,* 94); *Pacem in Terris,* nos. 55–59 (*CST,* 140). For Pope John Paul II's understanding of the common good, cf. *Centesimus Annus,* no. 47.2 (*EJP2,* 637).

18. Bellah et al., *The Good Society* (New York: Alfred Knopf, 1991).

19. For a traditional treatment of the three kinds of justice, cf. *M&C,* vol. 2, 36–38.

20. *Quadragesimo Anno,* no. 57 (*CST,* 55).

21. Pope Paul VI, *Octogesima Adveniens,* no. 23 (*CST,* 273).

22. *ERD,* no. 3.

23. For the tradition of the Jubilee, cf. Lev 25:8–18; for debt forgiveness, cf. Deut 15:1–11; for Jesus and the children, cf. Mark 10:13–16.

24. My position on rationing is described in *HCR,* 144–48. Cf. also the CHA's pamphlet *With Justice for All? The Ethics of Health Care Rationing* (St. Louis, 1991).

25. According to the 2000 *Britannica Book of the Year* (Chicago: Encyclopaedia Britannica, 2000), 778–82, thirty-six countries are listed as having a lower infant mortality rate than the United States for the most recent reported year. These include all the Western European countries, as well as Canada, Japan, Taiwan, Australia, and several of the Caribbean Islands.

26. Authors who mention the high rationing that is part of U.S. health care include Daniel Callahan, *What Kind of Life? The Limits of Medical Progress* (New York: Simon and Schuster, 1990), 18, and

Larry R. Churchill, *Rationing Health Care in America: Principles and Perceptions of Justice* (Notre Dame, Indiana: University of Notre Dame Press, 1987), 14.

27. Cf., e.g., Murray's treatment of censorship in his classic *We Hold These Truths* (Garden City, New York: Doubleday, 1964), 158–63. Cf. also Charles E. Curran, "Civil Law and Christian Morality: Abortion and the Churches," in *Ongoing Revision: Studies in Moral Theology* (Notre Dame, Indiana: Fides Press, 1976), 129–34.

28. Leo XIII, *Rerum Novarum,* no. 4 (*CST,* 15–16).

29. *Quadragesimo Anno,* nos. 45–46, 113 (*CST* 51–52, 67).

30. John XXIII, *Mater et Magistra,* nos. 59–67 (*CST,* 93–95). See also Second Vatican Council, *Pastoral Constitution on the Church in the Modern World (Gaudium et Spes),* nos. 6, 25 (*DV2,* 204, 224).

31. Cited in *CST,* 82–83.

32. The text can be found in *American Catholic Thought and Social Questions* (Indianapolis: Bobbs-Merrill, 1968), 325–48.

33. *CST,* 572–680.

34. For a classic example of a defense of fee-for-service, cf. Robert M. Sade, "Medical Care as a Right: A Refutation," *EM,* 573–76.

35. *Quadragesimo Anno,* no. 79 (*CST,* 60).

36. *Mater et Magistra,* nos. 59–67 (*CST,* 93–95). To be completely precise it should be noted that, while the earliest English versions of *Mater et Magistra* used the term "socialization," it later emerged that the term was not used in the official Latin version of the encyclical, so that modern translations do not use that term. But John XXIII clearly addressed the reality of an increasingly complex world in which the state suitably regulates and fosters the undertakings of individuals and groups. I have used the term socialization because I think that in English it stands as a helpful way to express John XXIII's concept about the need for increasing state involvement in many matters of social policy.

37. Cited in *CST*'s introductory comments to *Mater et Magistra,* 82–83.

38. Cf., e.g., Bradford Gray "Commentary," *ECMC,* 175. *M&MP,* 97–114.

39. Judith Shindul-Rothschild, "Commentary," *ECMC,* 195–96.

40. Besides the differences between for-profits and not-for-profits noted in the text, tax law considerations are an important issue here. Not-for-profit health providers are given significant tax benefits because of the services they provide. What would happen to the tax status of a not-for-profit health provider if it linked with a for-profit provider?

41. In 1999, both Cardinal Anthony Bevilacqua of Philadelphia and Bishop Donald Wuerl of Pittsburgh issued protocols on partnerships between Catholic and other health-care providers. Both protocols rule out Catholic partnerships with investor-owned, for-profit hospitals. Cardinal Anthony Bevilacqua, "Catholic Health Care Collaborative Relationships," *Origins* 28 (1999), 657, 659–60. Bishop Wuerl's protocol is described in Rick Stouffer, "Pittsburgh Bishop Draws Line on Hospital Mergers," *Pittsburgh Tribune Review*, November 30, 1999.

42. *Rerum Novarum*, no. 34 (*CST*, 31).

43. This was the figure (actually $601.03) given by John A. Ryan in 1906 in his *The Living Wage: Its Ethical and Economic Aspects* (New York: The Macmillan Company, 1912), 123–30.

44. This was a clear theme in Ryan's work, but we would view the matter very differently today.

45. NCCB, *Economic Justice for All,* nos. 68–76 (*CST*, 595–96).

46. United States Catholic Conference Domestic Policy Committee, *FJW*. Cf. also John Paul II, *Laborem Exercens*, nos. 24–27 *(EJP2)*, 206–14.

47. *CST*, 183.

48. Vatican II quotes Gal 3:28 most notably in its assertion of the equality of all the members of the church in *Lumen Gentium*, no. 32 (*DV2*, 58).

49. *ERD*, no. 7.

50. *FJW*, 185.

51. Charles Morris's *American Catholic: The Saints and Sinners Who Built America's Most Powerful Church* (New York: Random House, 1997) is a very helpful new history of the Catholic Church in the United States. Morris treats the Knights of Labor issue (including Gibbons's impact on *Rerum Novarum*) on pages 88–93.

52. For an explanation of this concept of autonomy, cf. Jacques Maritain, *Man and the State* (Chicago: University of Chicago Press, 1951), esp. 153, 159. Maritain roots his treatment of autonomy in Leo XIII's encyclical *Immortali Dei*.

53. I hesitate to give a full definition of the term "qualified." More normally it involves high-level study and practice in a field such as law or medicine. But sometimes persons go through a unique set of life experiences and/or nontraditional learning modes that can render them qualified to speak on a given subject.

54. *Gaudium et Spes*, no. 62 (*DV2*, 270).

55. *CJC*, no. 212, §, 63.

56. Quoted in *EM*, 5.

57. W. H. S. Jones, "From the Oath According to Hippocrates in So Far as a Christian May Swear It," *EM,* 10.

58. William F. May, *The Physician's Covenant* (Philadelphia: Westminster Press, 1983). Paul Ramsey, *The Patient as Person* (New Haven: Yale University Press, 1970).

59. In speaking about the sixteenth century, I am referring to the beginning of Catholic writing on specific case issues in the ethics of care for the dying. But from another perspective, the Catholic focus on care for the dying goes back even further, since the earliest Catholic hospitals (actually institutions much more like today's hospices) date back to the early part of the Middle Ages.

60. For a summary of this earlier history, cf. John Paris and Richard McCormick, "The Catholic Tradition on the Use of Nutrition and Fluids," *America* 156 (1987), 358.

61. Ibid.

62. Two key difficulties with the ordinary/extraordinary distinction can be mentioned. *First,* whose viewpoint is used to decide what is ordinary, the viewpoint of the so-called person in the street or the viewpoint of the modern, highly technologized hospital? *Second,* how can we determine whether or not we ought to use a health-care means unless we know something about the specific circumstances of the patient?

63. For the Vatican's use of proportionality in the death and dying context, the most important source is the Congregation for the Doctrine of the Faith, "Declaration on Euthanasia," June 26, 1980, esp. part IV (*Origins* 10, 1980, 156–57). For the U.S. Bishops' use of benefit/burden language, cf. *ERD,* no. 57.

64. *EV,* nos. 7–28 (*EJP2,* 797–818).

65. Note that my wording here leaves the decision in the hands of the patient or the person who speaks for the patient. There is an important debate about whether health-care providers might be permitted to make the decision about cases that are overridingly clear. This debate, often called the debate about medical futility, needs to continue. But whatever happens, in the great majority of cases these decisions should remain in the hands of the patient or the person who speaks for the patient.

66. Edwin F. Healy, S.J., *Medical Ethics* (Chicago: Loyola University Press, 1956), 68.

67. Paul Ramsey developed this theme of company keeping with special elegance in his classic book *The Patient as Person,* esp. 113–64.

68. The quote appears both on the back of the statue of Trudeau that was executed by Gutzon Borglum (perhaps most famous for his

work on Mt. Rushmore) and on the mantelpiece of the reception room at the Trudeau Institute at Saranac Lake. It is hard not to also add that Dr. Trudeau had a son and grandson who became physicians and worked on TB at Saranac Lake. His great grandson, Gary Trudeau, is the well-known cartoonist. The study of TB remains crucial today both because of the continued presence of this terrible disease and because it can help us grasp many issues related to AIDS.

69. Mark Hanson and Daniel Callahan, *The Goals of Medicine: The Forgotten Issue in Health Care Reform* (Washington, D.C.: Georgetown University Press, 1999).

70. The 4th edition of the *ERD*, issued in 2001, makes relatively few changes from the 3rd edition (1995). Here I am clearly discussing my experience with the 3rd edition. For comments on the 4th edition, cf. chapter 4, note 34.

71. *EV* (*EJP2*, 792–894).

72. *ERD*, 2, 5.

## 2. MANAGED CARE: DEFINITION, HISTORY, AND MORAL SUCCESSES

1. I take my own responsibility for this definition and those that follow. A very helpful lexicon or glossary of health care terms is *MCR*. Another glossary of terms can be found in Donald L. Madison, "Paying for Medical Care in America," *SMR*, 415–46.

2. *STAM*, esp. 301–6.

3. Ibid., 395.

4. The term does not appear in the index of the book, and I was not able to spot it anywhere on a recent rereading. Starr's final chapter, "The Coming of the Corporation," 420–49, surely foresaw much of the reality of the managed-care marketplace, including the problems faced by teaching hospitals.

5. Cf. Cathie Jo Martin, "Markets, Medicare and Making Do: Business Strategies after National Health Care Reform," in *Healthy Markets: The New Competition in Medical Care,* ed. by Mark A. Peterson (Durham, North Carolina: Duke University Press, 1998), 232. One also sees the terms "covered persons" and "eligibles."

6. Later, in the chapter on mergers and acquisitions, we will comment further on the values of primary care providers concentrating their strength to deal with the large managed-care providers.

7. Ellwood and Lundberg, "Managed Care: A Work in Progress," *JAMA* 276 (1996), 383–86.

8. For a seminal article on the managed competition model, cf. Alain Enthoven and Richard Kronick, "A Consumer Choice Plan for the 1990s: Universal Health Insurance in a System Designed to Promote Quality and Economy," *NEJM* 320 (1989), 29–37, 94–101.

9. Even in this descriptive phase of the book, it is hard not to at least mention some of the more formal ethical issues such as conflict of interest. These issues will be considered in more detail later in the book. For physicians and conflict of interest, cf. Edmund D. Pellegrino, "Allocation of Resources at the Bedside: The Intersections of Economics, Law, and Ethics," *Kennedy Institute of Ethics Journal* 4 (1994), 309–17; Arnold S. Relman, "Physicians and Business Managers: A Clash of Cultures," *Health Management Quarterly* 16 (1994), 11–14.

10. Cf. Robert Kuttner, "Must Good HMOs Go Bad?" *NEJM* 338: 21–22 (1998), 1558–63, 1635–59, esp. 1562–63.

11. For some comments on stop-loss insurance, cf. Kuttner, "Good HMOs," 1561.

12. For a summary of the recent trend of HMOs getting away from employing physicians or contracting with exclusive groups, cf. *MDHC*, 109–10. The more this trend develops, the more HMOs become utilization and financial control entities.

13. For an account of Deming's life and work, cf. *1994 Britannica Book of the Year* (Chicago: Encyclopaedia Britannica), 60.

14. Cf. Thomas Bodenheimer, "The American Health Care System—The Movement for Improved Quality in Health Care," *NEJM* 340 (1999), 488–92.

15. *MCR*, 19.

16. For comments on DRGs, cf. Marc A. Rodwin, *Medicine, Money, and Morals: Physicians' Conflicts of Interest* (New York: Oxford University Press, 1993), 15–16, 148–49.

17. Health-care economist Uwe Reinhardt comments on the decline of traditional charity care in today's complex health-care scene in "Reforming the Health Care System," *SMR*, 453. For the increase in Medicaid funding for the poor, cf. John K. Inglehart, "The American Health Care System—Medicaid," *NEJM* 340 (1999), 403–8.

18. For a description of the current scene in Canada, cf. Peggy Leatt and A. Paul Williams, "Canada," in *Health Care and Reform in Industrialized Countries*, ed. by Marshall W. Raffel (University Park, Pennsylvania: Pennsylvania State University Press, 1997), 1–23. This work is a follow-up to *CHS*.

19. My own thoughts on this issue are stated at the end of this book.

20. Cf. *STAM*, esp. 295–334.

21. Two helpful recent histories of Kaiser Permanente are Rickey Hendricks, *A Model for National Health Care: The History of Kaiser Permanente* (Rutgers, New Jersey: Rutgers University Press, 1993), and John G. Smillie, *PMG*. Dr. Smillie writes from his long years as a physician/administrator at Kaiser.

22. *PMG*, 38.

23. *Encyclopaedia Britannica*, 15th ed. (Chicago: Encyclopaedia Britannica, 1989), Micropedia 6, 686.

24. *PMG*, 42–43.

25. *Newsweek*, November 8, 1999, 69–72.

26. Walt Crowley, *To Serve the Greatest Number: A History of the Group Health Cooperative of Puget Sound* (Seattle: University of Washington Press, 1996), 28–29.

27. Ibid., ix.

28. Ibid., 65

29. *STAM*, 305.

30. Ibid., 295–310.

31. Ibid., 322.

32. David Allen, "England," *CHS*, 200–206.

33. For helpful contemporary assessments of both Medicare and Medicaid, cf. John K. Inglehart, "The American Health Care System—Medicare," *NEJM* 340 (1999), 327–32; id., "American Health Care—Medicaid," 403–8.

34. *STAM*, 415. In 1970, there were only thirty-three HMOs in the United States.

35. For comments on Vorhis's later career, cf. *Crowley, Greatest Number*, 105.

36. For comments on these prominent nonprofit New England plans (before the failure of the Harvard Plan), cf. Kuttner, "Good HMOs," 1560–61.

37. *Newsweek*, November 8, 1999, 69–72. The news media in early 2000 were filled with news of the bankruptcy of Harvard Pilgrim. But the fact remains that it was a highly regarded plan for a long time.

38. Deborah Shapley, *Promise and Power: The Life and Times of Robert MacNamara* (Boston: Little, Brown, 1993), esp. 203.

39. Shapley, *Promise and Power*, refers to Enthoven numerous times in her account of MacNamara's years at the Pentagon, at one point describing him as the chief whiz kid (p. 452). Cf. also *MDHC*, 111–13.

40. This figure was reported by Reuters Health on November 16, 1999. The figure comes from the 1999 Health Confidence Survey, sponsored by the Consumer Health Education Council, the Employees Benefit Research Association, and Matthew Greenwald Associates.

Abigail Rian Evans, *Redeeming Marketplace Medicine: A Theology of Health Care* (Cleveland: Pilgrim Press, 1999) puts the figure at 85 percent of working Americans. Other lower figures are also reported. The key to a given figure may well be just what is meant by "managed care."

41. Cf. the sources cited in nn. 21, 26.

42. Pope John Paul II, *Laborem Exercens,* no. 19 (*EJP2,* 200).

43. This is especially clear in Dr. Smillie's account of the Grand Coulee years (*PMG,* 19–32).

44. Cf. n. 26.

45. *Quality of Care: Selections from the New England Journal of Medicine* (Waltham, Massachusetts: Massachusetts Medical Society, 1993–1997).

46. For comments on the HEDIS data and its use, cf. Bodenheimer, "American Health Care," 488–92.

47. For the Catholic sources on professionals, cf. ch. 1, nn. 51–52.

48. Some of my clearest personal memories of the great Protestant theologian Paul Ramsey have to do with his stress in his lectures on the importance of good health habits.

49. For a helpful theological overview of issues in environmental ethics, cf. Larry L. Rasmussen, *Earth Community Earth Ethics* (Maryknoll, New York: Orbis Books, 1996).

50. Rachel Carson, *The Silent Spring* (Boston: Houghton-Mifflin, 1993, orig. 1962). Bill McKibben, *The End of Nature* (New York: Random House), 1989.

51. James Gustafson, *A Sense of the Divine: The Natural Environment from a Theocentric Perspective* (Cleveland: Pilgrim Press, 1994). This book is best understood in light of Gustafson's classic *Ethics from a Theocentric Perspective* (Chicago: University of Chicago Press, 1981, 1984).

52. John Paul II, *Sollicitudo Rei Socialis,* esp. nos. 26, 34 (*EJP2,* 448, 458).

53. Cf. ch. 1, n. 66.

54. This figure is from the Treasury Department, as reported in the *Washington Post* on January 10, 2000.

55. The exact figure of 44.3 million uninsured persons in the United States was reported by the U.S. Census Bureau in October 1999. Cf. *Baltimore Sun,* January 21, 2000.

56. Eli Ginzberg, "Managed Care and the Competitive Market in Health Care: What They Can and Cannot Do," *JAMA* 277 (1997), 1812–13. Ginzberg cites a January 1997 Working Paper by A. B. Kruger and H. Levy entitled "Accounting for the Slowdown in Employer Health Care Costs," sponsored by the National Bureau of Economic Research.

## 3. MANAGED CARE: PROBLEMS
## AND POTENTIAL SOLUTIONS

1. The *Newsweek* cover story of November 8, 1999, is but one example.

2. For an example of a more scholarly attack on managed care, cf. George Anders, *Health Against Wealth: HMOs and the Breakdown of Medical Trust* (Boston: Houghton Mifflin Company, 1996).

3. Uwe E. Reinhardt, "Managed Care Is Still a Good Idea," *Wall Street Journal,* November 17, 1999.

4. *Newsweek,* November 8, 1999.

5. For a helpful reflection on the physician-patient relationship, including the place of negotiating the relationship, cf. James F. Childress and Mark Siegler, "Metaphors and Models of Doctor-Patient Relationships: Their Implications for Autonomy," in *Biomedical Ethics,* 5th ed., Thomas A. Mappes and David DeGrazia, eds. (New York: McGraw-Hill, 2001), 71–80.

6. While a complete theory of patients' rights is beyond the scope of this book, and while some limits on these rights are surely acceptable, the right to a second opinion seems to be a very basic human right as part of the whole process of informed consent. Reasonable access to specialists is surely part of this basic right to a second opinion.

7. I refer especially to the November 1999 decision of United Health Group, with its 14.5 million members, not to continue requiring advance approval of decisions by its medical doctors.

8. In the passivity days, it was very common for doctors not even to tell their patients that they were dying. Cf., for example, Joseph Collins, "Should Doctors Tell the Truth?" which was originally published in 1927 (*EM,* 220–24). In the article Dr. Collins refers to "lying as a fine art" (p. 221).

9. *DV2,* 675–96.

10. I still believe that one of the finest short, modern theological statements on freedom is Rahner's "Theology of Freedom," *TI* 6, 178–96.

11. For some reflections on the underlying notion of self-help—with both pros and cons—cf. Albert Carter, "Self-Help," *EB* 5, 2338–44.

12. Significant recent literature on professional ethics includes: Dennis Campbell, *Doctors, Lawyers, Ministers: Christian Ethics in Professional Practice* (Nashville: Abingdon Press, 1982); Karen Lebacqz, *Professional Ethics: Power and Paradox* (Nashville: Abingdon Press, 1985); Eric Mount, *Professional Ethics in Context* (Louisville: Westminster/

John Knox Press, 1990); and Richard M. Gula, *Ethics in Pastoral Ministry* (New York: Paulist Press, 1996).

13. Reuters Health, November 16–17, 1999.

14. Rahner's Thomist/intellectualist bent is perhaps best seen in his doctoral dissertation, *Geist in Welt* (Munich: Kösel-Verlag, 1957). The English translation is *Spirit in the World,* trans. by William Dych (New York: Herder and Herder, 1968). Cardinal Ratzinger wrote his doctoral dissertation on St. Bonaventure, which helps explain his strong voluntarism. Like Rahner, Ratzinger supplied a major theological impetus to the work of Vatican II. During this period the two of them jointly authored *The Episcopate and the Primacy* (New York: Herder and Herder, 1963).

15. This decision of the United Health Group was very widely reported in the media. For one account, cf. Milt Freudenham, "Big H.M.O. to Give Decisions on Care Back to Doctors," *NYT,* November 9, 1999.

16. Robert Kuttner, "Must Good HMOs Go Bad?" *NEJM* 338 (1998), 1561.

17. Ezekiel Emanuel, Steven Pearson, and James Sabin, "Ethical Guidelines for Physician Compensation Based on Capitation," *NEJM* 339 (1998), 689–93. The table accompanying the article indicates the desirability of a less than 10 percent figure to reduce the risk of a conflict of interest. I have heard Dr. Emanuel use this 10 percent figure in public lectures.

18. Linda Greenhouse, "H.M.O.'s Win Crucial Ruling on Liability for Doctors' Acts," *NYT,* June 13, 2000.

19. For a thoughtful description of the changing tone of medical education, cf. *TTH,* esp. 349–99. See also Sharon Bernstein, "Managed Care Forcing Doctors to Be Even More Conservative/Medical Culture More Mindful of Costs Than Ever," *San Francisco Chronicle,* November 30, 1999.

20. Much recent publicity has been devoted to the Harvard Pilgrim Health Plan, which went into receivership on January 4, 2000. The Massachusetts Hospital Association estimates that Harvard owes its members $265 million, some of which will never be recovered, even if there is a large bailout of Harvard by the state of Massachusetts. (Cf. Lin Kowalcyzk, "HMO Problems Seen Hitting Providers, Consumers," *Boston Globe,* January 25, 2000.) While this is a more spectacular case, hospitals throughout the United States are regularly troubled by slow payments and failures of the managed-care companies.

21. As a counterbalance to this, while Daniel Callahan clearly acknowledges the importance of the tradition of solidarity in

European countries, he also points out that the pressures of recent years have led many European countries to turn toward market mechanisms and privatization of their health-care systems (*FH,* 15, 168, 231).

22. For Regina Herzlinger, cf. *MDHC.* For some of Reinhardt's most recent thinking, cf. his "Consumer Choice under 'Private Health Care Regulation,'" *RMC,* 1999, 91–116. Reinhardt ends with the analogy of a "farmer's market" to regulate managed care. Cf. also Alain Enthoven and Richard Kronick, "A Consumer Choice Plan for the 1990s: Universal Health Insurance in a System Designed to Promote Quality and Economy," *NEJM* 320 (1989), 29–37, 94–101.

23. For an application of the stakeholder theory to managed care, cf. *M&MP,* 143–55.

24. For some helpful comments on the interaction of technology and market forces in health care, cf. *FH,* 88–90.

25. *MCR,* 48. It is interesting to note how matter-of-factly this definition is presented, with no indication of there being any value issues at stake.

26. *FH,* esp. 275–89.

27. Cardinal Anthony Bevilacqua, "Catholic Health Care Collaborative Relationships," *Origins* 28 (1999), 657, 659–60. Bishop Wuerl's protocol is described in Rick Stouffer, "Pittsburgh Bishop Draws Line on Hospital Mergers," *Pittsburgh Tribune Review,* November 30, 1999.

28. For some eloquent comments on the needs of and for teaching hospitals, cf. the op-ed reflection by Sen. Daniel Patrick Moynihan, "How Medicine Became Just Another Product," *NYT,* November 27, 1999.

29. For a very thoughtful review of how some of the current systems of managed care have failed to achieve the original goals of managed competition, cf. Reinhardt, "Consumer Choice," 91–116. Reinhardt argues that only a Martian might believe that the early hopes for managed competition—that consumers could readily choose between competing managed-care plans based on readily accessible information about the plans' cost and quality—have been achieved in recent years.

30. Studies of patient satisfaction were a significant factor in United Health Group's decision to drop advance approvals of the decisions made by its medical doctors.

31. Cf., for example, Kevin Clarke, "A System Sick at Heart," *U.S. Catholic,* December 1999.

32. Gina Kolata, "For Those Who Can Afford It, Old-Style Medicine Returns," *NYT,* March 17, 2000.

33. Milt Freudenheim, "California Medical Association Files a Suit Against Three Insurers," *NYT,* May 26, 2000.

34. Robert Pear, "After Doctors' Antitrust Triumph, Lott Puts Up Roadblock in Senate," *NYT,* July 1, 2000.

35. For a report on some of the moves toward unionization for doctors, cf. Charles Orenstein, "Doctors/Owners," *Dallas Morning News,* November 29, 1999.

36. In the *Baltimore Sun* on January 5, 2000, Gerard Anderson, Director of Johns Hopkins' Center for Hospital Finance and Management, is quoted as saying that a main reason for hospital mergers today is to give hospitals more leverage when they are negotiating contracts with managed-care companies. Anderson was commenting on the purchase of eight hospitals of the Franciscan Health Partnership by the Bon Secours Health System. Anderson is quoted in a report on the Bon Secours transaction by Kristine Henry.

37. On this theme, cf. Joshua Fendel, "Mental-Health Bias" (Letter to the Editor), *NYT,* November 13, 1999.

38. In 1999, 27,000 of the 140,000 bills introduced in state legislatures were on health care. Of the 104,000 bills introduced at the beginning of 2000, 16,000 were on health care. *NYT,* January 23, 2000.

39. For an explanation of the unintended way in which ERISA protects managed-care plans from lawsuits, cf. Ronald F. Pollack, "Regulation from a Consumer's Perspective," *RMC,* 269–72.

40. The bill passed the House on October 8, 1999, by a vote of 275 to 151, with sixty-eight House Republicans breaking with the Republican leadership to vote with the Democrats. Reported in *NYT,* October 8, 1999.

41. *NYT,* June 9, 2000.

42. Carey Goldberg, "State Initiatives Seek Overhaul of Health Care," *NYT,* June 11, 2000.

## 4. THE ETHICS OF MERGERS, JOINT VENTURES, AND OTHER RECONFIGURATIONS

1. Cf. the article "Spinoffs, Big Deals Dominate in 1999: Despite Some High Volume Mergers, Total Hospital Transactions Dipped 28% Compared with the Previous Year," *Modern Healthcare,* January 10, 2000, 36–47.

2. "Part Six: Forming New Partnerships with Health Care Organizations and Providers," *ERD.*

3. The recent acquisition of the Franciscan Health Partnership by the Bon Secours Health System is an excellent example of a courageous and well-planned transaction. Cf. the article by Kristine Henry in the January 5, 2000, *Baltimore Sun*.

4. This could be done in various ways. Perhaps a charitable foundation might be set up. Perhaps new programs of health care for the poor might be established. Perhaps a medical school might be strengthened by the sale of a hospital. And there is always the concern to provide for the retirement of the members of a religious community who, for good reasons, need to sell a hospital.

5. For a recent example of a hospital-physician partnership, cf. Dan Thanh Dang, "St. Agnes Health Care Buys 25% of Maryland Physicians Care," *Baltimore Sun,* January 18, 2000. For the perhaps more common trend of divestiture of physicians' practices, cf. David Jakubiak "Tenet Healthcare Gets Out of Doctor Business," *Beaufort Gazette,* January 10, 2000.

6. In the Richmond, Virginia, area, the recent struggle between Columbia/HCA and Bon Secours Health System is an example of this distasteful conflict. The issue was whether Bon Secours should be given state approval to build a new hospital in Chesterfield County. Cf. the long cover article in the business section of the *Richmond Times-Dispatch* by Bob Rayner on January 17, 2000, as well as earlier *Times-Dispatch* articles by Rayner on January 15, 2000, October 20, 1999, and September 21, 1999. Rayner's articles are full of military and sports terms ("battleground," "going into overtime," "first couple of rounds," "first salvo,"), which surely helped make a difficult situation even more heated.

7. Mercy Health Services in Baltimore is a remarkably successful example of a Catholic hospital that retained its local autonomy.

8. I refer to the merger of the Daughters of Charity National Health System and the Sisters of St. Joseph Health System, Ann Arbor, Michigan. These two systems formed Ascension Health, which is based in St. Louis. The other example is the merger of Mercy Health Services of Farmington, Michigan, with the Holy Cross Health System of South Bend, Indiana, to form Trinity Health Services.

9. For an account of some of the labor issues related to Catholic Healthcare West, including the role of famed social activist Msgr. George G. Higgins, cf. Jean P. Fisher, "Clash of Principles, Profits at Mercy? Divisive Labor Issues at Catholic Health Care System Raise Ethical Questions," *Sacramento Bee,* December 16, 1999.

10. For the canonical approach to the public juridic person, cf. canons 113–23 (*CJC*, 31–36).

11. Canons 638, 1290–98 (*CJC*, 207–8, 399–402).

12. For a description of the status of doctors in the late nineteenth century, cf. *STAM*, 78–92. For Starr on the development of antiseptics and anesthesia, cf. *STAM*, 154–62.

13. For a very helpful study of the efforts to address tuberculosis, cf. Frank Ryan, M.D., *The Forgotten Plague: How the Battle Against Tuberculosis Was Won–and Lost* (Boston: Little, Brown and Company, 1993).

14. Cf. *TTH*, 180–82.

15. Karl Rahner, "Reflections on Dialogue within Pluralistic Society," *TI* 6, 35.

16. In January 2000, Governor John Kitzhaber of Oregon, who is a physician, proposed a plan to limit the number of different drugs that could be prescribed by Oregon's physicians. This seems to be an intriguing way to help control the proliferation of "Me too" drugs. Cf. Kristina Brenneman, "Kitzhaber's List Would Limit Choices," *Health Care Journal*, January 31, 2000.

17. During the period in which I have been writing this book, a great deal of publicity has been given to finding ways to help reduce medical errors, mostly because of the celebrated Institute of Medicine report that was published in the fall of 1999. Even if the human condition makes it impossible to eliminate every single medical error, efforts to do so are surely worthwhile. I have not given this issue any major attention herein because I do not see this issue—important as it may be—as immediately germane to my main focus, which is how to deliver health care more justly in a country whose highly productive economy still leaves 44.3 million persons without health insurance.

18. Cf. the comments of Johns Hopkins executive Gerard Anderson cited in ch. 3, n. 36.

19. For some background comments, cf. Steven Syre and Charles Stein, "Mergers of Health Care Firms Often Just Don't Work Out," *Boston Globe*, January 12, 2000.

20. For a fascinating and refreshing account of one recent effort to integrate these basic values, cf. Sharon Richardt, D.C., "A Clearing in the Woods: Retreat House Aids Mission Integration at Indianapolis Hospital," *Health Progress*, March–April 2000, 20–21.

21. Many important scholars could be mentioned here, but it is difficult not to mention the great Jesuit moralist, Richard A. McCormick, who died on February 12, 2000. In the context of biomedical ethics,

McCormick's works of note include *How Brave a New World? Dilemmas in Bioethics* (Garden City, New York: Doubleday, 1981) and *The Critical Calling: Reflections on Moral Dilemmas Since Vatican II* (Washington, D.C.: Georgetown University Press, 1989).

22. Much of the most recent discussion has concerned the Vatican document *Ex Corde Ecclesiae* and its use in the United States. Cf. NCCB "Ex Corde Ecclesiae: An Application to the United States," *Origins* 29 (1999), 401, 403–9. But substantive dialogue between bishops and theologians goes back considerably further. Cf. the joint document of the Catholic Biblical Association, The Catholic Theological Society of America, and the College Theology Society entitled "Report of the Intersocietal Committee on Academic Freedom and Ecclesial Responsibility," in *Proceedings of the Catholic Theological Society of America* 43 (1988), 190–92. These groups were later joined by the Canon Law Society of America. See also the response of U.S. bishops entitled "Doctrinal Responsibilities: Approaches to Promoting Cooperation and Resolving Misunderstandings Between Bishops and Theologians," June 17, 1989: Washington, D.C.: United States Catholic Conference, 1989.

23. For a presentation of the traditional Catholic approach to cooperation, cf. *M&C*, vol. 1, 603–28.

24. *ERD*, Part Six.

25. Karl Rahner, "The Dignity and Freedom of Man," *TI* 2 (1963), 254.

26. Cf. *Origins* 20 (1990), 103.

27. For the *ERD* on scandal, cf. *ERD*, no. 71. The significance of scandal in the traditional ethics of cooperation is such that scandal might have been listed along with the four key themes to be considered when determining whether or not there is a proportionate reason to justify the material cooperation. But the question of scandal remains extrinsic to the actual structure of the cooperation. Hence my approach is to note the importance of scandal, but not list it as one of the intrinsic elements in the search for proportionate reason in cooperation decisions.

28. I think, for instance, of a situation in one of the states in which it was clear to everyone that the sterilizations were the activity of a partner hospital. No one doubted this. However, because of some complications in state regulations, the sterilizations were listed under the same provider number as the activities of the newly merged entity. This technical fact did not seem to me to rule out the clarity and the lack of scandal in the arrangement that structured the sterilizations as an activity of a partner hospital.

NOTES TO PAGES 132–45   221

29. My sense is that the position taken on these matters by groups such as Merger Watch and Catholics for a Free Choice is not accurate on a number of specific points, especially as regards the overall goals of Catholic health care. As I write there is much discussion about the CBS program *60 Minutes*, which aired a segment on Catholicism and health-care mergers. The CHA and others have criticized some aspects of the *60 Minutes* segment.

30. *ERD*, nos. 47–49.

31. Any form of material cooperation in direct abortion is explicitly rejected by the *ERD*, no. 45.

32. Congregation for the Doctrine of the Faith, *Instruction on Respect for Human Life in its Origin and on the Dignity of Procreation* (February 22, 1987), nos. 5, 8 (*Origins* 16 [1987], 707–8).

33. Reported in *Modern Healthcare,* October 4, 1999, 17.

34. As this book was being completed, the USCCB began a process of substantive revision of the *ERD,* specifically on the issues of mergers and material cooperation. Three successive drafts of the revisions were circulated in the second half of the year 2000, and the bishops formally adopted the new *ERD* on June 15, 2001. Only Part Six has been  changed and the Appendix to the *ERD* has been dropped. Three points about the new *ERD* seem very clear. *First,* the bishops strongly oppose Catholic hospitals providing immediate material cooperation in practices such as tubal ligations. I described the bishops' mind on this matter in the text. *Second,* the bishops are strongly concerned to avoid poorly designed merger agreements, particularly agreements in which the Catholic party appears very closely involved in a partner's activities that are contrary to the *ERD. Third,* the bishops do not wish to close off the possibility of reasonable mergers (those I described in the text?), nor can they offer a complete description of all the concrete circumstances that might or might not justify a particular merger. Instead these concrete matters will need to be addressed by individual diocesan bishops and their advisers. The decision  to drop the Appendix to the *ERD* instead of trying to rewrite it more completely shows the bishops' awareness that as a body they cannot fully clarify every local issue about the acceptability of material cooperation in health-care mergers.

35. Cf. ch. 1, n. 41.

## 5. PUBLIC POLICY AND CONTEMPORARY HEALTH CARE

1. *NYT,* January 23, 2000.
2. Cf. abbreviation *C&C.*
3. *C&C,* 45–82.
4. In the United States, in the latter part of the twentieth century, the theologian John Howard Yoder (1927–1997) was probably the most eloquent spokesperson for the Mennonite position. Cf. especially Yoder's *The Politics of Jesus* (Grand Rapids, Michigan: Wm. B. Eerdmans, 1972).
5. The actual dates of disestablishment were 1818 for Connecticut and 1833 for Massachusetts. Virginia's disestablishment, inspired by Jefferson and Madison, took place in 1785.
6. *C&C,* 190–229.
7. Plato, *The Republic,* Book V, in *The Works of Plato,* selected and edited by Irwin Edman (New York: Modern Library, 1956), 431.
8. Martin Luther, "On Secular Authority: To What Extent It Must Be Obeyed," in *Martin Luther: Selections from His Writings* (Garden City, New York: Doubleday and Co., 1961), 363–402.
9. Ibid., 369–70, 73.
10. Ibid., 389.
11. Ibid., 374–75.
12. Probably the best source for Bonhoeffer's sense of the world as under God's judgment is his *Ethics,* ed. by Eberhard Bethge (New York: The MacMillan Company, 1955). But see also Dietrich Bonhoeffer, *Letters and Papers from Prison,* rev. ed., ed. by Eberhard Bethge (New York: The Macmillan Company, 1967), especially p. 188, with the famous and puzzling "Before God and with God we live without God." Bethge, who did so much to bring Bonhoeffer's work to the world, died on March 18, 2000.
13. True to form, one of Niebuhr's very last published articles was "The King's Chapel and the King's Court," a scathing critique of the religious services held in the White House during the Nixon administration. (In *Christianity and Crisis* 29 [1969], 211–12.)
14. For the classic twentieth-century account of Thomas's brilliant retrieval of the natural law tradition, cf. Odin Lottin, *Le Droit Naturel chez Thomas d'Acquin et ses prédécesseurs,* 2nd. ed. (Bruges: Charles Beyart, 1931). John Courtney Murray's *We Hold These Truths: Catholic Reflections on the American Proposition* (Garden City, New York: Doubleday and Co., 1964) remains the most helpful modern articulation of a Thomistic philosophy of government.

15. John Calvin, *Institutes of the Christian Religion,* Book 2, Chapter 8, no. 5, in Library of Christian Classics Edition (Philadelphia: Westminster Press, 1960), vol. 1, 372.

16. Cf. ch. 1, n. 27.

17. If it is carefully defined and understood, incremental change can be helpful. Cf. the use of the term in Michael D. Connelly, "Ending the Chaos in Our Health Care System," *Health Progress* (March–April 2000), 42. But on the whole I think there is a good case for moving to other adjectives such as *sequential.* Cf. n. 32.

18. For a summary of the plans proposed by candidates Gore, McCain, and Bradley, cf. Kristen Hallam, "Three Candidates Focus on Health Policy," *Modern Healthcare* (January 24, 2000), 32ff.

19. The already famous Institute of Medicine Report on Medical Errors was issued on November 28, 1999. Cf. Lawrence K. Altman, "Policing Health Care," *NYT,* December 1, 1999.

20. Similarly, Brazoria County, Texas, home of House Republican whip Tom DeLay, is deemed to be part of Houston, even though it is 45 miles away. Cf. Robert Pear, "Health Industry Sees Wish List Made into Law," *NYT,* December 6, 1999.

21. This figure was used by the CHA in its nationally run advertisements (in the fall of 1999) calling for relief from the excesses of the Balanced Budget Amendment. For a description of CHA's efforts to expand the CHIP program, cf. the CHA Working Proposal, "Building an Infrastructure for Universal Coverage: Expanding Coverage to America's Uninsured," 3–6.

22. For an account of Vermont's successes under its physician governor, Howard Dean, cf. David E. Rosenbaum, "Expansion of Medical Benefits Puts Vermont in the Vanguard," *NYT,* June 19, 2000.

23. Some recent published reports suggest that Minnesota may accept for-profit managed-care companies.

24. Two key arguments can be made of the success of Medicare. *First,* Medicare covers virtually everyone over sixty-five, so that it is the United States' one true universal access health-care program. *Second,* its administrative overhead remains the lowest of any segment of health care in the United States (only 2–3 percent). Of course there are problems. Some seniors have had disastrous experiences with Medicare HMOs. And there is, at least at the time of this writing, the lack of Medicare coverage for prescriptions. It is hoped that this last point will eventually change.

25. I have already referred to Daniel Patrick Moynihan's eloquent words on this subject. Cf. ch. 3, n. 28.

26. As the year 2000 unfolded, there seemed to be a wider realization that the Balanced Budget Amendment may have gone too far in its reduction of funding for health care. So it was easier to restore funding in late 2000 than in late 1999. What is unclear is whether this was a true conversion by Congress or only the practice of election year politics.

27. Shortly we will be discussing the CHA's new proposal on health-care reform. Even though the proposal urges a number of specific transitional steps, it clearly and prominently maintains the goal of universal access.

28. Throughout this book, I have regularly referred to Callahan's most recent book, *False Hopes (FH)*. But Callahan's asking the deeper questions goes back much further. See especially his *Troubled Dream of Life: In Search of a Peaceful Death* (New York: Simon and Schuster, 1993).

29. For an account of the HIAA working together with the other groups, cf. "Groups Express Common Themes for Addressing Uninsured," Reuters Health, January 13, 2000.

30. For the return of Harry and Louise, cf. Robert Pear, "'Harry and Louise' Return, with Health Insurance Plan," *NYT*, January 21, 2000. "Harry and Louise's New Attitude," *Chicago Tribune*, February 2, 2000. In their changed attitude about health-care reform, Harry and Louise even got to visit with President Clinton in the Oval Office.

31. For the shift in position by the drug companies, cf. Robert Pear, "Drug Company Executives Drop Opposition to Medicare Coverage of Prescription Drugs," *NYT*, January 14, 2000.

32. Rev. Michael Place, "Remarks on a Working Proposal by the Catholic Health Association of the United States," presentation by Fr. Place on January 13, 2000, at Health Coverage 2000, p. 2. Two weeks later, I had the opportunity to hear Fr. Place make very effective use of *sequential* in his address to the annual retreat of the Board of Trustees of the Bon Secours Health System.

33. "Building an Infrastructure of Universal Coverage: Expanding Coverage to America's Uninsured," A Working Proposal by the CHA of the United States, January 2000.

34. While Christian realism runs throughout Niebuhr's works, it is probably seen in its most classic form in his master work, *The Nature and Destiny of Man: A Christian Interpretation* (New York: Charles Scribner's Sons, 1941, 1943). Reprinted 1996 with introduction by Robin W. Lovin (Louisville: Westminster-John Knox Press).

35. Reinhold Niebuhr, *The Children of Light and the Children of Darkness: A Vindication of Democracy and a Critique of Its Traditional Defense* (New York: Charles Scribner's Sons, 1944), 144–45.

36.  In particular, the CHA deserves great credit for the way it has handled its role as an advocate for health-care reform.

## 6. SOME PARTICULAR PROBLEMS IN HEALTH-CARE JUSTICE

1.  Cf. the data I reported in *HCR,* 30.

2.  For a report of the 1998 data on health-care spending, cf. Alice Ann Lowe, "Health Care Bill Up 5.6% on Higher Drug Costs," *Washington Post,* January 10, 2000. For a first report on the 1999 data, cf. "Outpatient Prices Jump: Costs Rose 6.7%, Surpassing Increase in Prescription Prices," *Modern Healthcare,* January 31, 2000, 2. This article, based on the Labor Department Consumer Price Index, puts the 1999 increase in prescription costs at 6.7 percent.

3.  Kristina Brenneman, "Kitzhaber's List Would Limit Choices," *Health Care Journal,* January 31, 2000. Carey Goldberg, "Maine Gets Law to Reduce Cost of Drugs," *NYT,* May 12, 2000.

4.  According to the 2000 *Britannica Book of the Year* (Chicago: Encyclopaedia Britannica, 2000), life expectancy in Malawi is 35.9 years for men and 36.5 years for women (p. 653). In Zambia, life expectancy is 36.8 years for men and 37.3 years for women (p. 746). In Swaziland, life expectancy is 37.3 years for men and 39.8 years for women (p. 715). In Zimbabwe, life expectancy is 39.1 years for men and 39.2 years for women. Traffic accidents and malaria continue to be enormous problems in these countries, but it is the spread of AIDS that has significantly lowered life expectancy in recent years. The four countries mentioned are the only ones in the world where life expectancy is less than forty years.

5.  Donald G. McNeil, "Companies to Cut Cost of AIDS Drugs for Poor Nations," *NYT,* May 12, 2000.

6.  An example is the drug melarsoprol, much needed in some African countries for the treatment of sleeping sickness, but out of production because it is not needed elsewhere and not profitable to manufacture. Cf. Donald G. McNeil, "Drug Makers and the Third World: A Case Study in Neglect," *NYT,* May 21, 2000.

7.  Donald G. McNeil, "Prices for Medicine Are Exorbitant in Africa, Study Says," *NYT,* June 17, 2000.

8.  For a description of Medicaid's legal right to the highest discount rate (15.1 percent) for drugs, cf. "A Crisis in Credibility" (Editorial), *Modern Healthcare,* February 14, 2000.

9.  For the change of position by the drug industry, cf. ch. 5, n. 31. There continues to be a great deal of political infighting as to just how a Medicare drug program should work, so it remains to be seen

exactly what will happen. Cf. Ethan Wallison, "House Democrats Split on Strategy," *Roll Call*, February 19, 2000. This infighting was exacerbated by the White House's admission, only a week after President Clinton's 2000 State of the Union Address, that they had underestimated the cost of their Medicare drug funding proposal by $35–$40 billion. Cf. Lawrence O'Rourke, "Rx for Medicare Patients' Drug Bills Not Easy to Swallow," *Denver Rocky Mountain News*, February 19, 2000.

10. Robert Pear, "Care Providers and Elderly Fight over Health Funds," *NYT*, May 15, 2000.

11. Robert Pear, "G.O.P. Wants Government to Guarantee Drug Benefit," *NYT*, June 14, 2000.

12. While I have focused my remarks in the text on the burden of nursing care for seniors and their families, it should also be noted that the providers of nursing care are experiencing more and more stress, especially as those seniors who are able shift from nursing care to assisted living, leaving only the costliest cases in the nursing homes. In 1999 two major national nursing home chains filed for bankruptcy, and some of the others are in very difficult financial straits. Cf. the editorial, "Change and Crisis in Nursing Homes," *NYT*, December 13, 1999.

13. For an anthology of a number of important sources on religious ethics and mental health, cf. *OMM*, 817–82. Cf. also Laura Weiss Roberts, et al., "Persons with Mental Illness," *FLE*, 184–208; Michelle A Carter, "Mental-Health Services, II: Ethical Issues," *EB*, 1716–24.

14. Statistics for something like this might be developed in various ways. According to the major study sponsored by the World Health Organization, the World Bank, and the Harvard School of Public Health, of the total time that people in the developed countries spend living with disabilities, 43.9 percent of that time is spent living with neuro-psychiatric disabilities. For the world as a whole the figure is 28.5 percent. Cf. Christopher Murray and Alan Lopez, eds., *The Global Burden of Disease: A Comprehensive Assessment of Mortality and Disability from Diseases, Injuries, and Risk Factors in 1990 and Projected to 2000* (Cambridge, Massachusetts: Harvard University Press, 1996), 234.

15. For a report on managed care and mental health, cf. Steven Findlay, "Managed Behavioral Health Care in 1999: An Industry at the Crossroads," *Health Affairs*, September/October 1999.

16. On this theme, cf. Joshua Fendel, "Mental-Health Bias" (Letter to the Editor), *NYT*, November 13, 1999.

17. Cf. the concerns raised by Joseph Glenmullen, M.D., in *The Prozac Backlash: Overcoming the Dangers of Prozac, Zoloft, Paxil, and Other Antidepressants with Safe, Effective Alternatives* (New York: Simon and Schuster, 2000).

18. Cf. Menninger's now classic *Whatever Became of Sin?* (New York: Hawthorn Books, 1973), esp. 192–203.

19. Julie Magno Zito, et al., "Trends in the Prescribing of Psychotropic Drugs to Preschoolers," *JAMA* 283: 8 (February 23, 2000), 1025–30. For a report of White House follow-up activity, cf. Robert Pear, "White House Seeks to Curb Pills Used to Calm the Young," *NYT,* March 20, 2000.

20. The Joint Commission on the Accreditation of Healthcare Organizations (JCAHO) has established a Restraints Use Task Force and is in the process of revising its standards on the use of restraints. A summary of the input received by the Restraints Use Task Force may be found at the JCAHO Web site *(www.jcaho.org).*

21. On this theme of mental health and addictions, cf. Roberts, et al., "Persons with Mental Illness," 200–201.

22. In addition to *TTH,* cf. Edmund D. Pellegrino, "Medical Education," *EB* 3, 1435–39. On the role of women as medical educators, cf. Catherine DeAngelis, "Women in Academic Medicine: New Insights, Same Sad News," *NEJM* 342: 6 (February 10, 2000), 426–27.

23. Cf. Leon Eisenberg, "The Social Imperatives of Medical Research," *CIB,* 449–56.

## 7. TOWARD SOME OVERALL CONCLUSIONS ABOUT HEALTH-CARE JUSTICE TODAY

1. Søren Kierkegaard, *Concluding Unscientific Postscript to Philosophical Fragments* in *Kierkegaard's Writings* 12, ed. by Howard and Edna Fong (Princeton, New Jersey: Princeton University Press, 1992, orig. 1846).

2. Karl Rahner, "The Dignity and Freedom of Man," *TI* 2 (1963), 254.

3. For a summary of the probabilist tradition, cf. *M&C* vol.1, 194–270.

4. *FH,* 228–29.

5. Pope John XXIII, *Pacem in Terris,* no. 11 (CST, 132).

6. Cf. the works of the authors cited in ch. 3, n. 22.

7. I cannot refer to this notion of suspension of judgment without referring to the enormous contributions of the philosopher Paul

Ricoeur. For Ricoeur on suspension of judgment, cf. Paul Ricoeur, "The Metaphorical Process as Cognition, Imagination, and Feeling," *Critical Inquiry* 5 (1978), 143–59. Also Ricoeur, *Hermeneutics and the Human Sciences,* ed. and trans. by John B. Thompson (Cambridge: Cambridge University Press, 1981).

8.  In celebrating the year 2000, it was hard to raise these concerns about debt and so on without thinking about Jubilee traditions such as the forgiveness of debt. Cf. ch. 1, n. 23.

9.  Derrick A. Bell, *And We Are Not Saved: The Elusive Quest for Racial Justice* (New York: Basic Books, 1989).

10.  Particularly on the African continent, there are many small wars that receive very little attention from the U.S. media.

11.  My own view is that one of the problems with the Clinton health-care proposal of 1993–1994 was that it offered an overly romanticized view of what the health of individuals would be like if the United States had a better organized and more just health system. Much needs to be done in the United States, but no matter how good our health-care system becomes, people will still get sick and die.

12.  Genesis 49:26.

# GLOSSARY

Many of the more complex terms used in this book (e.g., managed care, managed competition, health maintenance organization) were explained in some detail in the text, especially in the first part of chapter 2. This glossary only defines those terms that were not explained in the text of the book. Readers are invited to use the Index to locate the definitions of the terms that are defined in the text.

*Alienation of Property.* Action by which a Catholic religious congregation or other sponsor of a Roman Catholic ministry sells or otherwise encumbers its assets (its "stable patrimony"). Alienations of more than $3,000,000 require the approval of the Holy See.

*American Medical Association.* Organized in 1848, the AMA is the principal national organization of doctors in the United States. It frequently takes positions on the major public policy issues related to health care.

*Balanced Budget Act* or *Balanced Budget Amendment.* Act passed by the U.S. Congress and signed by President Clinton in 1997 to bring the federal budget into balance, partly through very substantial cuts in Medicare and related programs. Because of its legislative origin as an amendment, popular parlance often describes it as the Balanced Budget Amendment, although it is officially an Act of Congress.

*Cardiopulmonary Resuscitation* (CPR). Combination of technologies used by modern medicine to restart a human heart that has stopped beating. Great progress has been made in the development of CPR techniques in recent decades. While CPR is good in itself, should it be used in case of someone who is very likely to die in the near future no matter what is done?

229

*Catholic Health Association of the United States.* Founded in 1915 as the Catholic Hospital Association, the CHA is the principal national organization representing the interests of Catholic health care. Headquartered in St. Louis, it has more than 2,000 member organizations, including religious sponsors of health care, health-care systems, individual health-care facilities, and related organizations.

*Children's Health Insurance Program.* More accurately called the State Children's Health Insurance Program (SCHIP), this program, which is Title 21 of the 1997 Balanced Budget Act, makes federal funds available to the states for qualifying state programs that provide health insurance to children. The program is administered by the Health Care Financing Administration.

*Diagnosis Related Group.* One of about 750 ways in which a Medicare-eligible person can be understood to need medical care. Once the person is placed in a DRG, the caregivers may only recover a fixed amount for the person's care, no matter what the care actually costs. This reimbursement system was established during the presidency of Ronald Reagan.

*Foundation for Accountability.* Established by Dr. Paul Ellwood, the coiner of the term "HMO," the foundation assembles and publishes data on the quality of various health-care plans.

*Health Insurance Association of America* (HIAA). Principal national organization of companies that provide health-care coverage and other insurance. Though an opponent of some earlier health-care reform proposals, the HIAA has recently become a supporter of a prescription drug benefit.

*Health Plan Employer Data and Information Set.* Database that offers employers information on the quality of a variety of health-care plans, so that the employers can make wise decisions about which health-care plans to offer to their employees.

*Joint Commission on the Accreditation of Healthcare Organizations* (JCAHO). The Joint Commission accredits all the activities of U.S. hospitals on a regular basis. In recent years, JCAHO has established very helpful accreditation standards on issues such as pain management, advance directives, patients' rights, and organizational ethics.

*Material Cooperation.* Activity in which a person or group offers support that helps enable a behavior that the person or group considers to be morally objectionable. The general principle is that material cooperation is acceptable when there is a sufficient reason for the cooperation.

*National Commission on Quality Assurance.* Agency that publishes the Health Plan Employer Data and Information Set. Much of its budget comes from the providers of the plans it evaluates, leaving some questions about its objectivity.

*Public Juridic Person.* Technical term through which Catholic Canon Law identifies the person or group who bears ultimate responsibility for a Catholic-sponsored activity, such as the administration of a Catholic hospital.

# SELECTED BIBLIOGRAPHY

Altman, Stuart, Reinhardt, Uwe, and Schactman, David. *Regulating Managed Care: Theory, Practice and Future Options*. San Francisco: Jossey-Bass, 1999.

Anders, George. *Health Against Wealth: HMOs and the Breakdown of Medical Trust*. Boston: Houghton Mifflin, 1996.

Bennahum, David A., ed. *Managed Care: Financial, Legal, and Ethical Issues*. Cleveland: The Pilgrim Press, 1999.

Bernardin, Joseph. *Celebrating the Ministry of Healing: Joseph Cardinal Bernardin's Reflections on Healthcare*. St. Louis: The Catholic Health Association of the United States, 1999.

Callahan, Daniel. *False Hopes: Why America's Quest for Perfect Health Care Is a Recipe for Failure*. New York: Simon and Schuster, 1998.

———. *The Terrible Dream of Life: Living with Mortality*. New York: Simon and Schuster, 1993.

———. *What Kind of Life: The Limits of Medical Progress*. New York: Simon and Schuster, 1990.

Churchill, Larry R. *Rationing Health Care in America: Perceptions and Principles of Justice*. Notre Dame, Indiana: University of Notre Dame Press, 1987.

Dougherty, Charles J. *American Health Care: Realities, Rights, and Reforms*. New York: Oxford University Press, 1988.

———. *Back to Reform: Values, Markets, and the Health Care System.* New York: Oxford University Press, 1996.

Evans, Abigail Rian. *Redeeming Marketplace Medicine: A Theology of Health Care.* Cleveland: The Pilgrim Press, 1999.

Gervais, Karen, et al., eds. *Ethical Challenges in Managed Care: A Casebook.* Washington, D.C.: Georgetown University Press, 1999.

Ginzberg, Eli. *Tomorrow's Hospital: A Look to the Twenty-First Century.* New Haven: Yale University Press, 1996.

Ginzberg, Eli, with Miriam Ostrow. *The Road to Reform: The Future of Health Care in America.* New York: Free Press, 1994.

Hansen, Mark J. and Callahan, Daniel, eds. *The Goals of Medicine: The Forgotten Issue in Health Care Reform.* Washington, D.C.: Georgetown University Press, 1999.

Henderson, Gail, et al. *The Social Medicine Reader.* Durham, North Carolina: Duke University Press, 1997.

Herzlinger, Regina M. *Market Driven Health Care.* Reading, Massachusetts: Perseus Books, 1997.

Keane, Philip S. *Health Care Reform: A Catholic View.* Mahwah, New Jersey: Paulist Press, 1993.

Kilner, John F. *Life on the Line: Ethics, Aging, Ending Patients' Lives and Allocating Vital Resources.* Grand Rapids, Michigan: William B. Eerdmans, 1992.

Kilner, John F., Orr, Robert D., and Shelly, Judith A., eds. *The Changing Face of Health Care: A Christian Appraisal of Managed Care, Resource Allocation, and Patient-Caregiver Relationships.* Grand Rapids, Michigan: William B. Eerdmans, 1998.

Lammers, Stephen E. and Verhey, Allen, eds. *On Moral Medicine: Theological Perspectives in Medical Ethics.* 2nd ed. Grand Rapids, Michigan: William B. Eerdmans, 1998.

LaPuma, John. *Managed Care Ethics: Essays on the Impact of Managed Care on Traditional Medical Ethics.* New York: Hatherleigh Books, 1998.

Lavastida, Jose. *Health Care and the Common Good: A Theory of Justice.* Lanham, Maryland: University Press of America, 1999.

Lundmerer, Kenneth M. *Time to Heal: American Medical Education from the Turn of the Century to the Era of Managed Care.* New York: Oxford University Press, 1999.

Macklin, Ruth. *Against Relativism: Cultural Diversity and the Search for Ethical Universals in Medicine.* New York: Oxford University Press, 1999.

Mann, Jonathan, et al., eds. *Health and Human Rights: A Reader.* New York: Routledge, 1999.

Mappes, Thomas A. and DeGrazia, David. *Biomedical Ethics.* 5th ed. New York: McGraw-Hill, 2001.

May, William F. *Testing the Medical Covenant: Active Euthanasia and Health Care Reform.* Grand Rapids, Michigan: William B. Eerdmans, 1996.

McCormick, Richard A., S.J. *Corrective Vision: Explorations in Moral Theology.* Kansas City, Missouri: Sheed and Ward, 1994.

————. *The Critical Calling: Reflections on Moral Dilemmas Since Vatican II.* Washington, D.C.: Georgetown University Press, 1989.

Menzel, Paul T. *Medical Costs, Moral Choices: A Philosophy of Health Care Economics in America.* New Haven: Yale University Press, 1983.

————. *Strong Medicine: The Ethical Rationing of Health Care.* New York: Oxford University Press, 1990.

Mooney, Gavin. *Economics, Medicine and Health Care.* 2nd ed. Lanham, Maryland: Rowman and Littlefield, 1992.

United States Conference of Catholic Bishops. *Ethical and Religious Directives for Catholic Health Care Services.* 4th ed. Washington, D.C., 2001.

Nelson, James L. and Nelson, Hilde L. *Meaning and Medicine: A Reader in the Philosophy of Health Care.* New York: Routledge, 1999.

O'Rourke, Kevin D. *Medical Ethics: Sources of Catholic Teachings.* 2nd ed. Washington, D.C.: Georgetown University Press, 1994.

Pellegrino, Edmund D. *Helping and Healing: Religious Commitment in Health Care.* Washington, D.C.: Georgetown University Press, 1997.

———. *The Christian Virtues in Medical Practice.* Washington, D.C.: Georgetown University Press, 1996.

Prather, Stephen E. *The New Health Partners: Renewing the Leadership of Physician Practice.* San Francisco: Jossey-Bass, 1999.

Raffel, Marshal W. *Health and Reform in Industrialized Countries.* University Park Pennsylvania: University of Pennsylvania Press, 1997.

Reich, Warren T., ed. *Encyclopedia of Bioethics.* 2nd ed. New York: Macmillan, 1995.

Starr, Paul. *The Social Transformation of American Medicine.* New York: Basic Books Inc., 1982.

Thomasma, David C. and Kissell, Judith Lee, eds. *The Health Care Professional as Friend and Healer: Building on the Work of Edmund D. Pellegrino.* Washington, D.C.: Georgetown University Press, 2000.

Walters, LeRoy and Joy, Tamar, eds. *Bibliography of Bioethics.* 23 vols. to date. Washington, D.C.: Georgetown University Press, 1975–1997.

Weiss, Lawrence D. *Private Medicine and Public Health: Profit, Politics, and Prejudice in the American Health Care Enterprise.* Boulder, Colorado: Westview Press, 1997.

Wong, Kenman L. *Medicine and the Marketplace: The Moral Dimensions of Managed Care.* Notre Dame, Indiana: University of Notre Dame Press, 1998.

# INDEX